art spiegelman

BREAKDOWNS
From Maus to Now. An anthology of strips by art spiegelman

BREAKDOWNS

PORTRAIT OF THE ARTIST AS A YOUNG %@?★!

FOR FRANÇOISE

(AND IN MEMORY OF WOODY GELMAN)

The author would like to raise a bottle of india ink and toast his enablers for making this new edition of *Breakdowns* possible:
to Pantheon's Andy Hughes, Altie Karper and Lisa Lucas;
to the Wylie Agency's Sarah Chalfant, Luke Ingram, Rebecca Nagel and Andrew Wylie;
to John Kuramoto for his digital remastering skills;
and to Françoise Mouly for her editorial acumen, tech support and love.

 PUBLISHED IN THE UNITED STATES BY PANTHEON BOOKS, A DIVISION OF PENGUIN RANDOM HOUSE LLC, NEW YORK, AND IN CANADA BY PENGUIN RANDOM HOUSE OF CANADA LIMITED, TORONTO.
PANTHEON BOOKS AND COLOPHON ARE REGISTERED TRADEMARKS OF PENGUIN RANDOM HOUSE LLC.
ORIGINALLY PUBLISHED IN HARDCOVER BY PANTHEON BOOKS, A DIVISION OF PENGUIN RANDOM HOUSE LLC, NEW YORK, IN 2008.
A PREVIOUS EDITION OF *BREAKDOWNS* WAS PUBLISHED IN DIFFERENT FORM BY BELIER PRESS, NEW YORK, IN 1977.
A CATALOGUING IN PUBLICATION RECORD FOR THIS WORK HAS BEEN ESTABLISHED BY THE LIBRARY OF CONGRESS.

art spiegelman

BREAKDOWNS

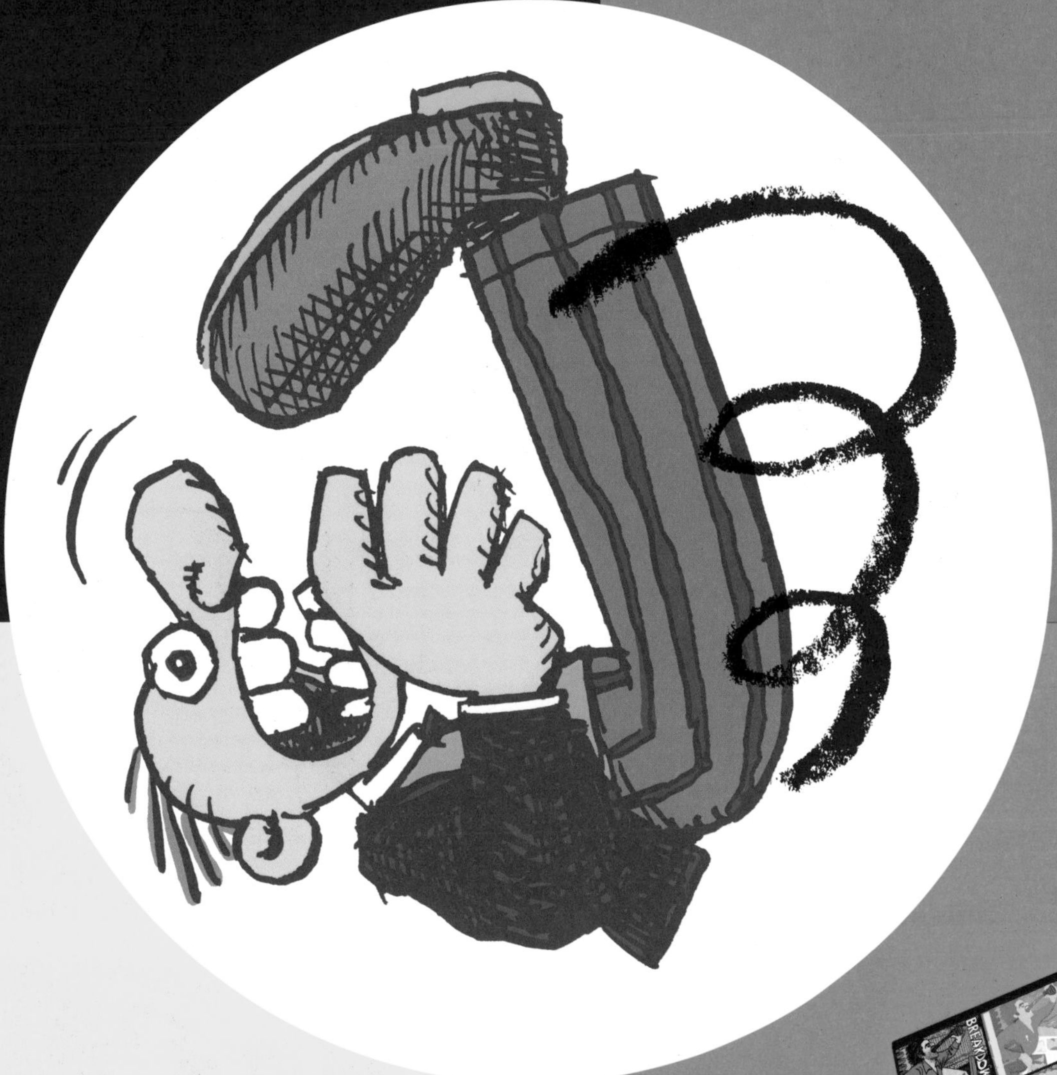

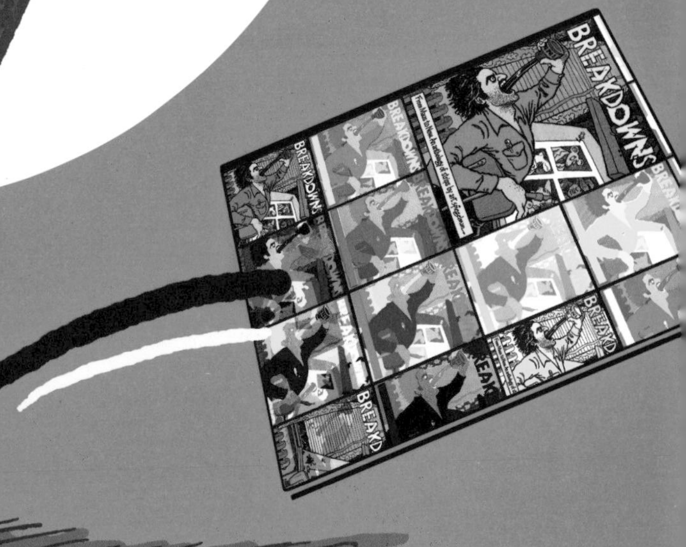

BREAKDOWNS

PORTRAIT OF THE ARTIST AS A YOUNG %@&*!

PANTHEON BOOKS • NEW YORK

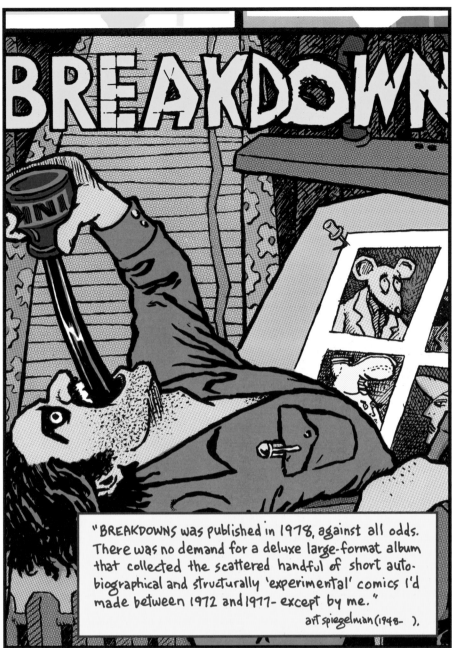

BREAKDOWN

"BREAKDOWNS was published in 1978, against all odds. There was no demand for a deluxe large-format album that collected the scattered handful of short auto-biographical and structurally 'experimental' comics I'd made between 1972 and 1977— except by me."

art spiegelman (1948–).

HA! TURN *THIS* ONE INTO SOMETHING!

HMMM...

AWW...

JEEZ, MOM! NO MATTER WHAT I SCRIBBLE, YOU JUST TURN IT INTO HAIR ON THE SAME OLD FACE!

OKAY— SO I'LL DO A SCRIBBLE FOR YOU!

TOO EASY, MOMMY— IT'S *ALREADY* A DUCK!

VERY GOOD, COOKIE!

GIVE ME ANOTHER!!

MAYBE LATER... I'M WORRIED YOUR FATHER ISN'T HOME YET!

YOU'RE WORRIED EVERY NIGHT!

"WHAT ME WORRY?" RIGHT, MOMMY?

UH-HUH.

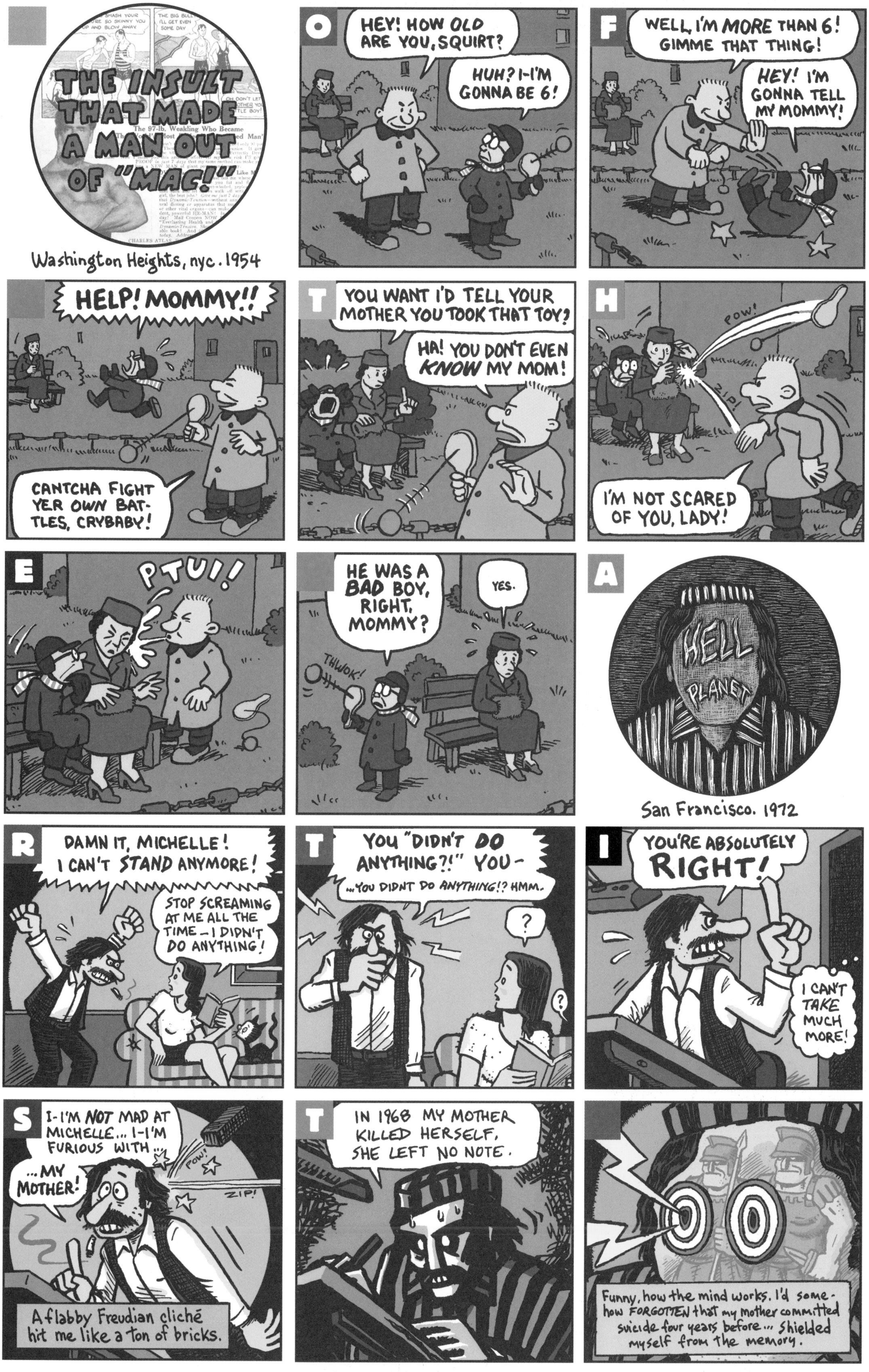
THE INSULT THAT MADE A MAN OUT OF "MAC!"
Washington Heights, nyc. 1954
O
HEY! HOW OLD ARE YOU, SQUIRT?
HUH? I-I'M GONNA BE 6!
F
WELL, I'M MORE THAN 6! GIMME THAT THING!
HEY! I'M GONNA TELL MY MOMMY!
HELP! MOMMY!!
CANTCHA FIGHT YER OWN BATTLES, CRYBABY!
T
YOU WANT I'D TELL YOUR MOTHER YOU TOOK THAT TOY?
HA! YOU DON'T EVEN KNOW MY MOM!
H
POW!
ZIP!
I'M NOT SCARED OF YOU, LADY!
E
PTUI!
HE WAS A BAD BOY, RIGHT, MOMMY?
YES.
THWOK!
A
HELL PLANET
San Francisco. 1972
R
DAMN IT, MICHELLE! I CAN'T STAND ANYMORE!
STOP SCREAMING AT ME ALL THE TIME – I DIDN'T DO ANYTHING!
T
YOU "DIDN'T DO ANYTHING?!" YOU–
...YOU DIDNT DO ANYTHING!? HMM.
?
?
I
YOU'RE ABSOLUTELY RIGHT!
I CAN'T TAKE MUCH MORE!
S
I-I'M NOT MAD AT MICHELLE... I-I'M FURIOUS WITH...
...MY MOTHER!
POW!
ZIP!
A flabby Freudian cliché hit me like a ton of bricks.
T
IN 1968 MY MOTHER KILLED HERSELF. SHE LEFT NO NOTE.
Funny, how the mind works. I'd somehow FORGOTTEN that my mother committed suicide four years before... Shielded myself from the memory.

Other work came to a halt while I feverishly brought "Hell Planet" into focus. At first I thought it might be too personal – too fraught – to publish... but comics just aren't complete 'til they're printed...

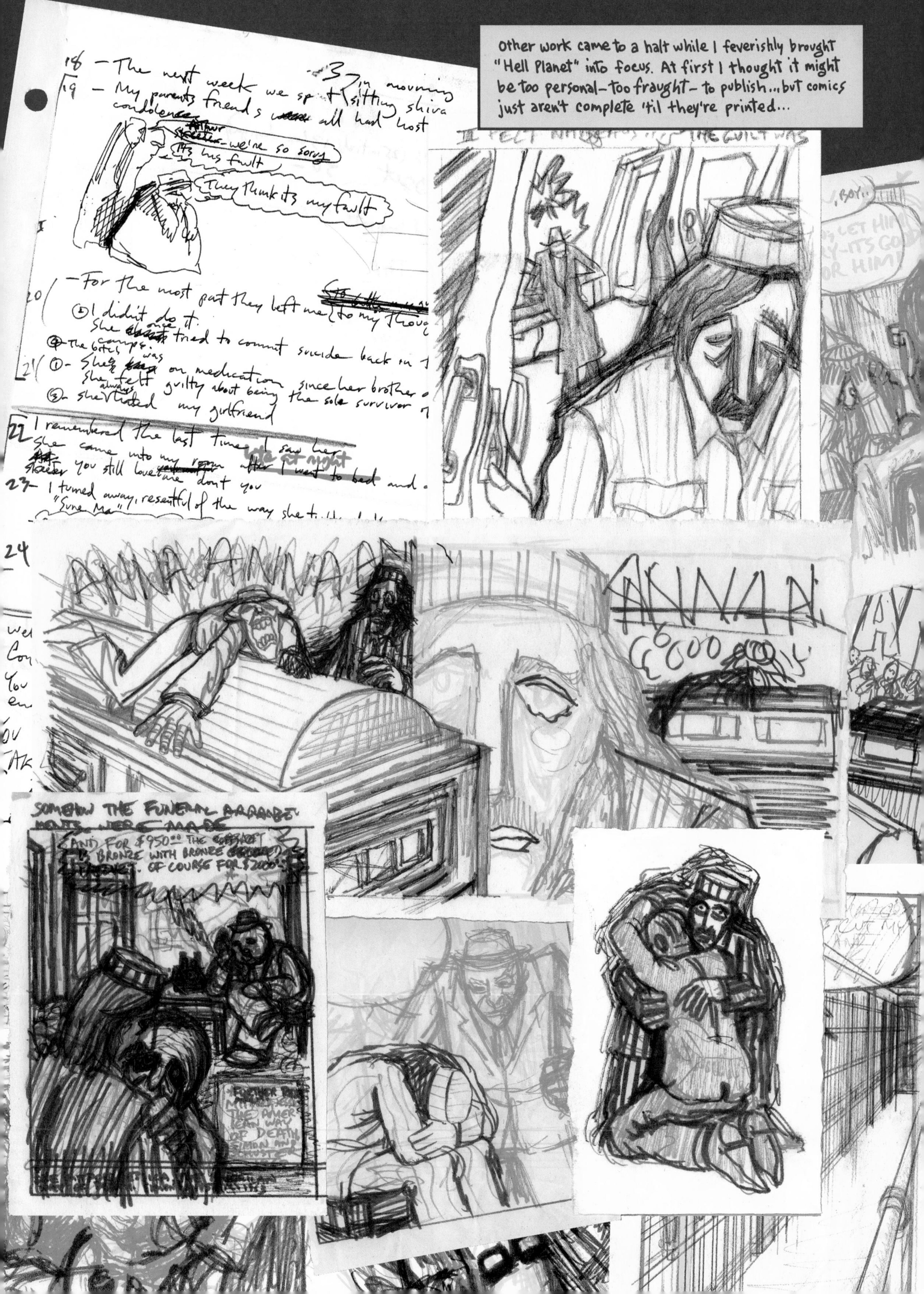

18 – The next week we spent sitting shiva in mourning
19 – My parents friend's condolences all had lost
we're so sorry
It's his fault
They think it's my fault
20 – For the most part they left me to my thoughts
① I didn't do it.
22 I remembered the last time I saw her
23 – I turned away, resentful of the way she
ANNA
SOMEHOW THE FUNERAL ARRANGEMENTS WERE MADE

A
*
I tossed aside the genuinely paltry Piece of Shit I'd been working on, and began to write as if I was possessed!
WHEN WALTER BUNG SPOKE, NOBODY LISTENED! AT BEACHES 13 YEAR OLD GIRLS WOULD KICK SAND IN HIS FACE! HE WAS JUST AN INCONSEQUENTIAL WIMP!...JUST ANOTHER ASSHOLE!...
JUST A PIECE O' SHIT!
INCONSEQUENTIAL WIMP
PIECE OF SHIT
...BUT ALL THIS WAS ABOUT TO CHANGE!!!...
JEEZIS! IT'S A QUARTER TO NINE! IF I'M LATE ONE MORE TIME MR. GONIFF WILL FIRE ME SURE!!!
GRUNT! UNNF!
EASY-TO-DIGEST
Short Order comix
No 1
OUR MOTTO: NO STORY OVER FOUR PAGES!!!!
PARDON ME, MISS... DO YOU SERVE CRABS HERE?
SURE, TOOTS... WE'LL SERVE ANYONE—JUST KEEP YER SHIRT ON!
Chat'n Chew
CHIM-CHIMI CHIM-CHIM
CRIME STOPPER! ALWAYS WIPE WITH THE LEFT!
ORKK?
?
H-HELLO? IS SOMEBODY THERE?
*
S
YOU COMIN' TO BED, ART?
N-NOT TONIGHT!
In the grip of my recovered memories, and an Expressionist art style that I associated with Real Art, I worked for weeks.
FINALLY! IT'S DONE!
WOW! THE DRAWINGS ARE REALLY PRETTY!
A
PRETTY?!! YOU'RE PRETTY! THIS HAS NOTHING TO DO WITH PRETTY!
JEEZ. I JUST MEANT-
IT'S NOT PRETTY!
I JUST CAN'T TAKE MUCH MORE!
Y
UNPACKING
Soho, nyc. 2005
O
Dear Diary, Thinking back on the days when I drew "Prisoner on the Hell Planet" I looked through a box of old family photos.
U
OW!
I don't tend to confuse Art and Therapy (making Art is cheaper), but I did think Hell Planet had helped me "deal" with Anja's suicide...
N
AOOOO!
33 years after drawing that strip, 37 years after my mother's death, I didn't expect the bolt of pain!

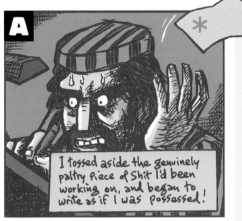

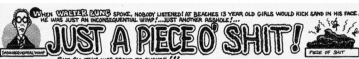

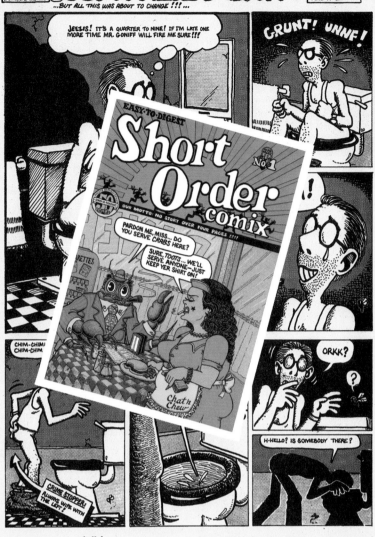

"Just a Piece o' Shit" (a four-page story about a talking turd), an aptly named specimen of the artist's early work. Inset: His cover for the underground comic where it and "Prisoner on the Hell Planet" were both first published.

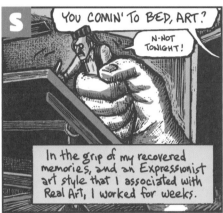

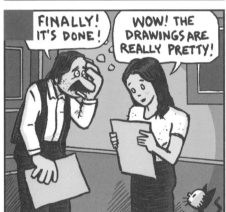

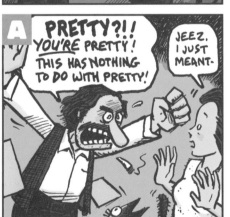

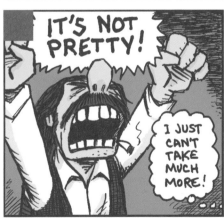

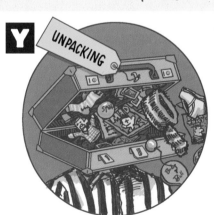

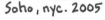

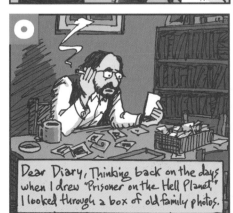

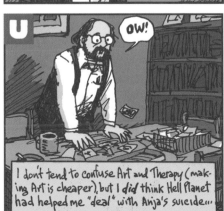

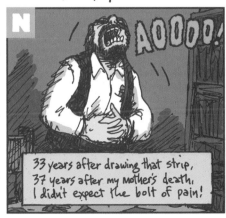

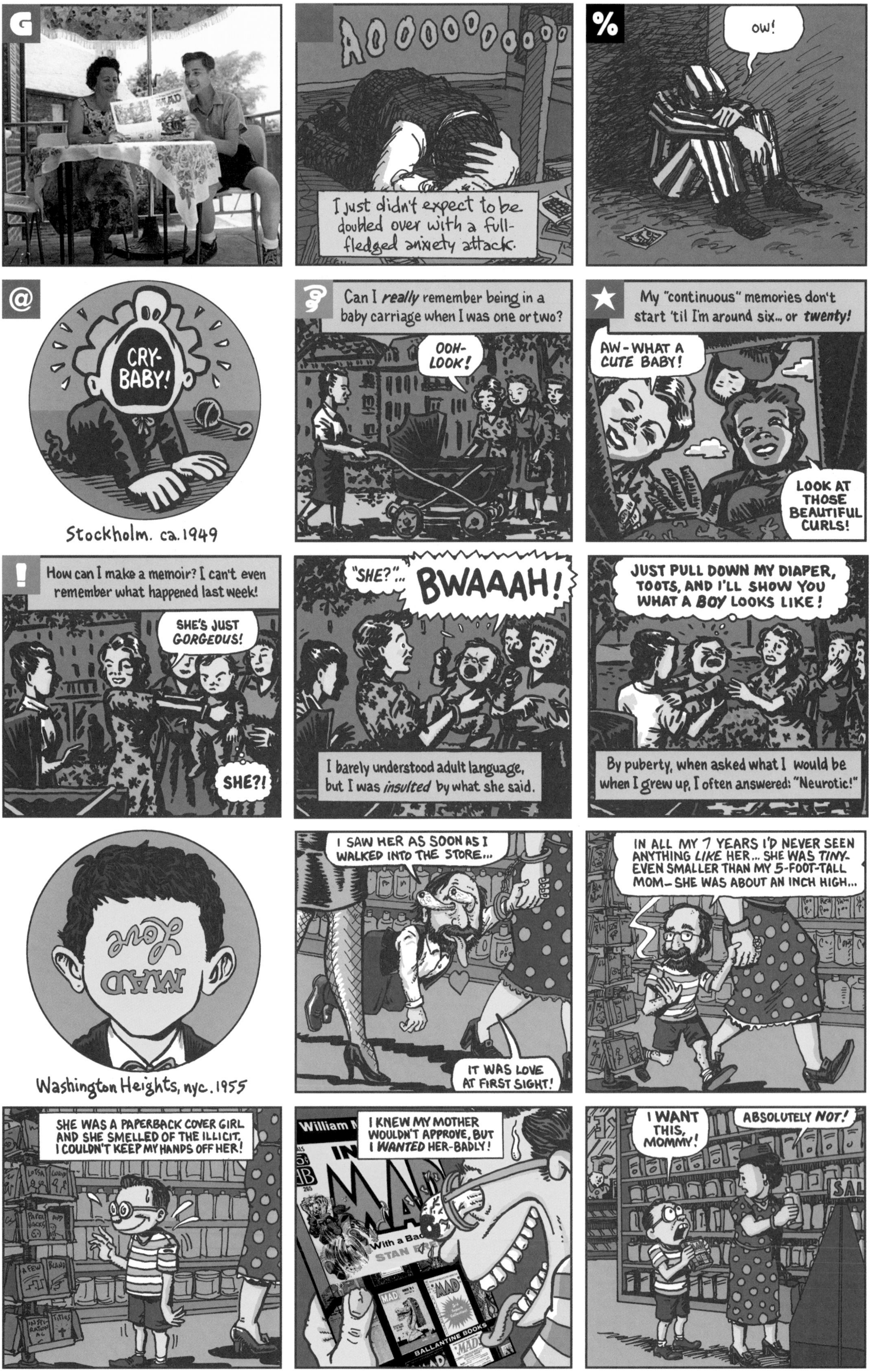
AOOOOOOooooo
I just didn't expect to be doubled over with a full-fledged anxiety attack.
OW!
CRY-BABY!
Stockholm. ca. 1949
Can I *really* remember being in a baby carriage when I was one or two?
OOH-LOOK!
My "continuous" memories don't start 'til I'm around six... or *twenty!*
AW-WHAT A CUTE BABY!
LOOK AT THOSE BEAUTIFUL CURLS!
How can I make a memoir? I can't even remember what happened last week!
SHE'S JUST *GORGEOUS!*
SHE?!
"SHE?"... BWAAAH!
I barely understood adult language, but I was *insulted* by what she said.
JUST PULL DOWN MY DIAPER, TOOTS, AND I'LL SHOW YOU WHAT A *BOY* LOOKS LIKE!
By puberty, when asked what I would be when I grew up, I often answered: "Neurotic!"
Love
MAD
Washington Heights, nyc. 1955
I SAW HER AS SOON AS I WALKED INTO THE STORE...
IT WAS LOVE AT FIRST SIGHT!
IN ALL MY 7 YEARS I'D NEVER SEEN ANYTHING *LIKE* HER... SHE WAS *TINY*-EVEN SMALLER THAN MY 5-FOOT-TALL MOM-SHE WAS ABOUT AN INCH HIGH...
SHE WAS A PAPERBACK COVER GIRL AND SHE SMELLED OF THE ILLICIT. I COULDN'T KEEP MY HANDS OFF HER!
I KNEW MY MOTHER WOULDN'T APPROVE, BUT I *WANTED* HER-BADLY!
MAD
BALLANTINE BOOKS
I WANT THIS, MOMMY!
ABSOLUTELY *NOT!*

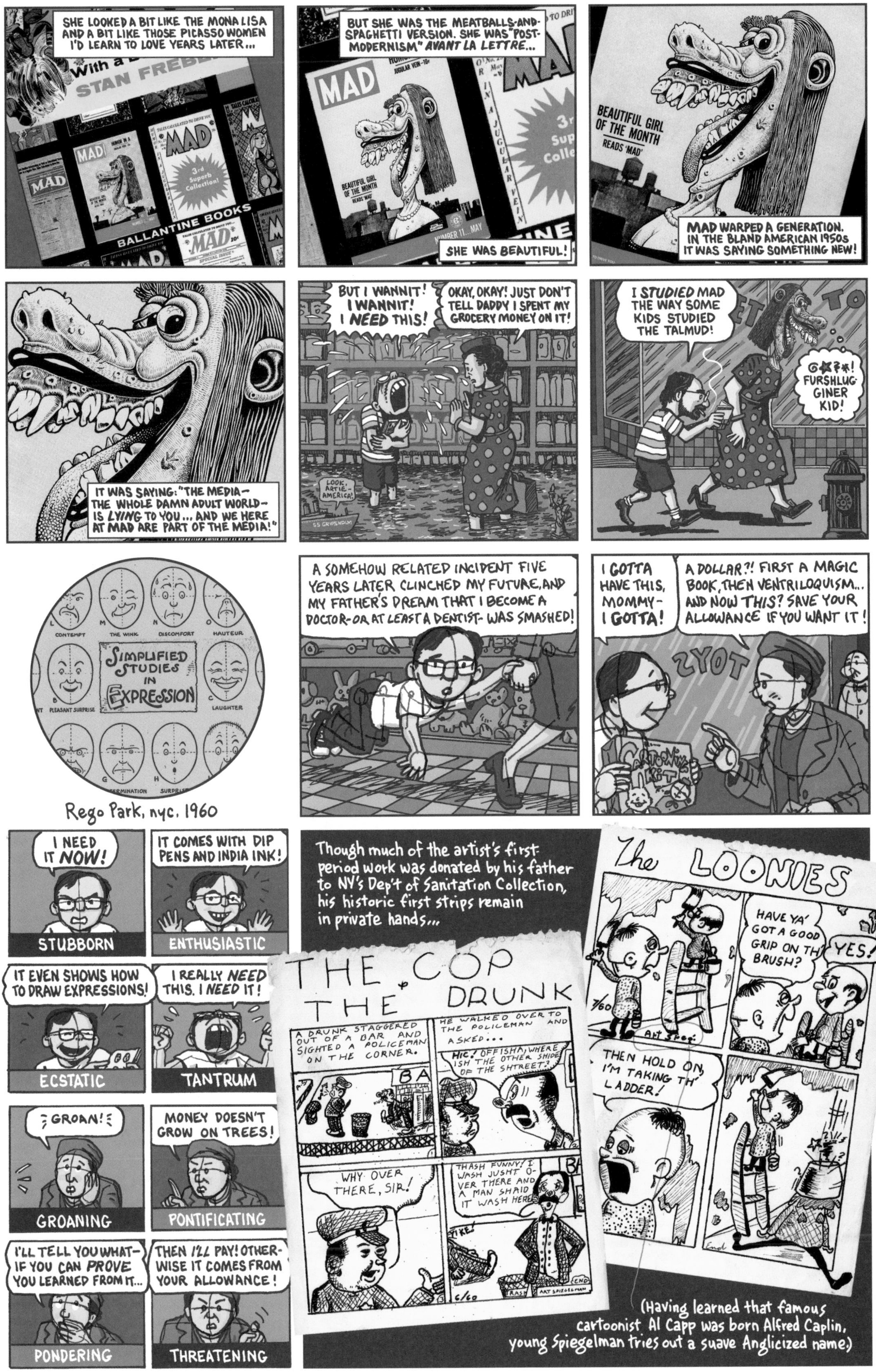
SHE LOOKED A BIT LIKE THE MONA LISA AND A BIT LIKE THOSE PICASSO WOMEN I'D LEARN TO LOVE YEARS LATER...
BUT SHE WAS THE MEATBALLS-AND-SPAGHETTI VERSION. SHE WAS "POST-MODERNISM" AVANT LA LETTRE...
SHE WAS BEAUTIFUL!
MAD WARPED A GENERATION. IN THE BLAND AMERICAN 1950s IT WAS SAYING SOMETHING NEW!
IT WAS SAYING: "THE MEDIA—THE WHOLE DAMN ADULT WORLD—IS LYING TO YOU... AND WE HERE AT MAD ARE PART OF THE MEDIA!"
BUT I WANNIT! I WANNIT! I NEED THIS!
OKAY, OKAY! JUST DON'T TELL DADDY I SPENT MY GROCERY MONEY ON IT!
LOOK, ARTIE—AMERICA!
SS GRIPSHOLM
I STUDIED MAD THE WAY SOME KIDS STUDIED THE TALMUD!
FURSHLUGGINER KID!
SIMPLIFIED STUDIES IN EXPRESSION
CONTEMPT
THE WINK
DISCOMFORT
HAUTEUR
PLEASANT SURPRISE
LAUGHTER
Rego Park, nyc, 1960
A SOMEHOW RELATED INCIDENT FIVE YEARS LATER CLINCHED MY FUTURE, AND MY FATHER'S DREAM THAT I BECOME A DOCTOR—OR AT LEAST A DENTIST—WAS SMASHED!
I GOTTA HAVE THIS, MOMMY—I GOTTA!
A DOLLAR?! FIRST A MAGIC BOOK, THEN VENTRILOQUISM... AND NOW THIS? SAVE YOUR ALLOWANCE IF YOU WANT IT!
TOYS
I NEED IT NOW!
STUBBORN
IT COMES WITH DIP PENS AND INDIA INK!
ENTHUSIASTIC
IT EVEN SHOWS HOW TO DRAW EXPRESSIONS!
ECSTATIC
I REALLY NEED THIS. I NEED IT!
TANTRUM
GROAN!
GROANING
MONEY DOESN'T GROW ON TREES!
PONTIFICATING
I'LL TELL YOU WHAT—IF YOU CAN PROVE YOU LEARNED FROM IT...
PONDERING
THEN I'LL PAY! OTHERWISE IT COMES FROM YOUR ALLOWANCE!
THREATENING
Though much of the artist's first-period work was donated by his father to NY's Dep't of Sanitation Collection, his historic first strips remain in private hands...
THE COP & THE DRUNK
A DRUNK STAGGERED OUT OF A BAR AND SIGHTED A POLICEMAN ON THE CORNER.
HE WALKED OVER TO THE POLICEMAN AND ASKED...
HIC! OFFISHA, WHERE ISH THE OTHER SHIDE OF THE SHTREET?
WHY OVER THERE, SIR!
THASH FUNNY! I WASH JUSHT OVER THERE AND A MAN SHAID IT WASH HERE!
YIKE!
END
6/60
ART SPIEGELMAN
The LOONIES
HAVE YA' GOT A GOOD GRIP ON TH' BRUSH?
YES!
7/60
Art Spog
THEN HOLD ON, I'M TAKING TH' LADDER!
End
(Having learned that famous cartoonist Al Capp was born Alfred Caplin, young Spiegelman tries out a suave Anglicized name.)

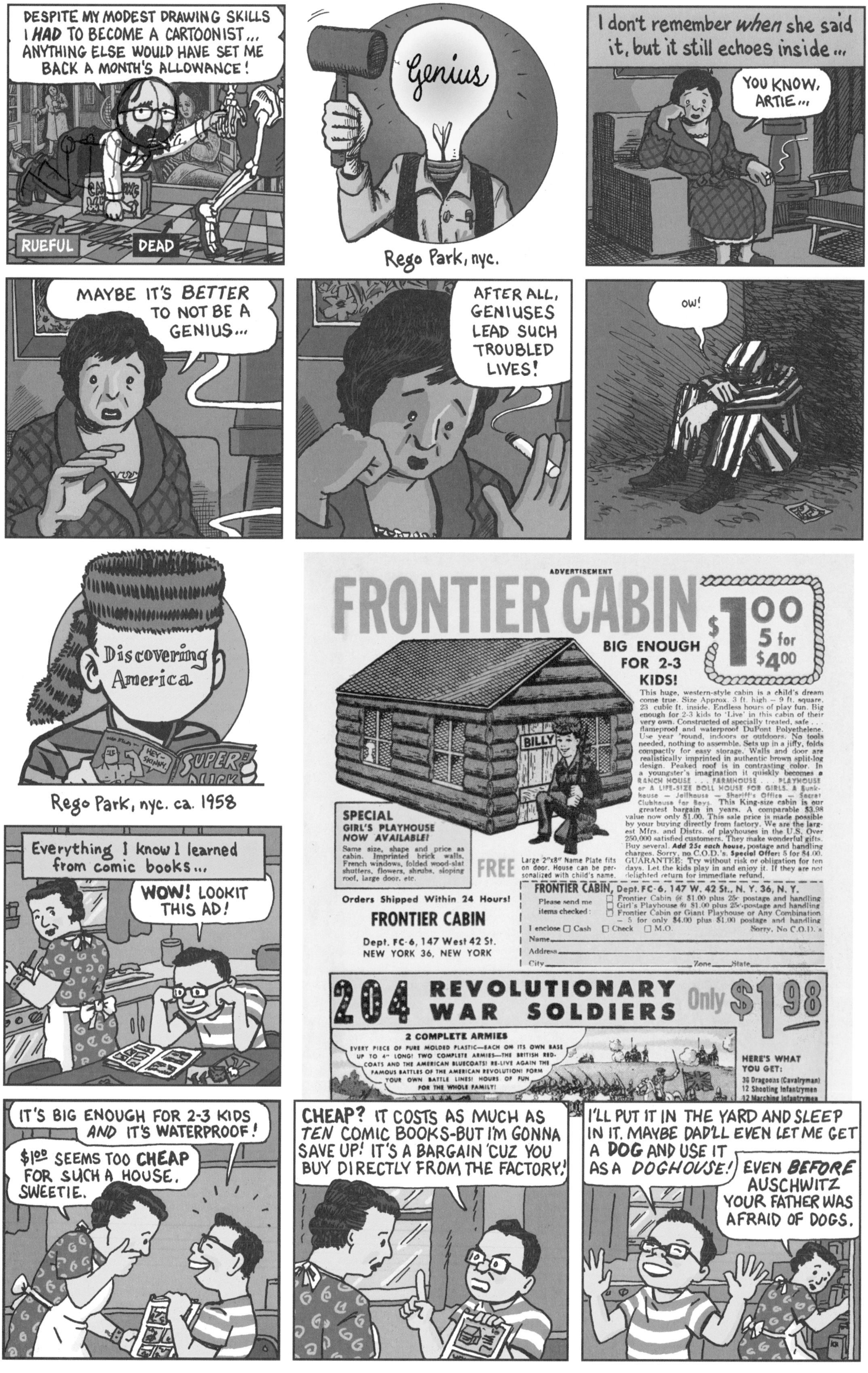
DESPITE MY MODEST DRAWING SKILLS I HAD TO BECOME A CARTOONIST... ANYTHING ELSE WOULD HAVE SET ME BACK A MONTH'S ALLOWANCE!
RUEFUL
DEAD
Genius
Rego Park, nyc.
I don't remember when she said it, but it still echoes inside...
YOU KNOW, ARTIE...
MAYBE IT'S BETTER TO NOT BE A GENIUS...
AFTER ALL, GENIUSES LEAD SUCH TROUBLED LIVES!
OW!
Discovering America
HEY- SKINNY
SUPER DUCK
Rego Park, nyc. ca. 1958
Everything I know I learned from comic books...
WOW! LOOKIT THIS AD!
ADVERTISEMENT
FRONTIER CABIN
$1.00
5 for $4.00
BIG ENOUGH FOR 2-3 KIDS!
This huge, western-style cabin is a child's dream come true. Size Approx. 3 ft. high – 9 ft. square. 23 cubic ft. inside. Endless hours of play fun. Big enough for 2-3 kids to 'Live' in this cabin of their very own. Constructed of specially treated, safe . . . flameproof and waterproof DuPont Polyethelene. Use year 'round, indoors or outdoors. No tools needed, nothing to assemble. Sets up in a jiffy, folds compactly for easy storage. Walls and door are realistically imprinted in authentic brown split-log design. Peaked roof is in contrasting color. In a youngster's imagination it quiskly becomes a RANCH HOUSE . . . FARMHOUSE . . . PLAYHOUSE or A LIFE-SIZE DOLL HOUSE FOR GIRLS. A Bunkhouse — Jailhouse — Sheriff's Office — Secret Clubhouse for Boys. This King-size cabin is our greatest bargain in years. A comparable $3.98 value now only $1.00. This sale price is made possible by your buying directly from factory. We are the largest Mfrs. and Distrs. of playhouses in the U.S. Over 250,000 satisfied customers. They make wonderful gifts. Buy several. Add 25¢ each house, postage and handling charges. Sorry, no C.O.D.'s. Special Offer: 5 for $4.00. GUARANTEE: Try without risk or obligation for ten days. Let the kids play in and enjoy it. If they are not delighted return for immediate refund.
BILLY
SPECIAL GIRL'S PLAYHOUSE NOW AVAILABLE!
Same size, shape and price as cabin. Imprinted brick walls, French windows, folded wood-slat shutters, flowers, shrubs, sloping roof, large door, etc.
FREE
Large 2"x8" Name Plate fits on door. House can be personalized with child's name.
Orders Shipped Within 24 Hours!
FRONTIER CABIN
Dept. FC-6, 147 West 42 St. NEW YORK 36, NEW YORK
FRONTIER CABIN, Dept. FC-6, 147 W. 42 St., N. Y. 36, N. Y.
Please send me items checked:
Frontier Cabin @ $1.00 plus 25¢ postage and handling
Girl's Playhouse @ $1.00 plus 25¢ postage and handling
Frontier Cabin or Giant Playhouse or Any Combination – 5 for only $4.00 plus $1.00 postage and handling
I enclose Cash Check M.O. Sorry, No C.O.D.'s
Name
Address
City Zone State
204 REVOLUTIONARY WAR SOLDIERS Only $1.98
2 COMPLETE ARMIES
EVERY PIECE OF PURE MOLDED PLASTIC—EACH ON ITS OWN BASE UP TO 4" LONG! TWO COMPLETE ARMIES—THE BRITISH RED-COATS AND THE AMERICAN BLUECOATS! RE-LIVE AGAIN THE FAMOUS BATTLES OF THE AMERICAN REVOLUTION! FORM YOUR OWN BATTLE LINES! HOURS OF FUN FOR THE WHOLE FAMILY!
HERE'S WHAT YOU GET:
36 Dragoons (Cavalryman)
12 Shooting Infantrymen
IT'S BIG ENOUGH FOR 2-3 KIDS AND IT'S WATERPROOF!
$1.00 SEEMS TOO CHEAP FOR SUCH A HOUSE, SWEETIE.
CHEAP? IT COSTS AS MUCH AS TEN COMIC BOOKS-BUT I'M GONNA SAVE UP! IT'S A BARGAIN 'CUZ YOU BUY DIRECTLY FROM THE FACTORY!
I'LL PUT IT IN THE YARD AND SLEEP IN IT. MAYBE DAD'LL EVEN LET ME GET A DOG AND USE IT AS A DOGHOUSE!
EVEN BEFORE AUSCHWITZ YOUR FATHER WAS AFRAID OF DOGS.

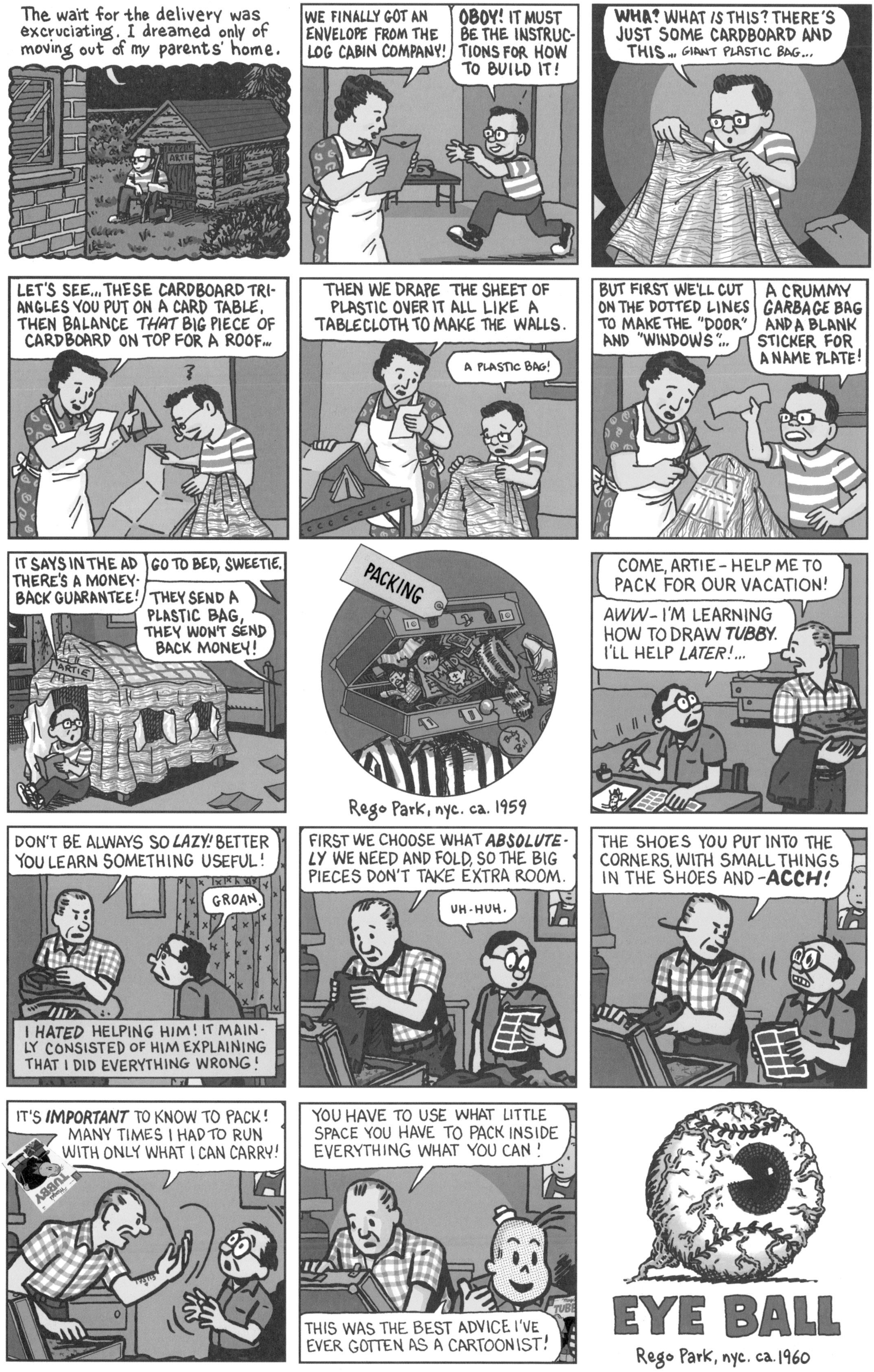
The wait for the delivery was excruciating. I dreamed only of moving out of my parents' home.
ARTIE
WE FINALLY GOT AN ENVELOPE FROM THE LOG CABIN COMPANY!
OBOY! IT MUST BE THE INSTRUCTIONS FOR HOW TO BUILD IT!
WHA? WHAT IS THIS? THERE'S JUST SOME CARDBOARD AND THIS... GIANT PLASTIC BAG...
LET'S SEE... THESE CARDBOARD TRIANGLES YOU PUT ON A CARD TABLE, THEN BALANCE THAT BIG PIECE OF CARDBOARD ON TOP FOR A ROOF...
?
THEN WE DRAPE THE SHEET OF PLASTIC OVER IT ALL LIKE A TABLECLOTH TO MAKE THE WALLS.
A PLASTIC BAG!
BUT FIRST WE'LL CUT ON THE DOTTED LINES TO MAKE THE "DOOR" AND "WINDOWS"...
A CRUMMY GARBAGE BAG AND A BLANK STICKER FOR A NAME PLATE!
IT SAYS IN THE AD THERE'S A MONEY-BACK GUARANTEE!
GO TO BED, SWEETIE.
THEY SEND A PLASTIC BAG, THEY WON'T SEND BACK MONEY!
ARTIE
PACKING
Rego Park, nyc. ca. 1959
COME, ARTIE - HELP ME TO PACK FOR OUR VACATION!
AWW - I'M LEARNING HOW TO DRAW TUBBY. I'LL HELP LATER!...
DON'T BE ALWAYS SO LAZY! BETTER YOU LEARN SOMETHING USEFUL!
GROAN
I HATED HELPING HIM! IT MAINLY CONSISTED OF HIM EXPLAINING THAT I DID EVERYTHING WRONG!
FIRST WE CHOOSE WHAT ABSOLUTELY WE NEED AND FOLD, SO THE BIG PIECES DON'T TAKE EXTRA ROOM.
UH-HUH.
THE SHOES YOU PUT INTO THE CORNERS, WITH SMALL THINGS IN THE SHOES AND -ACCH!
IT'S IMPORTANT TO KNOW TO PACK! MANY TIMES I HAD TO RUN WITH ONLY WHAT I CAN CARRY!
TUBBY
YOU HAVE TO USE WHAT LITTLE SPACE YOU HAVE TO PACK INSIDE EVERYTHING WHAT YOU CAN!
THIS WAS THE BEST ADVICE I'VE EVER GOTTEN AS A CARTOONIST!
EYE BALL
Rego Park, nyc. ca. 1960

Forged in a crucible of humiliation and trauma, cartoonists are made, not born...

The young misfit must escape into fantasy and/or develop a rarefied sense of humor to survive.

STRIKE ONE!

For a boy in 1950s America, baseball was not optional...

STRIKE TWO!

YER OUT, FAGGOT!

...and to be inept assured a place in the social hierarchy even lower than a girl's.

Boredom undercut my anxiety that a ball might come at me...

So I often kept some comic book handy!

Any comic would do, except those 3-D comics,

WHAT'S SO GREAT ABOUT SEEING PANELS IN RED?!

...since I'm virtually blind in my left eye.

HEADS UP, FOUR-EYES!

Amblyopia, a "lazy eye," made my whole world 2-D...

SPASTIC!

RETARD!

DOOFUS!

...so confusing 2-D comics with reality seems natural to me!

I started hiding in the library after school to avoid further ignominy...

JEEZ! HE TURNS INTO A GIANT BUG! THIS IS COOLER THAN THE TWILIGHT ZONE!

and learned that Kafka probably sucked at baseball too...

A FATHER'S GUIDING HAND

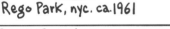

Rego Park, nyc. ca.1961

AGAIN WITH THE COMIC BOOKS?! YOU WASTE WITH THEM ALL YOUR TIME, NOT TO MENTION THE MONEY!

I JUST USE MY ALLOWANCE. I BUY TWO A WEEK AND HAVE ENOUGH LEFT OVER FOR A CANDY BAR!

TEN CENTS EACH THEY COST?!

PFEH—NEAR TO MY DIAMOND DEALERS' CLUB, IT'S TO BUY TWO OR THREE SUCH COMICS FOR A DIME!

GREAT! YOU BUY 'EM NEXT WEEK!

He kept forgetting, but eventually...

SO, DIDJA GET 'EM? DIDJA GET 'EM?!

YAH. YAH. HERE YOU HAVE MANY COMIC BOOKS FOR A QUARTER!

AWW—THESE ARE OLD ONES—SOME DON'T EVEN HAVE COVERS ON THEM!

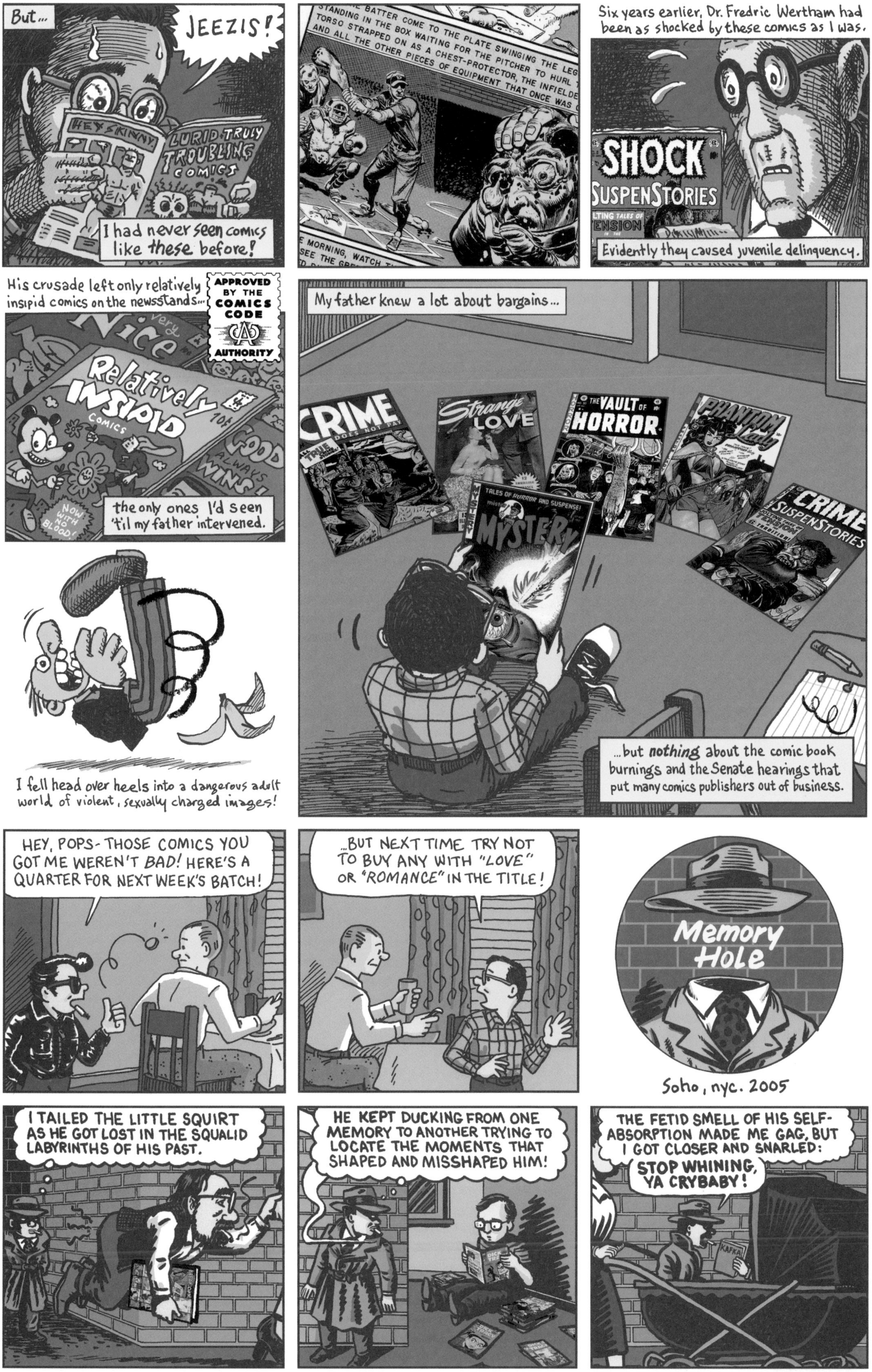

But...
JEEZIS!
HEY SKINNY
LURID TRULY TROUBLING COMICS
I had never seen comics like these before!
Six years earlier, Dr. Fredric Wertham had been as shocked by these comics as I was.
SHOCK SUSPENSTORIES
Evidently they caused juvenile delinquency.
His crusade left only relatively insipid comics on the newsstands...
APPROVED BY THE COMICS CODE AUTHORITY
Relatively INSIPID COMICS
NOW WITH NO BLOOD!
GOOD ALWAYS WINS!
the only ones I'd seen 'til my father intervened.
I fell head over heels into a dangerous adult world of violent, sexually charged images!
My father knew a lot about bargains...
CRIME DOES NOT PAY
Strange LOVE
THE VAULT OF HORROR
PHANTOM Lady
MYSTERY
CRIME SUSPENSTORIES
...but nothing about the comic book burnings and the Senate hearings that put many comics publishers out of business.
HEY, POPS- THOSE COMICS YOU GOT ME WEREN'T BAD! HERE'S A QUARTER FOR NEXT WEEK'S BATCH!
...BUT NEXT TIME TRY NOT TO BUY ANY WITH "LOVE" OR "ROMANCE" IN THE TITLE!
Memory Hole
Soho, nyc. 2005
I TAILED THE LITTLE SQUIRT AS HE GOT LOST IN THE SQUALID LABYRINTHS OF HIS PAST.
HE KEPT DUCKING FROM ONE MEMORY TO ANOTHER TRYING TO LOCATE THE MOMENTS THAT SHAPED AND MISSHAPED HIM!
THE FETID SMELL OF HIS SELF-ABSORPTION MADE ME GAG, BUT I GOT CLOSER AND SNARLED:
STOP WHINING, YA CRYBABY!
KAFKA

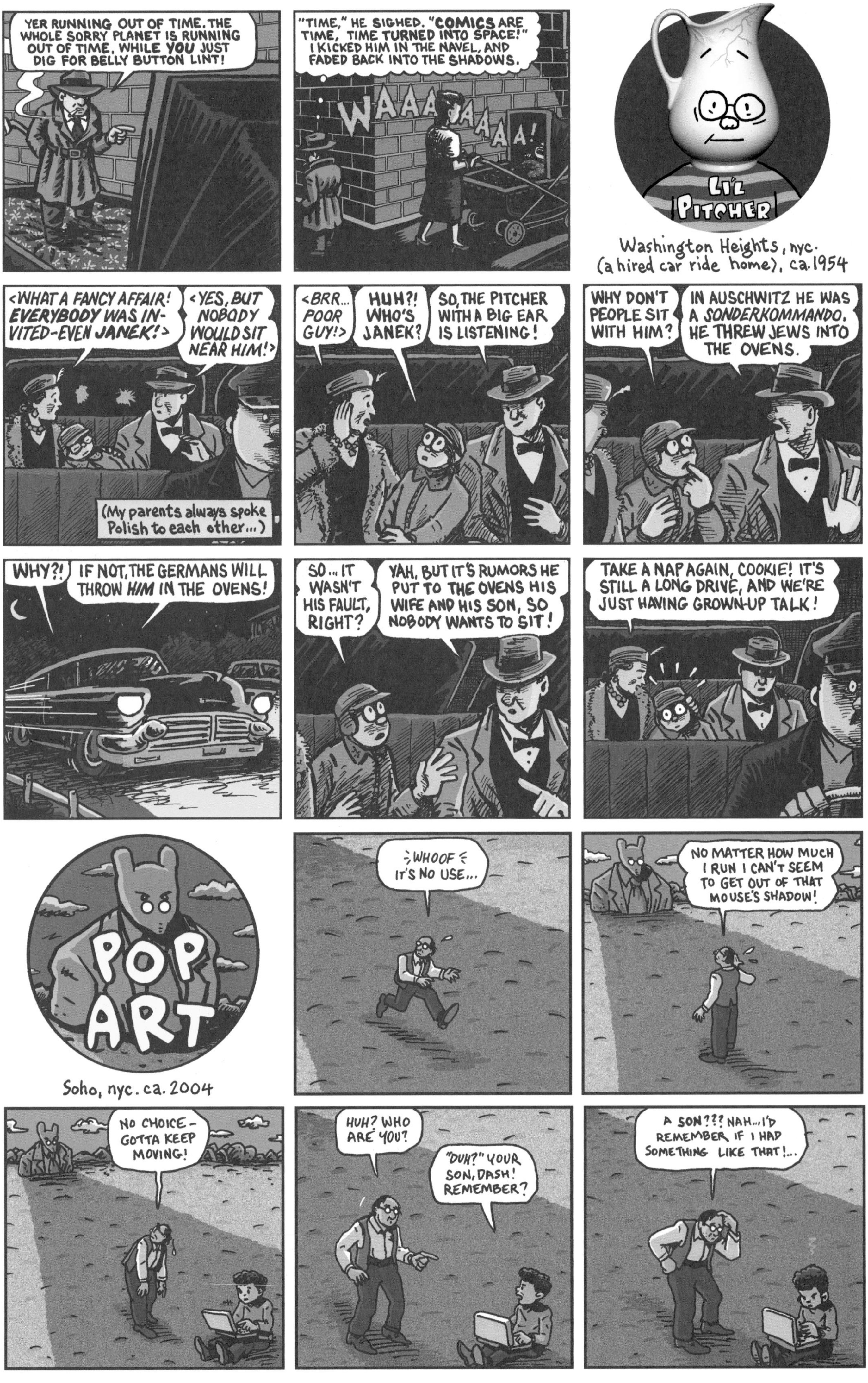
YER RUNNING OUT OF TIME. THE WHOLE SORRY PLANET IS RUNNING OUT OF TIME, WHILE YOU JUST DIG FOR BELLY BUTTON LINT!
"TIME," HE SIGHED. "COMICS ARE TIME, TIME TURNED INTO SPACE!" I KICKED HIM IN THE NAVEL, AND FADED BACK INTO THE SHADOWS.
WAAAAAAA!
LI'L PITCHER
Washington Heights, nyc. (a hired car ride home), ca. 1954
<WHAT A FANCY AFFAIR! EVERYBODY WAS INVITED-EVEN JANEK!>
<YES, BUT NOBODY WOULD SIT NEAR HIM!>
(My parents always spoke Polish to each other...)
<BRR... POOR GUY!>
HUH?! WHO'S JANEK?
SO, THE PITCHER WITH A BIG EAR IS LISTENING!
WHY DON'T PEOPLE SIT WITH HIM?
IN AUSCHWITZ HE WAS A SONDERKOMMANDO. HE THREW JEWS INTO THE OVENS.
WHY?!
IF NOT, THE GERMANS WILL THROW HIM IN THE OVENS!
SO... IT WASN'T HIS FAULT, RIGHT?
YAH, BUT IT'S RUMORS HE PUT TO THE OVENS HIS WIFE AND HIS SON, SO NOBODY WANTS TO SIT!
TAKE A NAP AGAIN, COOKIE! IT'S STILL A LONG DRIVE, AND WE'RE JUST HAVING GROWN-UP TALK!
POP ART
Soho, nyc. ca. 2004
WHOOF IT'S NO USE...
NO MATTER HOW MUCH I RUN I CAN'T SEEM TO GET OUT OF THAT MOUSE'S SHADOW!
NO CHOICE - GOTTA KEEP MOVING!
HUH? WHO ARE YOU?
"DUH?" YOUR SON, DASH! REMEMBER?
A SON??? NAH... I'D REMEMBER IF I HAD SOMETHING LIKE THAT!...

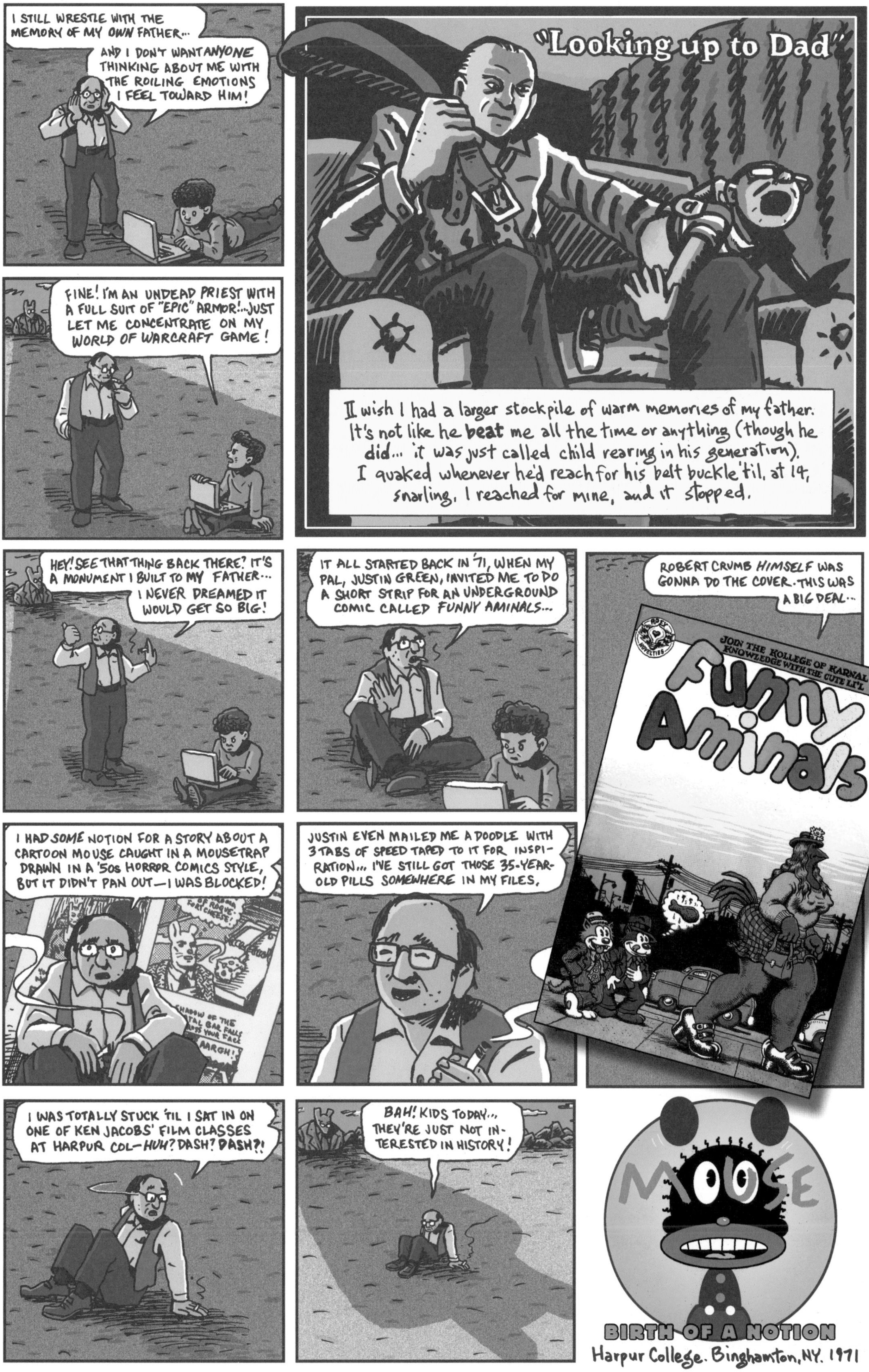
I STILL WRESTLE WITH THE MEMORY OF MY OWN FATHER...
AND I DON'T WANT ANYONE THINKING ABOUT ME WITH THE ROILING EMOTIONS I FEEL TOWARD HIM!
"Looking up to Dad"
I wish I had a larger stockpile of warm memories of my father. It's not like he **beat** me all the time or anything (though he did... it was just called child rearing in his generation). I quaked whenever he'd reach for his belt buckle 'til, at 14, snarling, I reached for mine, and it stopped.
FINE! I'M AN UNDEAD PRIEST WITH A FULL SUIT OF "EPIC" ARMOR!...JUST LET ME CONCENTRATE ON MY WORLD OF WARCRAFT GAME!
HEY! SEE THAT THING BACK THERE? IT'S A MONUMENT I BUILT TO MY FATHER...
I NEVER DREAMED IT WOULD GET SO BIG!
IT ALL STARTED BACK IN '71, WHEN MY PAL, JUSTIN GREEN, INVITED ME TO DO A SHORT STRIP FOR AN UNDERGROUND COMIC CALLED FUNNY AMINALS...
ROBERT CRUMB HIMSELF WAS GONNA DO THE COVER. THIS WAS A BIG DEAL...
JOIN THE KOLLEGE OF KARNAL KNOWLEDGE WITH THE CUTE LI'L
Funny Aminals
50¢
I HAD SOME NOTION FOR A STORY ABOUT A CARTOON MOUSE CAUGHT IN A MOUSETRAP DRAWN IN A '50s HORROR COMICS STYLE, BUT IT DIDN'T PAN OUT—I WAS BLOCKED!
AARGH!
JUSTIN EVEN MAILED ME A DOODLE WITH 3 TABS OF SPEED TAPED TO IT FOR INSPIRATION... I'VE STILL GOT THOSE 35-YEAR-OLD PILLS SOMEWHERE IN MY FILES.
I WAS TOTALLY STUCK 'TIL I SAT IN ON ONE OF KEN JACOBS' FILM CLASSES AT HARPUR COL—HUH? DASH? DASH?!
BAH! KIDS TODAY... THEY'RE JUST NOT INTERESTED IN HISTORY!
MOUSE
BIRTH OF A NOTION
Harpur College. Binghamton, NY. 1971

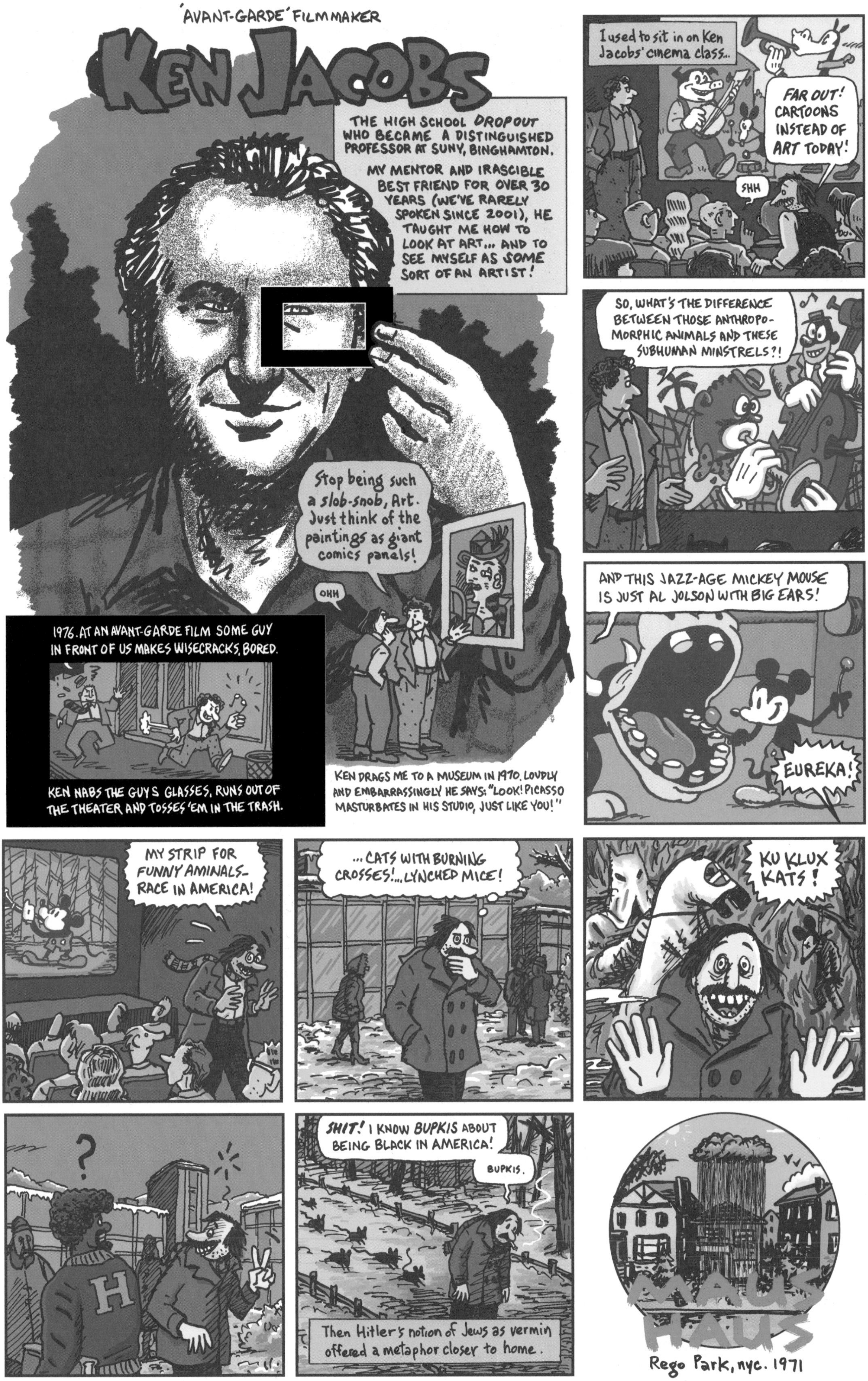

'AVANT-GARDE' FILMMAKER
KEN JACOBS
THE HIGH SCHOOL DROPOUT WHO BECAME A DISTINGUISHED PROFESSOR AT SUNY, BINGHAMTON.
MY MENTOR AND IRASCIBLE BEST FRIEND FOR OVER 30 YEARS (WE'VE RARELY SPOKEN SINCE 2001), HE TAUGHT ME HOW TO LOOK AT ART... AND TO SEE MYSELF AS SOME SORT OF AN ARTIST!
Stop being such a slob-snob, Art. Just think of the paintings as giant comics panels!
OHH
KEN DRAGS ME TO A MUSEUM IN 1970. LOUDLY AND EMBARRASSINGLY HE SAYS: "LOOK! PICASSO MASTURBATES IN HIS STUDIO, JUST LIKE YOU!"
1976. AT AN AVANT-GARDE FILM SOME GUY IN FRONT OF US MAKES WISECRACKS, BORED.
KEN NABS THE GUY'S GLASSES, RUNS OUT OF THE THEATER AND TOSSES 'EM IN THE TRASH.
I used to sit in on Ken Jacobs' cinema class...
FAR OUT! CARTOONS INSTEAD OF ART TODAY!
SHH
SO, WHAT'S THE DIFFERENCE BETWEEN THOSE ANTHROPOMORPHIC ANIMALS AND THESE SUBHUMAN MINSTRELS?!
AND THIS JAZZ-AGE MICKEY MOUSE IS JUST AL JOLSON WITH BIG EARS!
EUREKA!
MY STRIP FOR FUNNY AMINALS- RACE IN AMERICA!
...CATS WITH BURNING CROSSES!... LYNCHED MICE!
KU KLUX KATS!
?
SHIT! I KNOW BUPKIS ABOUT BEING BLACK IN AMERICA!
BUPKIS.
Then Hitler's notion of Jews as vermin offered a metaphor closer to home.
MAUS HAUS
Rego Park, nyc. 1971

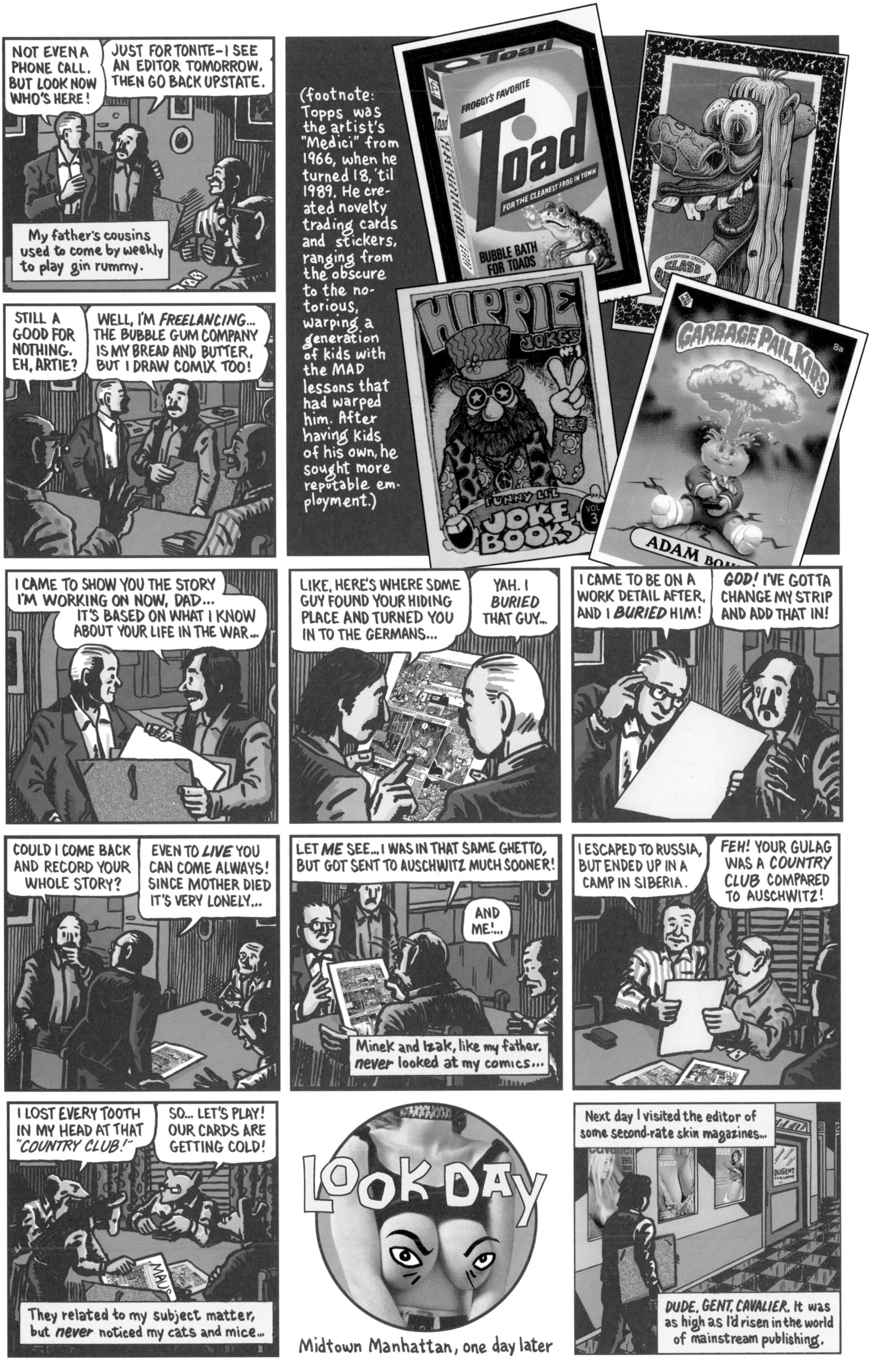

NOT EVEN A PHONE CALL. BUT LOOK NOW WHO'S HERE!
JUST FOR TONITE–I SEE AN EDITOR TOMORROW, THEN GO BACK UPSTATE.
My father's cousins used to come by weekly to play gin rummy.
STILL A GOOD FOR NOTHING, EH, ARTIE?
WELL, I'M FREELANCING... THE BUBBLE GUM COMPANY IS MY BREAD AND BUTTER, BUT I DRAW COMIX TOO!
(footnote: Topps was the artist's "Medici" from 1966, when he turned 18, 'til 1989. He created novelty trading cards and stickers, ranging from the obscure to the notorious, warping a generation of kids with the MAD lessons that had warped him. After having kids of his own, he sought more reputable employment.)
Toad
FROGGY'S FAVORITE
FOR THE CLEANEST FROG IN TOWN
BUBBLE BATH FOR TOADS
HIPPIE JOKES No1
FUNNY LI'L JOKE BOOKS
VOL 3
GARBAGE PAIL KIDS
8a
I CAME TO SHOW YOU THE STORY I'M WORKING ON NOW, DAD... IT'S BASED ON WHAT I KNOW ABOUT YOUR LIFE IN THE WAR...
LIKE, HERE'S WHERE SOME GUY FOUND YOUR HIDING PLACE AND TURNED YOU IN TO THE GERMANS...
YAH. I BURIED THAT GUY...
I CAME TO BE ON A WORK DETAIL AFTER, AND I BURIED HIM!
GOD! I'VE GOTTA CHANGE MY STRIP AND ADD THAT IN!
COULD I COME BACK AND RECORD YOUR WHOLE STORY?
EVEN TO LIVE YOU CAN COME ALWAYS! SINCE MOTHER DIED IT'S VERY LONELY...
LET ME SEE... I WAS IN THAT SAME GHETTO, BUT GOT SENT TO AUSCHWITZ MUCH SOONER!
AND ME!...
Minek and Izak, like my father, never looked at my comics...
I ESCAPED TO RUSSIA, BUT ENDED UP IN A CAMP IN SIBERIA.
FEH! YOUR GULAG WAS A COUNTRY CLUB COMPARED TO AUSCHWITZ!
I LOST EVERY TOOTH IN MY HEAD AT THAT "COUNTRY CLUB!"
SO... LET'S PLAY! OUR CARDS ARE GETTING COLD!
They related to my subject matter, but never noticed my cats and mice...
LOOK DAY
Midtown Manhattan, one day later
Next day I visited the editor of some second-rate skin magazines...
DUDE, GENT, CAVALIER. It was as high as I'd risen in the world of mainstream publishing.

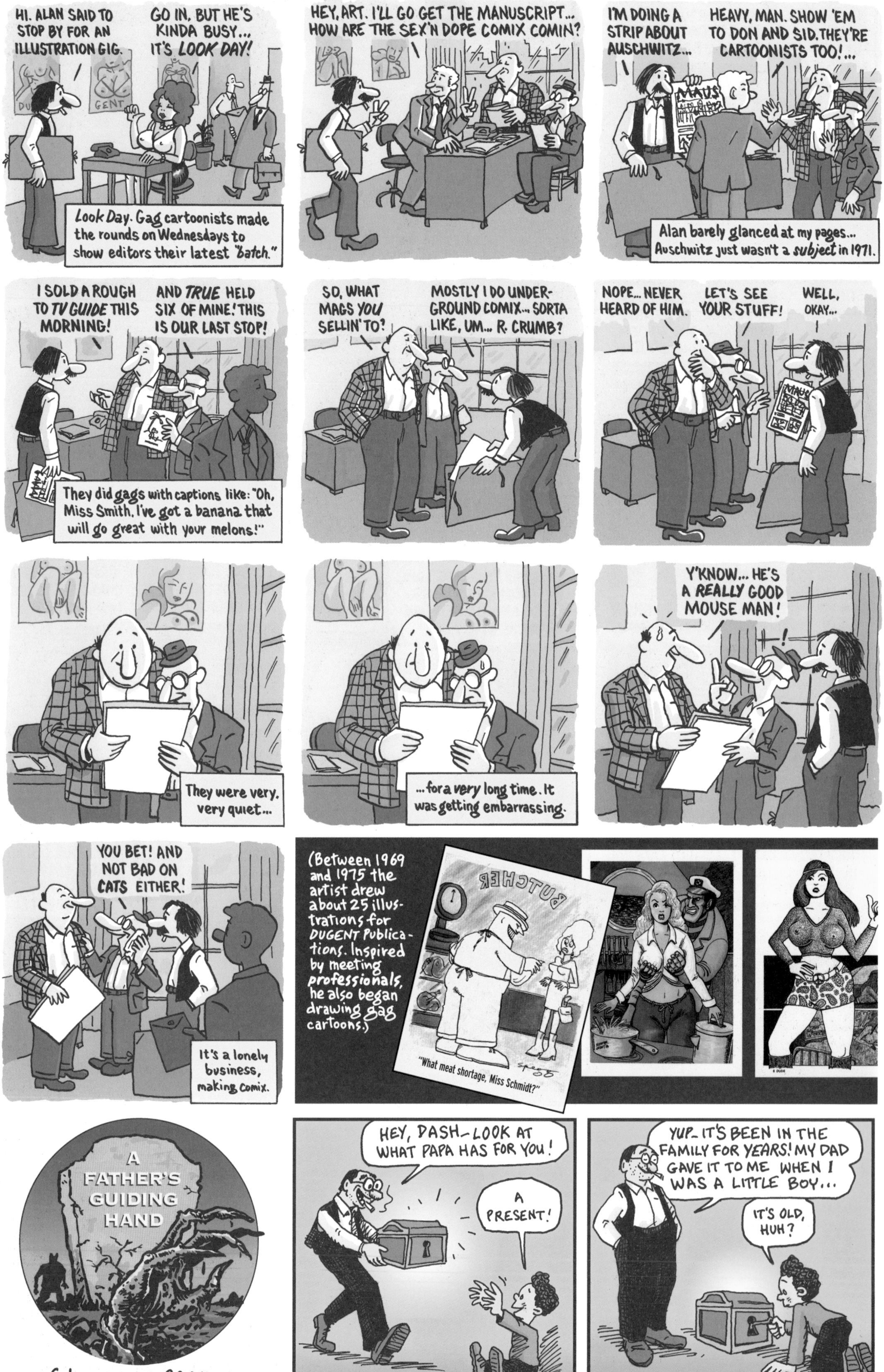
HI. ALAN SAID TO STOP BY FOR AN ILLUSTRATION GIG.
GO IN, BUT HE'S KINDA BUSY... IT'S LOOK DAY!
Look Day. Gag cartoonists made the rounds on Wednesdays to show editors their latest "batch."
HEY, ART. I'LL GO GET THE MANUSCRIPT... HOW ARE THE SEX'N DOPE COMIX COMIN?
I'M DOING A STRIP ABOUT AUSCHWITZ...
HEAVY, MAN. SHOW 'EM TO DON AND SID. THEY'RE CARTOONISTS TOO!...
MAUS
Alan barely glanced at my pages... Auschwitz just wasn't a subject in 1971.
I SOLD A ROUGH TO TV GUIDE THIS MORNING!
AND TRUE HELD SIX OF MINE! THIS IS OUR LAST STOP!
They did gags with captions like: "Oh, Miss Smith, I've got a banana that will go great with your melons!"
SO, WHAT MAGS YOU SELLIN' TO?
MOSTLY I DO UNDERGROUND COMIX... SORTA LIKE, UM... R. CRUMB?
NOPE... NEVER HEARD OF HIM.
LET'S SEE YOUR STUFF!
WELL, OKAY...
They were very, very quiet...
...for a very long time. It was getting embarrassing.
Y'KNOW... HE'S A REALLY GOOD MOUSE MAN!
YOU BET! AND NOT BAD ON CATS EITHER!
It's a lonely business, making comix.
(Between 1969 and 1975 the artist drew about 25 illustrations for DUGENT Publications. Inspired by meeting professionals, he also began drawing gag cartoons.)
"What meat shortage, Miss Schmidt?"
A FATHER'S GUIDING HAND
Soho, nyc. ca. 2004
HEY, DASH– LOOK AT WHAT PAPA HAS FOR YOU!
A PRESENT!
YUP– IT'S BEEN IN THE FAMILY FOR YEARS! MY DAD GAVE IT TO ME WHEN I WAS A LITTLE BOY...
IT'S OLD, HUH?

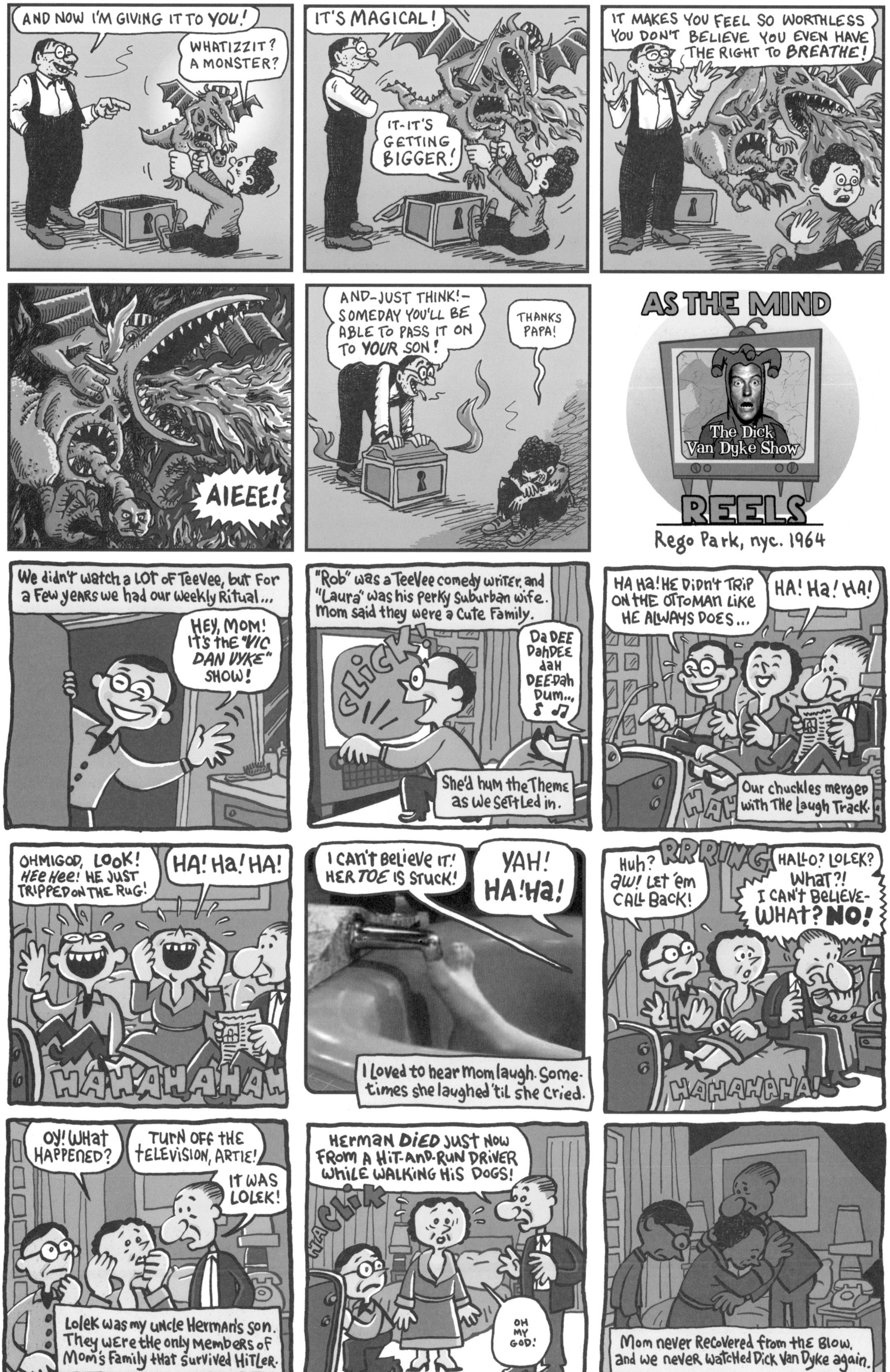
AND NOW I'M GIVING IT TO YOU!
WHATIZZIT? A MONSTER?
IT'S MAGICAL!
IT-IT'S GETTING BIGGER!
IT MAKES YOU FEEL SO WORTHLESS YOU DON'T BELIEVE YOU EVEN HAVE THE RIGHT TO BREATHE!
AIEEE!
AND-JUST THINK!- SOMEDAY YOU'LL BE ABLE TO PASS IT ON TO YOUR SON!
THANKS PAPA!
AS THE MIND
The Dick Van Dyke Show
REELS
Rego Park, nyc. 1964
We didn't watch a LOT of TeeVee, but For a Few years we had our weekly Ritual...
HEY, MOM! IT'S THE "VIC DAN VYKE" SHOW!
"Rob" was a TeeVee comedy writer, and "Laura" was his perky suburban wife. Mom said they were a Cute Family.
CLICK!
Da DEE DahDEE dah DEE-Dah Dum...
She'd hum the Theme as we settled in.
HA Ha! HE DIDN'T TRIP ON THE OTTOMAN LIKE HE ALWAYS DOES...
HA! Ha! HA!
HAH
Our chuckles merged with the Laugh Track.
OHMIGOD, LOOK! HEE HEE! HE JUST TRIPPED ON THE RUG!
HA! Ha! HA!
HAHAHAHAHAH
I CAN'T BELIEVE IT! HER TOE IS STUCK!
YAH! HA! Ha!
I loved to hear mom laugh. Sometimes she laughed 'til she cried.
RRRING
Huh? aw! Let 'em CALL Back!
HALLO? LOLEK? WHAT?! I CAN'T BELIEVE- WHAT? NO!
HAHAHAHA!
OY! WHAT HAPPENED?
TURN OFF THE TELEVISION, ARTIE!
IT WAS LOLEK!
Lolek was my uncle Herman's son. They were the only members of Mom's Family that survived Hitler.
HERMAN DIED JUST NOW FROM A HIT-AND-RUN DRIVER WHILE WALKING HIS DOGS!
HA CLIK
OH MY GOD!
Mom never Recovered from the Blow, and we never watched Dick Van Dyke again.

THE POWER OF NARRATIVE!

Washington Heights, nyc. ca.1952

"What a curious feeling," said Alice. "I must be shutting up like a telescope!"

YAWN

I guess I was three or four, a bit old to still be in a crib.

did so indeed, and much sooner than she ha
d: before she had drunk half the bottle she

SLEEP TIGHT, SWEETIE. WE'LL READ AGAIN TOMORROW!

G'NIGHT, MOMMY.

HUNH? BWAAAAAAA AAIEEAIEEE

I'M SHRINKING! I'M GETTING SMALLER! I'M GONNA DISAPPEAR!

SHH! IT'S ONLY A DREAM!

HELP ME! BWAAH!

I-I'LL GET A SLICE OF BREAD. IT'LL MAKE YOU BIGGER!

BUT MY PARENTS HAD TO KEEP BRINGING FOOD 'TIL DAWN BEFORE I'D EVEN TRY TO CLOSE MY EYES AGAIN.

And Lewis Carroll still leaves me unhinged.

THE ART of FICTION ILLUSTRATED

Charles stared vacantly out the window of his Hamburg hotel.

LENI WARNED ME TO STAY AWAY SO HORST DOESN'T FIND OUT ABOUT US.

AND IF LUCILLE EVEN SUSPECTED, SHE'D SLASH MY DAMN THROAT!

Herald Tribune
Terrorists Regroup in Germany

He glared at the wall clock...

IT'S TOO HARD, KEEPING ALL THESE LIES STRAIGHT.

and he browsed the comics in his Herald Tribune...

But all he could think about were Leni's lips... and comics

HOW ABOUT MY LIPS?!
I'VE LOST INTEREST IN EVERYTHING.

and now that he'd turned 50, even those didn't excite him that much!

He should've stayed in Chicago with Lucille and the kids...

HE'S GONE TOO FAR!

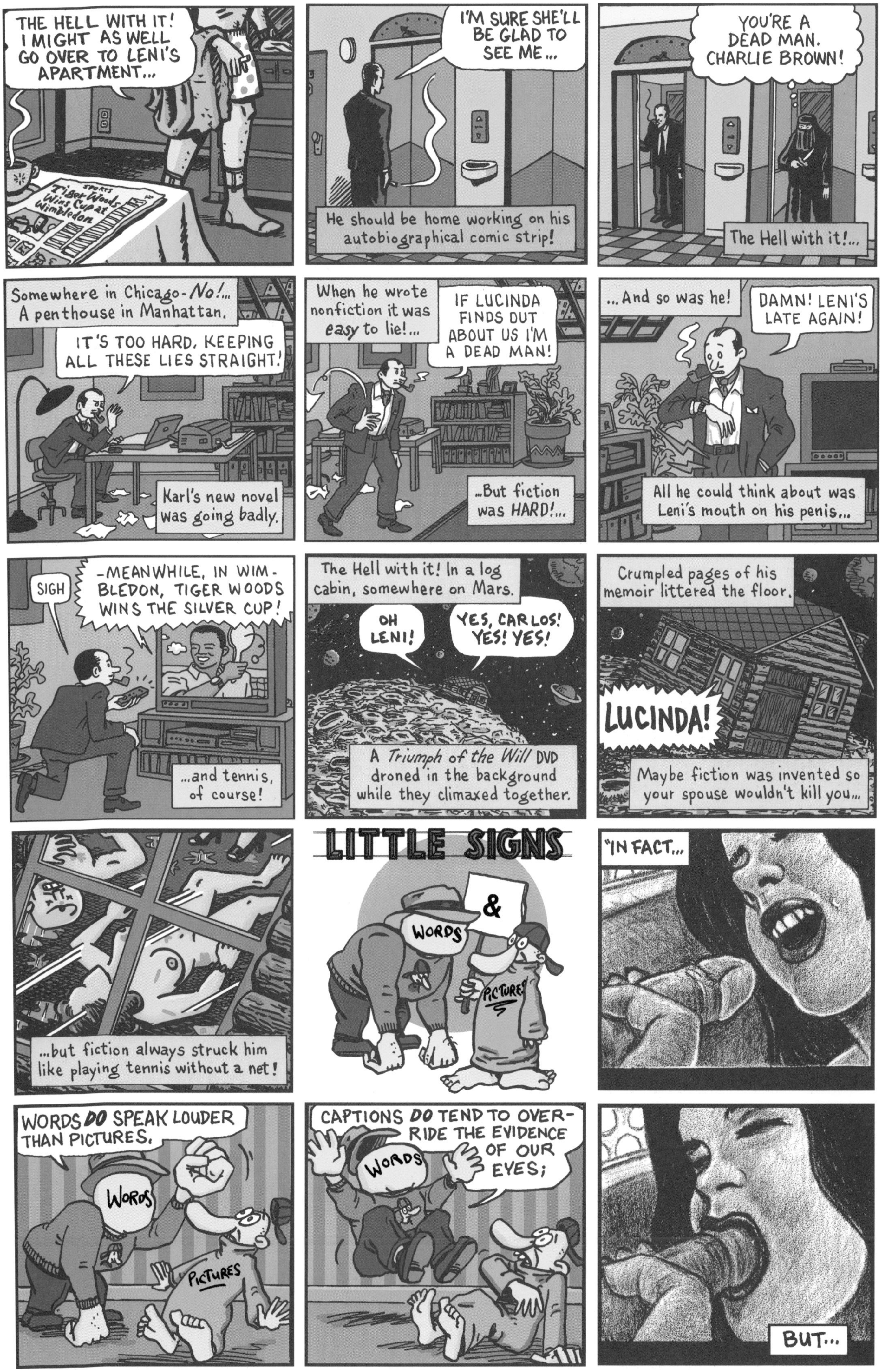
THE HELL WITH IT! I MIGHT AS WELL GO OVER TO LENI'S APARTMENT...
SPORTS Tiger Woods Wins Cup at Wimbledon
I'M SURE SHE'LL BE GLAD TO SEE ME...
He should be home working on his autobiographical comic strip!
YOU'RE A DEAD MAN. CHARLIE BROWN!
The Hell with it!...
Somewhere in Chicago-No!... A penthouse in Manhattan.
IT'S TOO HARD, KEEPING ALL THESE LIES STRAIGHT!
Karl's new novel was going badly.
When he wrote nonfiction it was easy to lie!...
IF LUCINDA FINDS OUT ABOUT US I'M A DEAD MAN!
..But fiction was HARD!...
...And so was he!
DAMN! LENI'S LATE AGAIN!
All he could think about was Leni's mouth on his penis...
SIGH
-MEANWHILE, IN WIMBLEDON, TIGER WOODS WINS THE SILVER CUP!
...and tennis, of course!
The Hell with it! In a log cabin, somewhere on Mars.
OH LENI!
YES, CARLOS! YES! YES!
A Triumph of the Will DVD droned in the background while they climaxed together.
Crumpled pages of his memoir littered the floor.
LUCINDA!
Maybe fiction was invented so your spouse wouldn't kill you...
...but fiction always struck him like playing tennis without a net!
LITTLE SIGNS
&
WORDS
PICTURES
"IN FACT...
WORDS DO SPEAK LOUDER THAN PICTURES,
WORDS
PICTURES
CAPTIONS DO TEND TO OVERRIDE THE EVIDENCE OF OUR EYES;
WORDS
BUT...

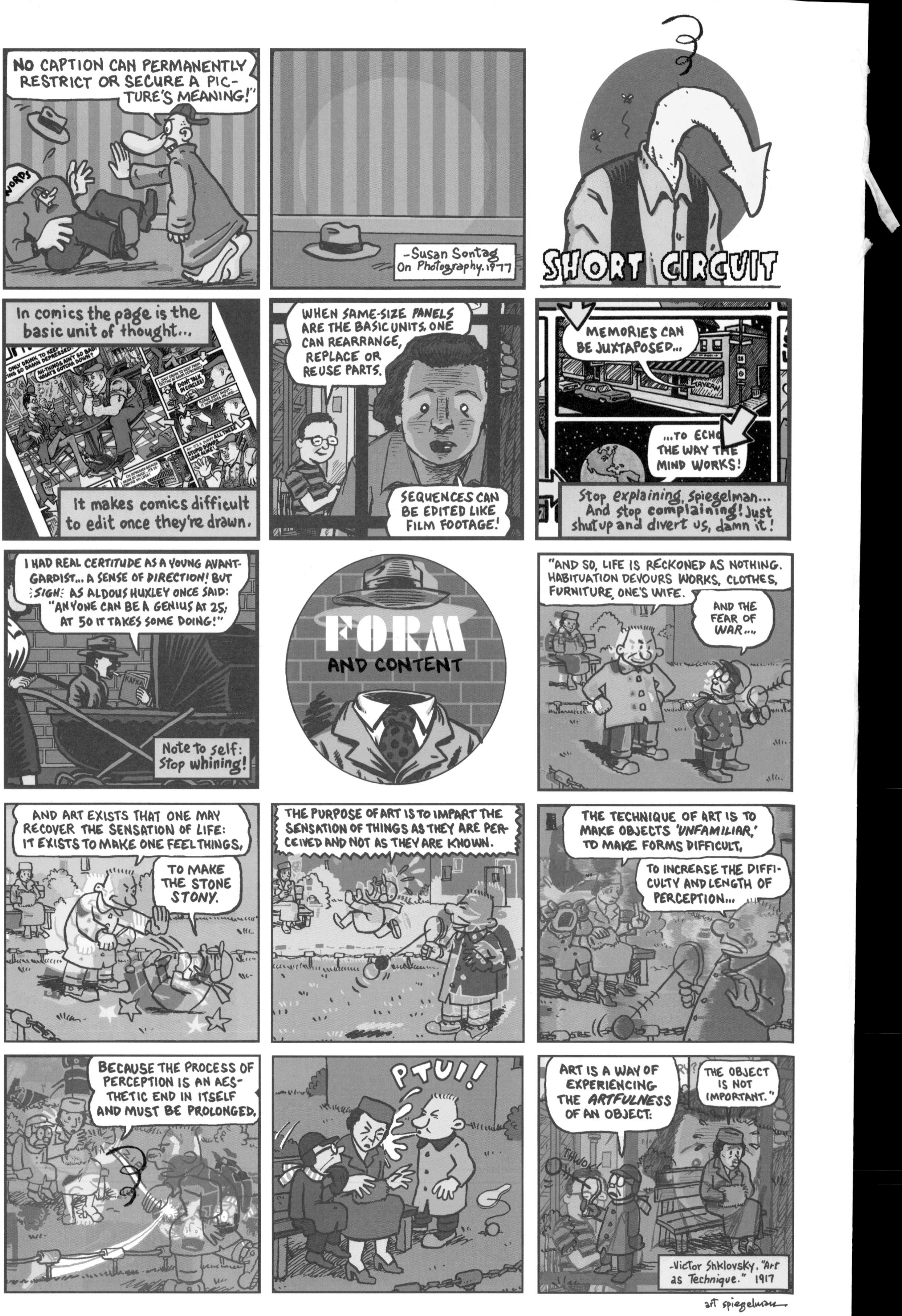
NO CAPTION CAN PERMANENTLY RESTRICT OR SECURE A PIC- TURE'S MEANING!"
WORDS
-Susan Sontag On Photography. 1977
SHORT CIRCUIT
In comics the page is the basic unit of thought...
It makes comics difficult to edit once they're drawn.
WHEN SAME-SIZE PANELS ARE THE BASIC UNITS, ONE CAN REARRANGE, REPLACE OR REUSE PARTS.
SEQUENCES CAN BE EDITED LIKE FILM FOOTAGE!
MEMORIES CAN BE JUXTAPOSED...
TAVERN
...TO ECHO THE WAY THE MIND WORKS!
Stop explaining, Spiegelman... And stop complaining! Just shut up and divert us, damn it!
I HAD REAL CERTITUDE AS A YOUNG AVANT-GARDIST... A SENSE OF DIRECTION! BUT SIGH: AS ALDOUS HUXLEY ONCE SAID: "ANYONE CAN BE A GENIUS AT 25; AT 50 IT TAKES SOME DOING!"
KAFKA
Note to self: Stop whining!
FORM AND CONTENT
"AND SO, LIFE IS RECKONED AS NOTHING. HABITUATION DEVOURS WORKS, CLOTHES, FURNITURE, ONE'S WIFE,
AND THE FEAR OF WAR....
AND ART EXISTS THAT ONE MAY RECOVER THE SENSATION OF LIFE: IT EXISTS TO MAKE ONE FEEL THINGS,
TO MAKE THE STONE STONY.
THE PURPOSE OF ART IS TO IMPART THE SENSATION OF THINGS AS THEY ARE PERCEIVED AND NOT AS THEY ARE KNOWN.
THE TECHNIQUE OF ART IS TO MAKE OBJECTS 'UNFAMILIAR,' TO MAKE FORMS DIFFICULT,
TO INCREASE THE DIFFICULTY AND LENGTH OF PERCEPTION...
BECAUSE THE PROCESS OF PERCEPTION IS AN AESTHETIC END IN ITSELF AND MUST BE PROLONGED.
PTUI!
ART IS A WAY OF EXPERIENCING THE ARTFULNESS OF AN OBJECT:
THE OBJECT IS NOT IMPORTANT."
THWOK
-Victor Shklovsky, "Art as Technique." 1917
art spiegelman

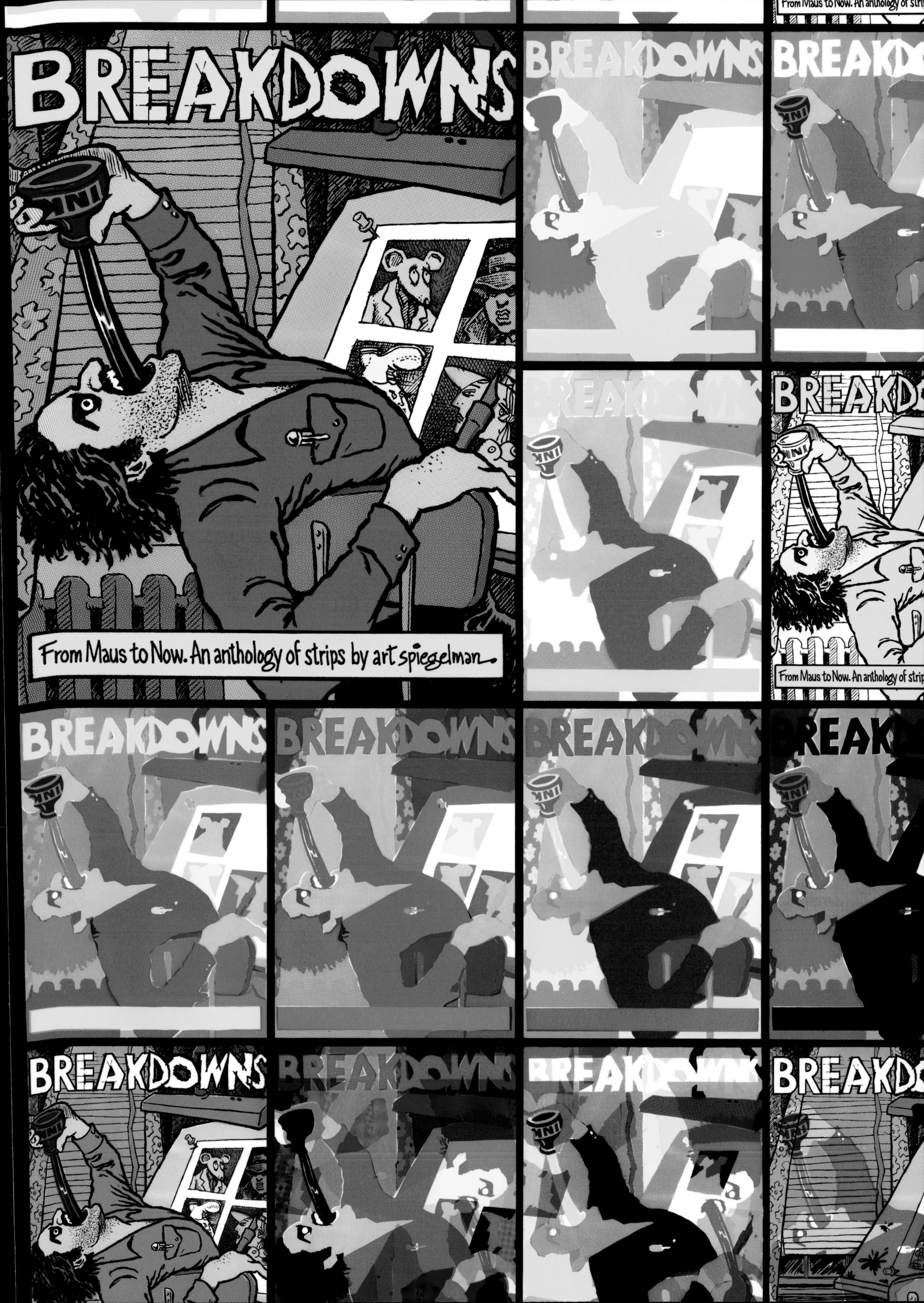
BREAKDOWNS
INK
From Maus to Now. An anthology of strips by art spiegelman

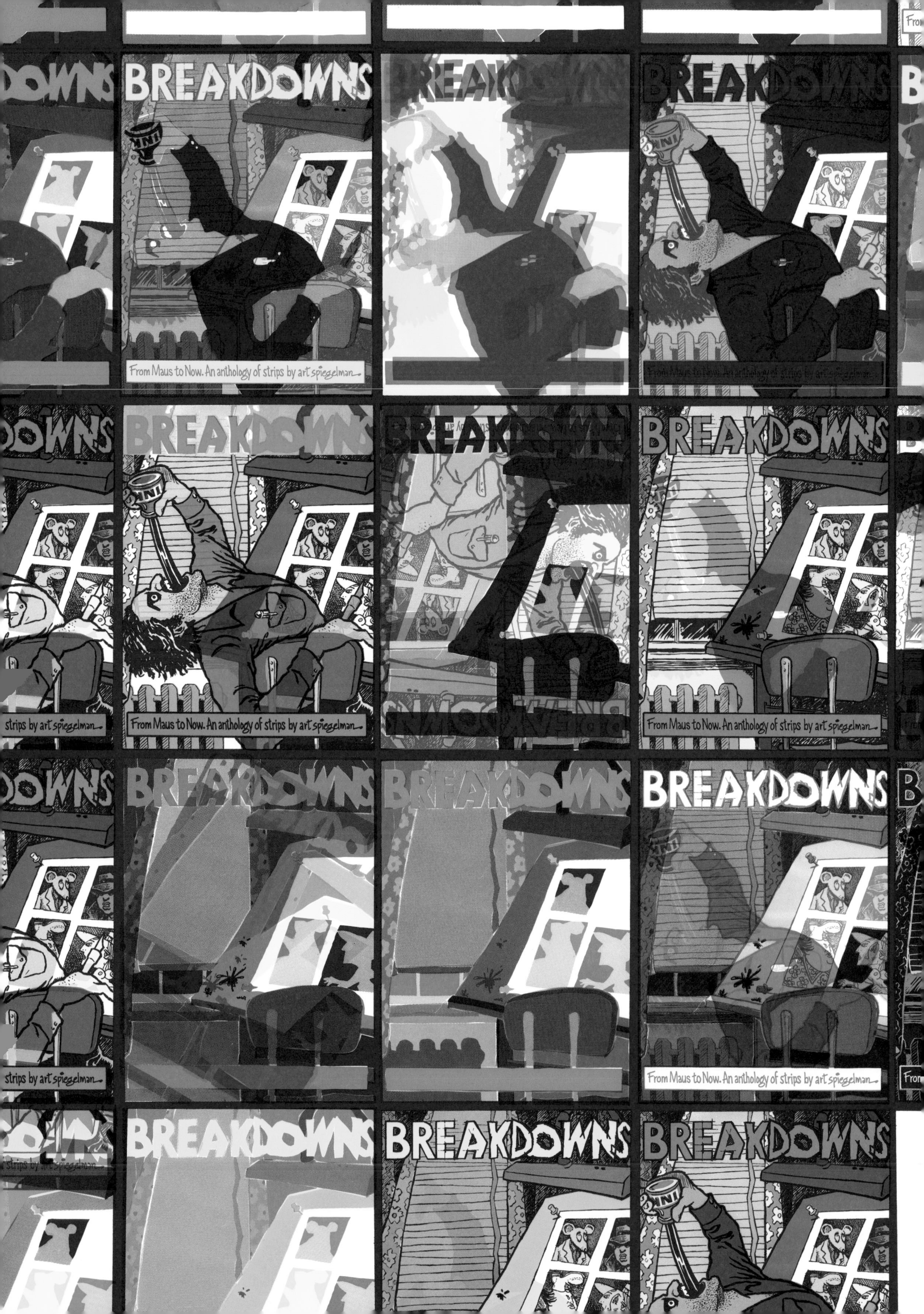
BREAKDOWNS
From Maus to Now. An anthology of strips by art spiegelman

DON'T BELIEVE EVERYTHING YOU READ!...

The publishing information on the following two pages is *incorrect*.

This book is *not* published by NOSTALGIA PRESS.

(Therein hangs a tale, one better left untold. Just let it be known that this book could not have been more aptly named...)

BREAKDOWNS. Published by:

BELIER PRESS

P.O. BOX 'C'
GRACIE STATION
NEW YORK, N.Y. 10028

(Additional copies available from Bélier Press for $8.95 post paid.)

International Standard Book Number: 0-914646-14-1

Library of Congress Catalogue Card Number: 77-93591

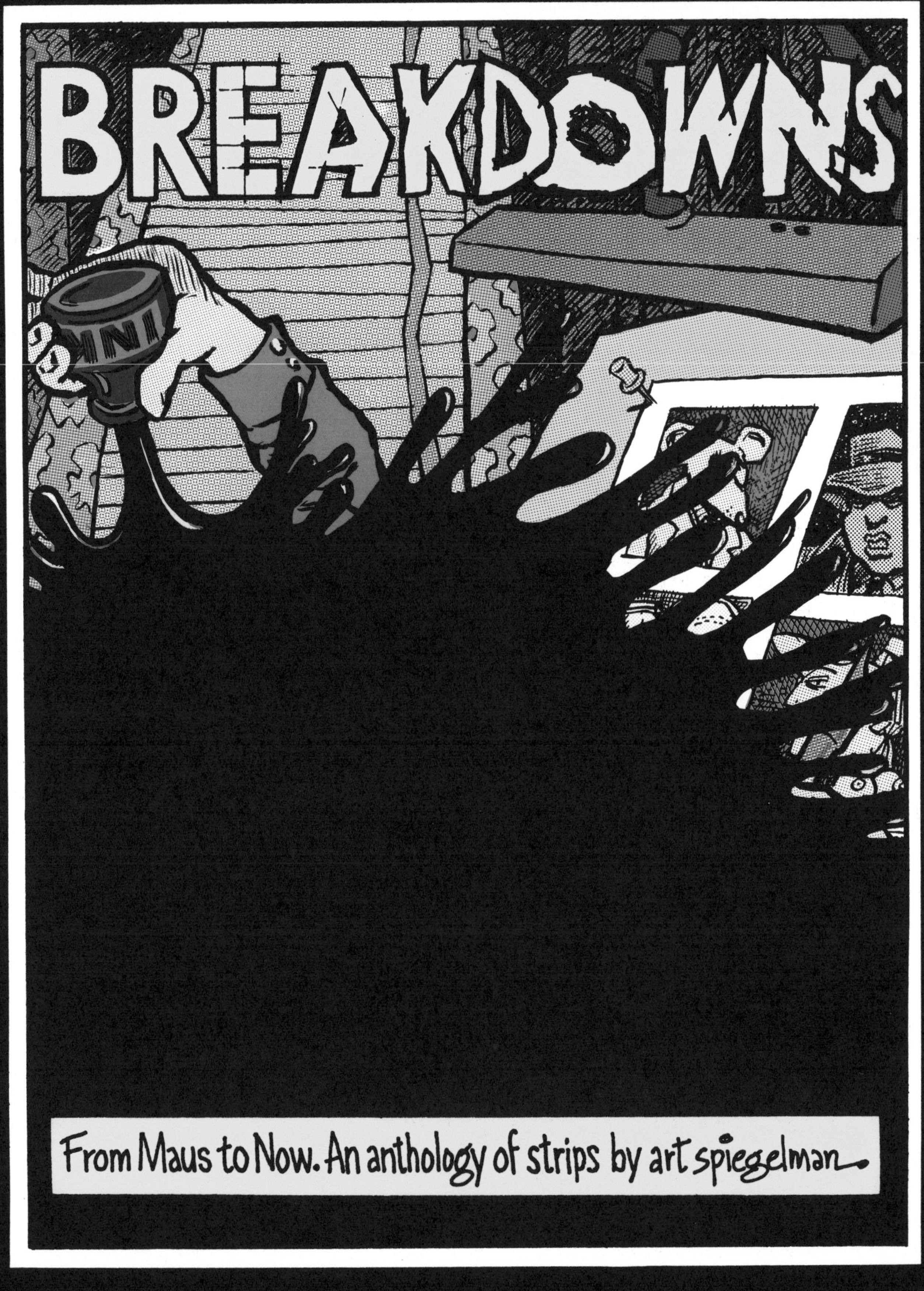
BREAKDOWNS
From Maus to Now. An anthology of strips by art spiegelman

NOSTALGIA PRESS INC. NEW YORK

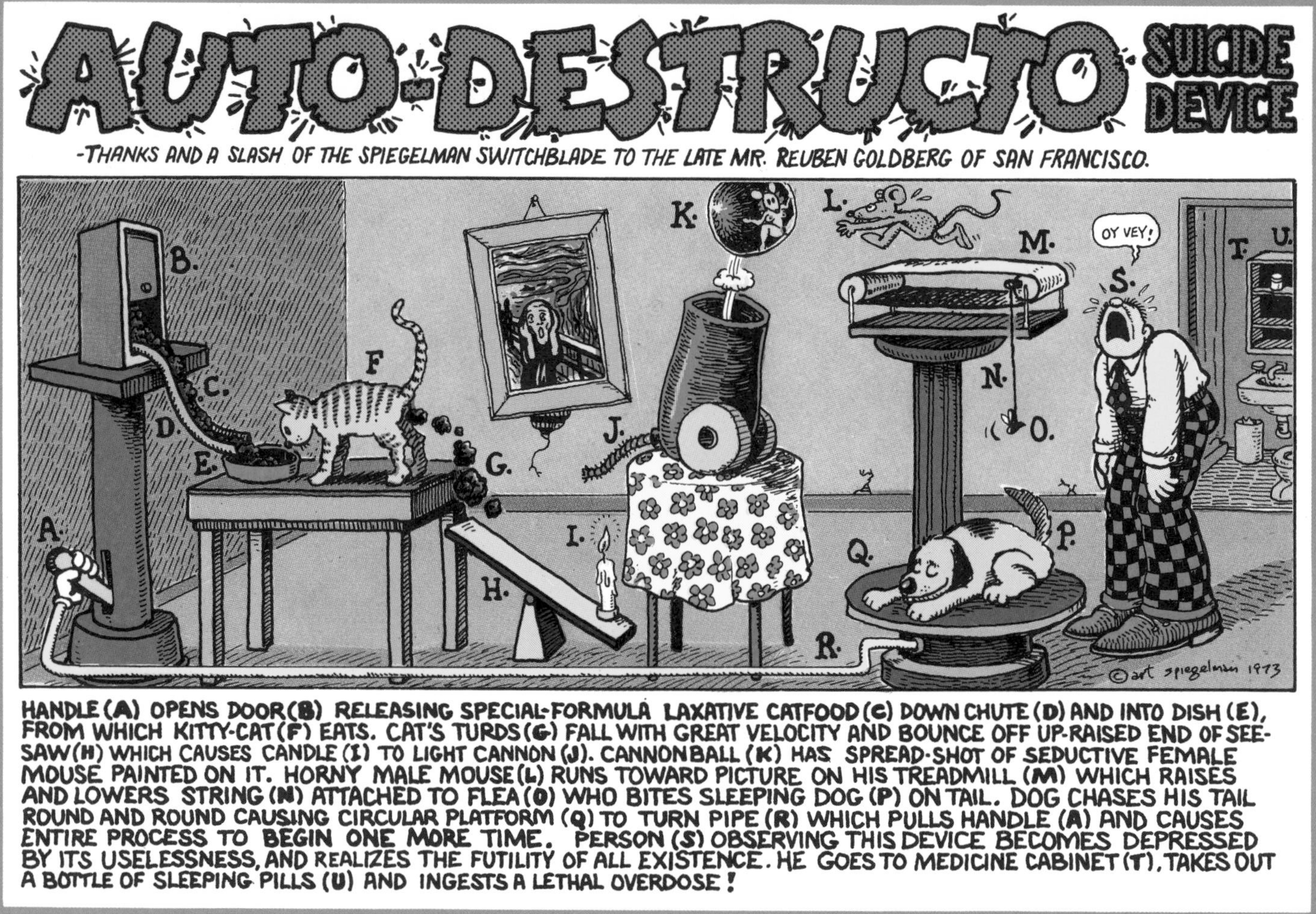
AUTO-DESTRUCTO SUICIDE DEVICE
-THANKS AND A SLASH OF THE SPIEGELMAN SWITCHBLADE TO THE LATE MR. REUBEN GOLDBERG OF SAN FRANCISCO.
OY VEY!
©art spiegelman 1973
HANDLE (A) OPENS DOOR (B) RELEASING SPECIAL-FORMULA LAXATIVE CATFOOD (C) DOWN CHUTE (D) AND INTO DISH (E), FROM WHICH KITTY-CAT (F) EATS. CAT'S TURDS (G) FALL WITH GREAT VELOCITY AND BOUNCE OFF UP-RAISED END OF SEE-SAW (H) WHICH CAUSES CANDLE (I) TO LIGHT CANNON (J). CANNONBALL (K) HAS SPREAD-SHOT OF SEDUCTIVE FEMALE MOUSE PAINTED ON IT. HORNY MALE MOUSE (L) RUNS TOWARD PICTURE ON HIS TREADMILL (M) WHICH RAISES AND LOWERS STRING (N) ATTACHED TO FLEA (O) WHO BITES SLEEPING DOG (P) ON TAIL. DOG CHASES HIS TAIL ROUND AND ROUND CAUSING CIRCULAR PLATFORM (Q) TO TURN PIPE (R) WHICH PULLS HANDLE (A) AND CAUSES ENTIRE PROCESS TO BEGIN ONE MORE TIME. PERSON (S) OBSERVING THIS DEVICE BECOMES DEPRESSED BY ITS USELESSNESS, AND REALIZES THE FUTILITY OF ALL EXISTENCE. HE GOES TO MEDICINE CABINET (T), TAKES OUT A BOTTLE OF SLEEPING PILLS (U) AND INGESTS A LETHAL OVERDOSE!

International Standard Book Number: 0-87897-052-5

First printing: December 1977
Printed in the United States of America.

Published by Nostalgia Press Inc., Box 293, Franklin Sq., New York. 11010
Additional copies available from the Publisher for $ 8.95, post paid.

Printed by Quad Offset Corporation, 250 Hudson St., N.Y.C., N.Y. 10013.
Bound by Publishers Book Bindery, Inc., Long Island City, N.Y. 11101.

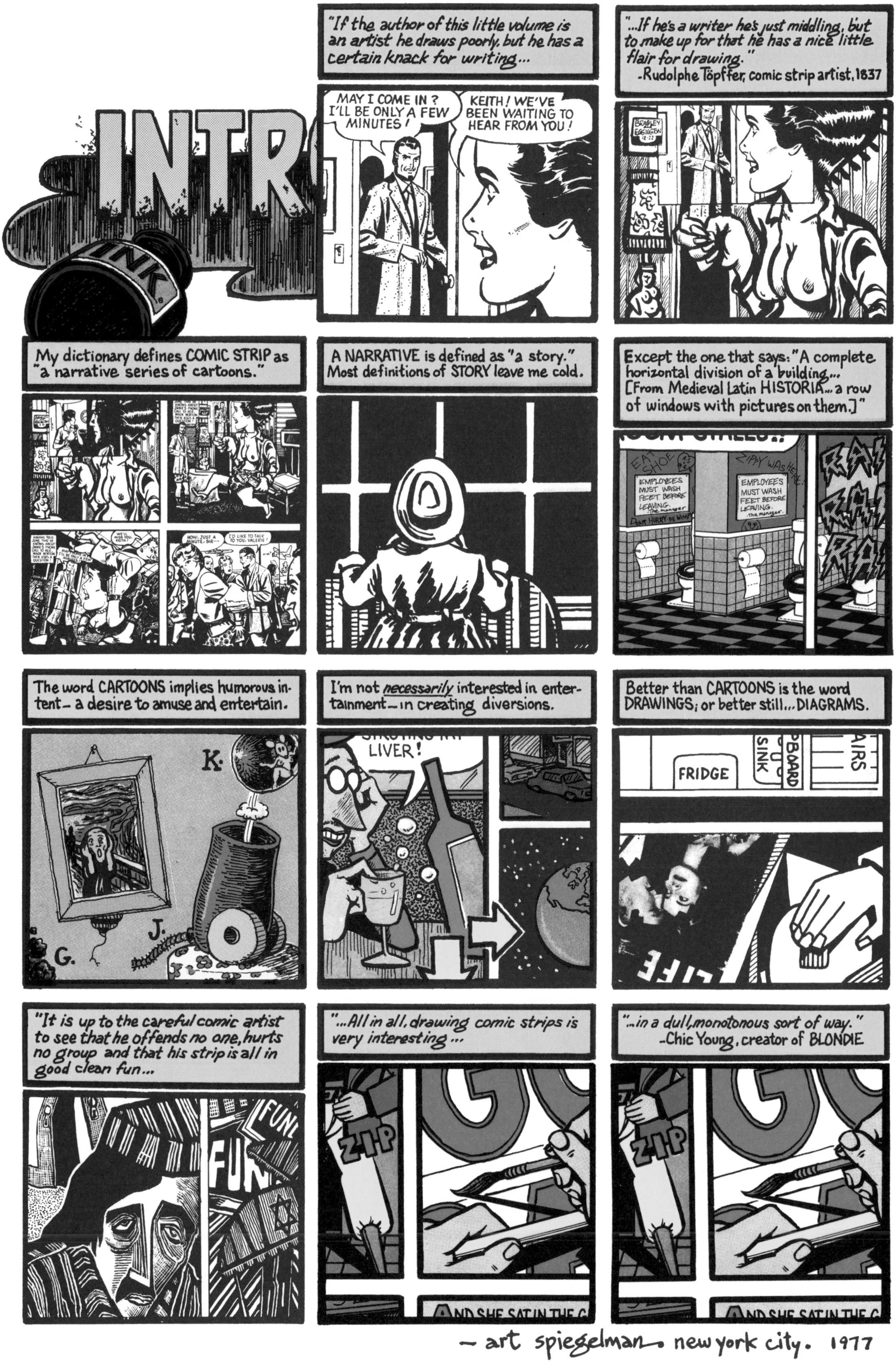
"If the author of this little volume is an artist he draws poorly, but he has a certain knack for writing...
"...If he's a writer he's just middling, but to make up for that he has a nice little flair for drawing."
-Rudolphe Töpffer, comic strip artist, 1837
INTRO
INK
MAY I COME IN? I'LL BE ONLY A FEW MINUTES!
KEITH! WE'VE BEEN WAITING TO HEAR FROM YOU!
My dictionary defines COMIC STRIP as "a narrative series of cartoons."
A NARRATIVE is defined as "a story." Most definitions of STORY leave me cold.
Except the one that says: "A complete horizontal division of a building... [From Medieval Latin HISTORIA... a row of windows with pictures on them.]"
EMPLOYEES MUST WASH FEET BEFORE LEAVING. -The manager
ZIPPY WAS HERE
The word CARTOONS implies humorous intent - a desire to amuse and entertain.
I'm not necessarily interested in entertainment - in creating diversions.
Better than CARTOONS is the word DRAWINGS; or better still... DIAGRAMS.
LIVER!
FRIDGE
SINK
"It is up to the careful comic artist to see that he offends no one, hurts no group and that his strip is all in good clean fun...
"...All in all, drawing comic strips is very interesting...
"...in a dull, monotonous sort of way."
-Chic Young, creator of BLONDIE
FUN
ZIP
AND SHE SAT IN THE C
- art spiegelman. new york city. 1977

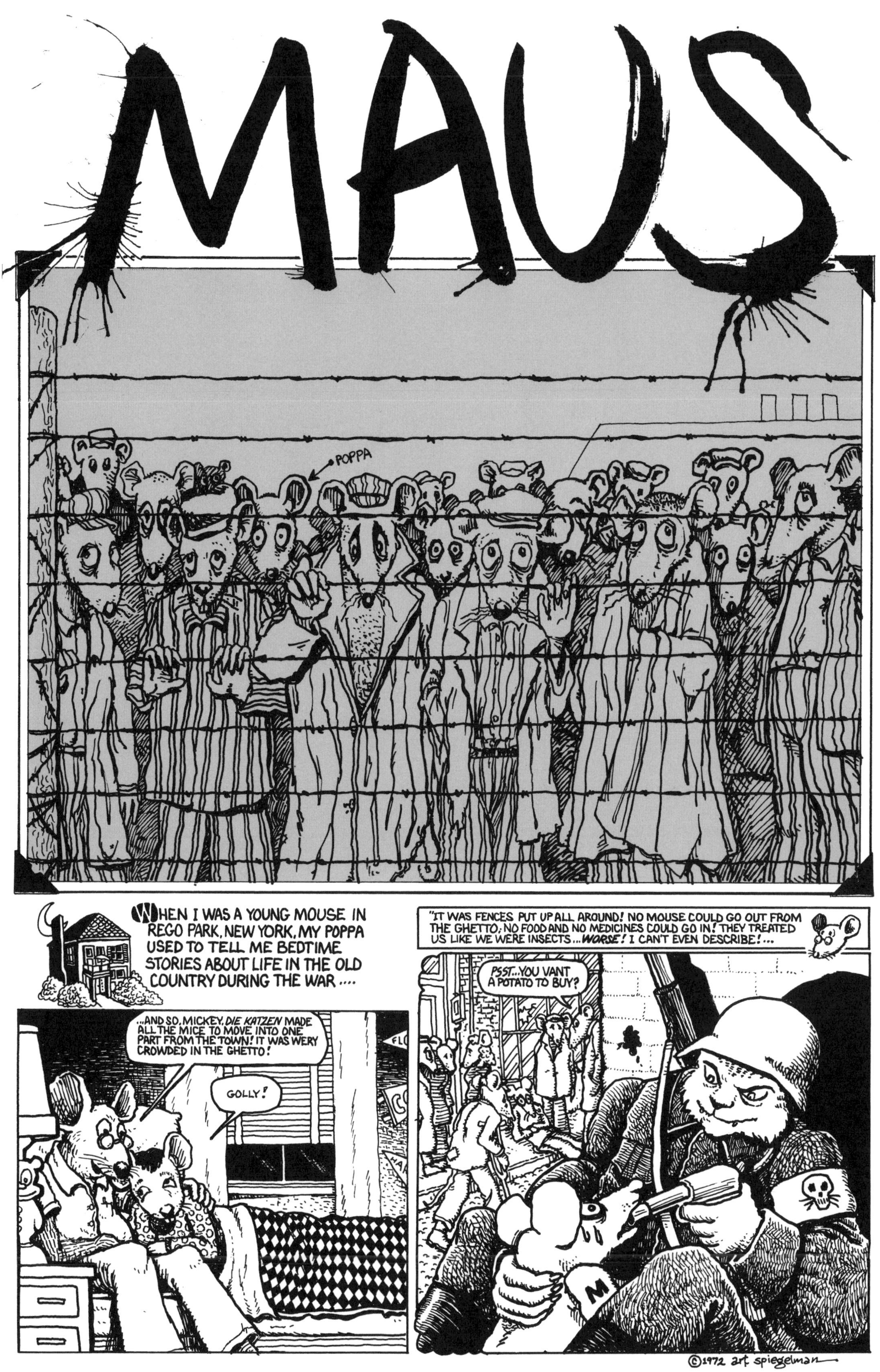
MAUS
POPPA
WHEN I WAS A YOUNG MOUSE IN REGO PARK, NEW YORK, MY POPPA USED TO TELL ME BEDTIME STORIES ABOUT LIFE IN THE OLD COUNTRY DURING THE WAR ....
...AND SO, MICKEY, DIE KATZEN MADE ALL THE MICE TO MOVE INTO ONE PART FROM THE TOWN! IT WAS WERY CROWDED IN THE GHETTO!
GOLLY!
"IT WAS FENCES PUT UP ALL AROUND! NO MOUSE COULD GO OUT FROM THE GHETTO; NO FOOD AND NO MEDICINES COULD GO IN! THEY TREATED US LIKE WE WERE INSECTS...WORSE! I CAN'T EVEN DESCRIBE!...
PSST...YOU VANT A POTATO TO BUY?
M
©1972 art spiegelman

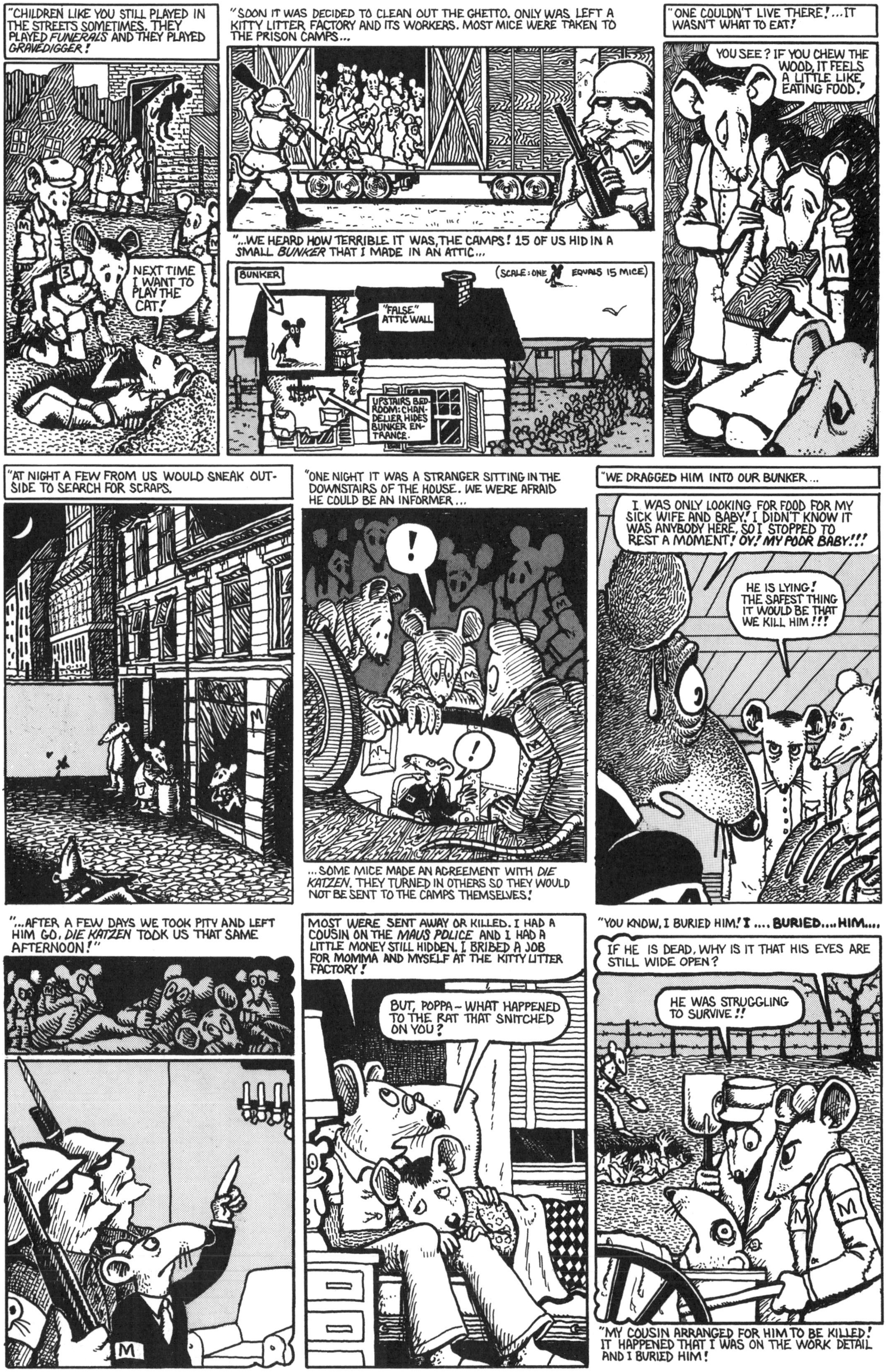
"CHILDREN LIKE YOU STILL PLAYED IN THE STREETS SOMETIMES. THEY PLAYED FUNERALS AND THEY PLAYED GRAVEDIGGER!
NEXT TIME I WANT TO PLAY THE CAT!
"SOON IT WAS DECIDED TO CLEAN OUT THE GHETTO. ONLY WAS LEFT A KITTY LITTER FACTORY AND ITS WORKERS. MOST MICE WERE TAKEN TO THE PRISON CAMPS...
"...WE HEARD HOW TERRIBLE IT WAS, THE CAMPS! 15 OF US HID IN A SMALL BUNKER THAT I MADE IN AN ATTIC...
BUNKER
(SCALE: ONE EQUALS 15 MICE)
"FALSE" ATTIC WALL
UPSTAIRS BEDROOM: CHANDELIER HIDES BUNKER ENTRANCE.
"ONE COULDN'T LIVE THERE!... IT WASN'T WHAT TO EAT!
YOU SEE? IF YOU CHEW THE WOOD, IT FEELS A LITTLE LIKE EATING FOOD.
M
"AT NIGHT A FEW FROM US WOULD SNEAK OUTSIDE TO SEARCH FOR SCRAPS.
M
"ONE NIGHT IT WAS A STRANGER SITTING IN THE DOWNSTAIRS OF THE HOUSE. WE WERE AFRAID HE COULD BE AN INFORMER...
!
!
...SOME MICE MADE AN AGREEMENT WITH DIE KATZEN. THEY TURNED IN OTHERS SO THEY WOULD NOT BE SENT TO THE CAMPS THEMSELVES!
"WE DRAGGED HIM INTO OUR BUNKER...
I WAS ONLY LOOKING FOR FOOD FOR MY SICK WIFE AND BABY! I DIDN'T KNOW IT WAS ANYBODY HERE, SO I STOPPED TO REST A MOMENT! OY! MY POOR BABY!!!
HE IS LYING! THE SAFEST THING IT WOULD BE THAT WE KILL HIM!!!
"...AFTER A FEW DAYS WE TOOK PITY AND LEFT HIM GO. DIE KATZEN TOOK US THAT SAME AFTERNOON!"
M
MOST WERE SENT AWAY OR KILLED. I HAD A COUSIN ON THE MAUS POLICE AND I HAD A LITTLE MONEY STILL HIDDEN. I BRIBED A JOB FOR MOMMA AND MYSELF AT THE KITTY LITTER FACTORY!
BUT, POPPA – WHAT HAPPENED TO THE RAT THAT SNITCHED ON YOU?
"YOU KNOW, I BURIED HIM! I .... BURIED.... HIM....
IF HE IS DEAD, WHY IS IT THAT HIS EYES ARE STILL WIDE OPEN?
HE WAS STRUGGLING TO SURVIVE!!
M
"MY COUSIN ARRANGED FOR HIM TO BE KILLED! IT HAPPENED THAT I WAS ON THE WORK DETAIL AND I BURIED HIM!

"SO... IN TIME THE FACTORY WAS LIQUIDATED TOO, AND THE WHOLE GHETTO WAS CLOSED! AGAIN SOME FROM US MANAGED TO HIDE IN A CORNER...

"DIE KATZEN MADE GUARDS AROUND TO STARVE OUT THOSE LEFT IN THE GHETTO...

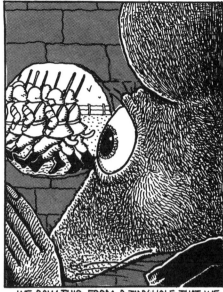

"AFTER SOME WEEKS THE GUARDS LEFT US FOR DEAD...

...WE SAW THIS FROM A TINY HOLE THAT WE MADE IN THE WALL WITH A SMALL PIECE WOOD AND OUR NAILS!

"THERE WAS NO FOOD AT ALL! WE LEFT THE BUNKER, BUT WHERE TO GO? WHERE TO GO?...

"YOUR MOMMA AND I SNEAKED TO HER OLD HOME TOWN....LOCAL CATS SHE KNEW BEFORE THE WAR WERE AFRAID TO HIDE US!

GO AWAY! QUICKLY!!!

"WITH MY LAST MONEY I MADE A DEAL WITH ONE CAT TO SNEAK US OUT FROM THE COUNTRY...

OKAY—MEET ME HERE TOMORROW MORNING! I'LL HIDE YOU IN MY WAGON!

THANK YOU, THANK YOU!

"THE NEXT MORNING WAS ONLY WAITING DIE KATZEN!....

...THEY SENT US TO MAUSCHWITZ....

"...MAUSCHWITZ..."

...AND SO IT WAS.... I CAN TELL YOU NO MORE NOW....

...I CAN TELL YOU NO MORE.... IT'S TIME TO GO TO SLEEP, MICKEY!

UH-HUH... G'NIGHT, POPPA!

Zip·a·Tones
and Moiré Melodies
featuring
Skeeter Grant's
SKINLESS PERKINS
*MOIRÉ (MŌ-RAY): A wavy, rippled pattern.
A "SOMERSAULT" FOR YOUR AMUSEMENT!
D-D-Dot's all, folks!
Zip·a·Tones
© art spiegelman 1972

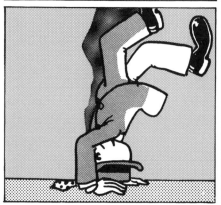

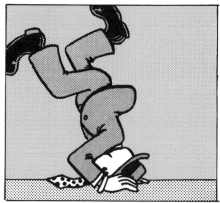

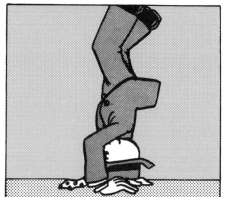

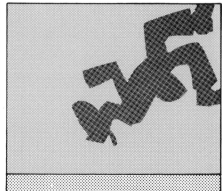

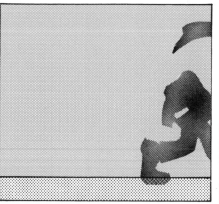

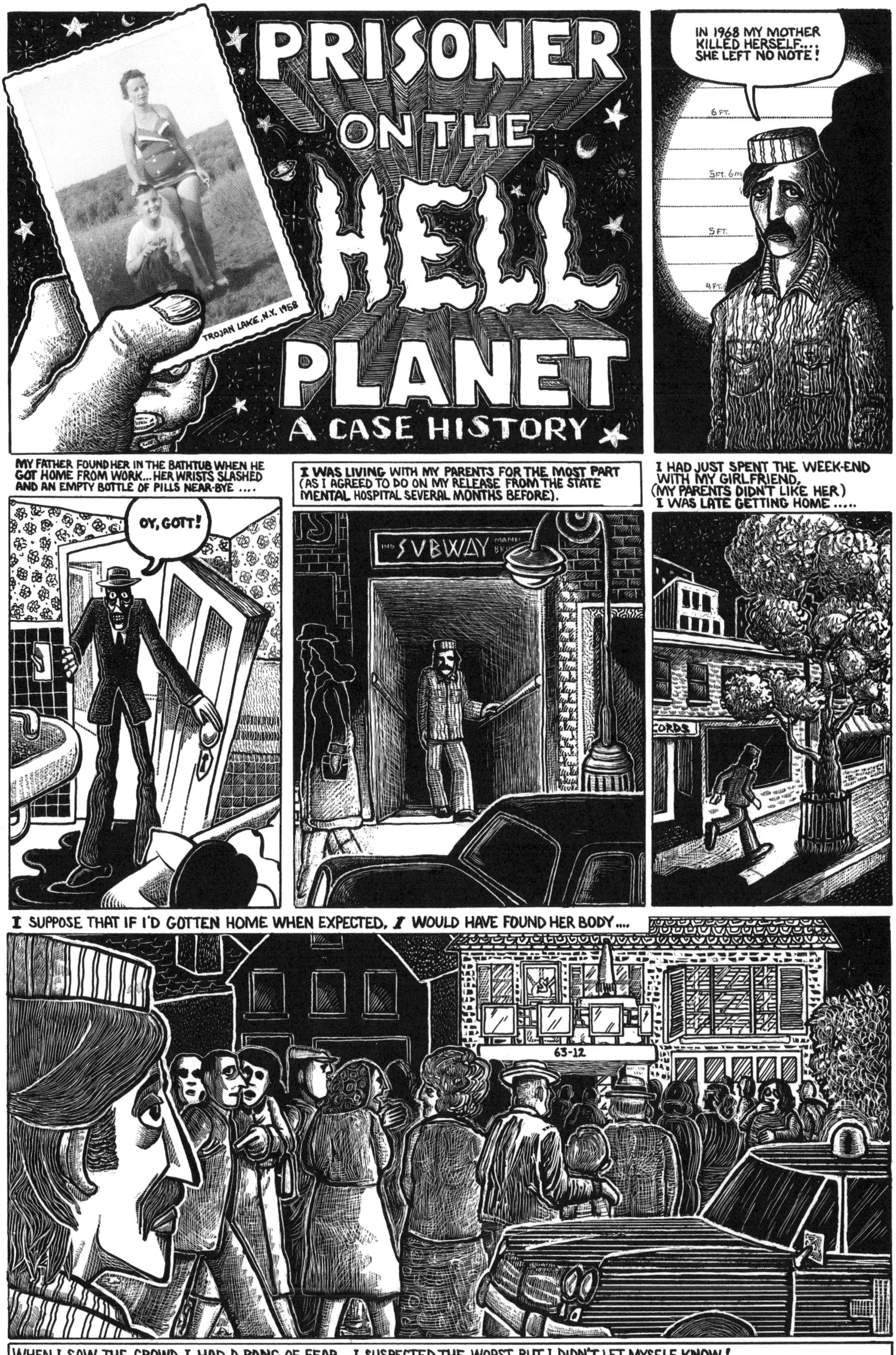

PRISONER ON THE HELL PLANET
A CASE HISTORY
TROJAN LAKE, N.Y. 1958
IN 1968 MY MOTHER KILLED HERSELF... SHE LEFT NO NOTE!
MY FATHER FOUND HER IN THE BATHTUB WHEN HE GOT HOME FROM WORK... HER WRISTS SLASHED AND AN EMPTY BOTTLE OF PILLS NEAR-BYE ....
OY, GOTT!
I WAS LIVING WITH MY PARENTS FOR THE MOST PART (AS I AGREED TO DO ON MY RELEASE FROM THE STATE MENTAL HOSPITAL SEVERAL MONTHS BEFORE).
SUBWAY
I HAD JUST SPENT THE WEEK-END WITH MY GIRLFRIEND, (MY PARENTS DIDN'T LIKE HER) I WAS LATE GETTING HOME .....
I SUPPOSE THAT IF I'D GOTTEN HOME WHEN EXPECTED, I WOULD HAVE FOUND HER BODY....
63-12
WHEN I SAW THE CROWD I HAD A PANG OF FEAR... I SUSPECTED THE WORST, BUT I DIDN'T LET MYSELF KNOW!

A COUSIN HERDED ME AWAY FROM THE SCENE:

COME TO THE DOCTOR'S.... YOUR MOTHER IS -AH- SICK!... HE WILL EXPLAIN ......

DOCTOR ORENS LIVED NEARBYE.....

SIT DOWN, ARTHUR... I THOUGHT I SHOULD BE THE ONE TO TELL YOU...

YOUR MOTHER KILLED HER- SELF—SHE'S DEAD!

I COULD AVOID THE TRUTH NO LONGER—THE DOCTOR'S WORDS CLATTERED INSIDE ME.... I FELT CONFUSED; I FELT ANGRY; I FELT NUMB!... I DIDN'T EXACTLY FEEL LIKE CRYING, BUT FIGURED I SHOULD!....

SHE'S DEAD! A SUICIDE!

NOW, NOW BOY...

NO, LET HIM CRY— IT'S GOOD FOR HIM!

WE WENT HOME...MY FATHER HAD COM- PLETELY FALLEN APART! ....

OY, ARTIE! WHY? WHY! SUCH A TRAGEDY! AND NOT EVEN A NOTE!!!

I WAS EXPECTED TO COMFORT HIM!

MOTHER... MOTHER...

SOMEHOW THE FUNERAL ARRANGE- MENTS WERE MADE...

...AND FOR $950°° WE HAVE A BRONZE CASKET WITH BRONZE COLORED VELVET- OF COURSE, FOR $2,000°° WE CAN...

PROTECT WHAT YOU HAVE

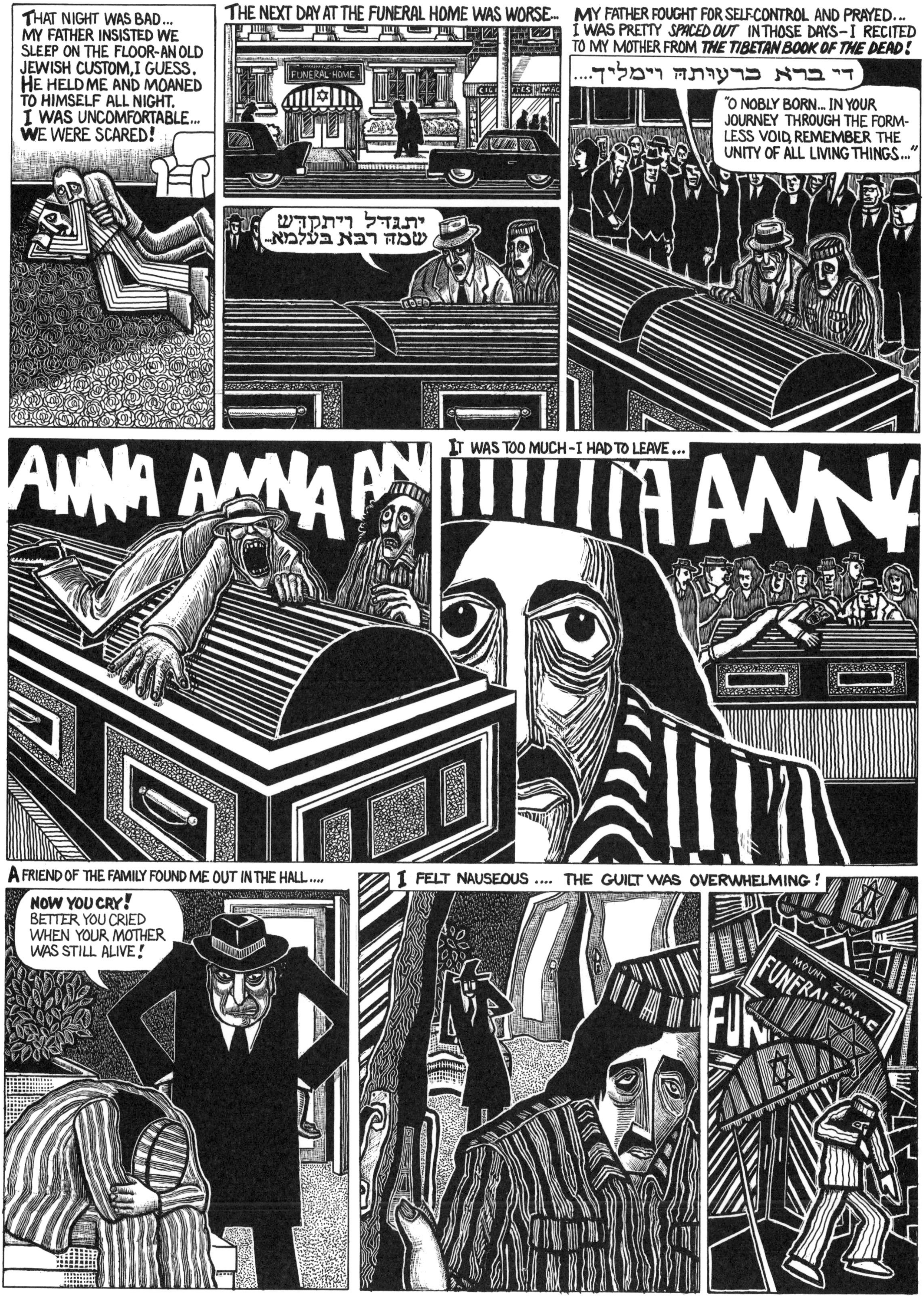
THAT NIGHT WAS BAD... MY FATHER INSISTED WE SLEEP ON THE FLOOR-AN OLD JEWISH CUSTOM, I GUESS. HE HELD ME AND MOANED TO HIMSELF ALL NIGHT. I WAS UNCOMFORTABLE... WE WERE SCARED!
THE NEXT DAY AT THE FUNERAL HOME WAS WORSE...
MOUNT ZION FUNERAL HOME
CIGARETTES
יתגדל ויתקדש שמה רבא בעלמא...
MY FATHER FOUGHT FOR SELF-CONTROL AND PRAYED... I WAS PRETTY *SPACED OUT* IN THOSE DAYS - I RECITED TO MY MOTHER FROM ***THE TIBETAN BOOK OF THE DEAD!***
די ברא כרעותה וימליך....
"O NOBLY BORN... IN YOUR JOURNEY THROUGH THE FORMLESS VOID, REMEMBER THE UNITY OF ALL LIVING THINGS..."
ANNA ANNA AN
IT WAS TOO MUCH - I HAD TO LEAVE...
A ANNA
A FRIEND OF THE FAMILY FOUND ME OUT IN THE HALL....
NOW YOU CRY! BETTER YOU CRIED WHEN YOUR MOTHER WAS STILL ALIVE!
I FELT NAUSEOUS .... THE GUILT WAS OVERWHELMING!
MOUNT ZION FUNERAL HOME
FUN

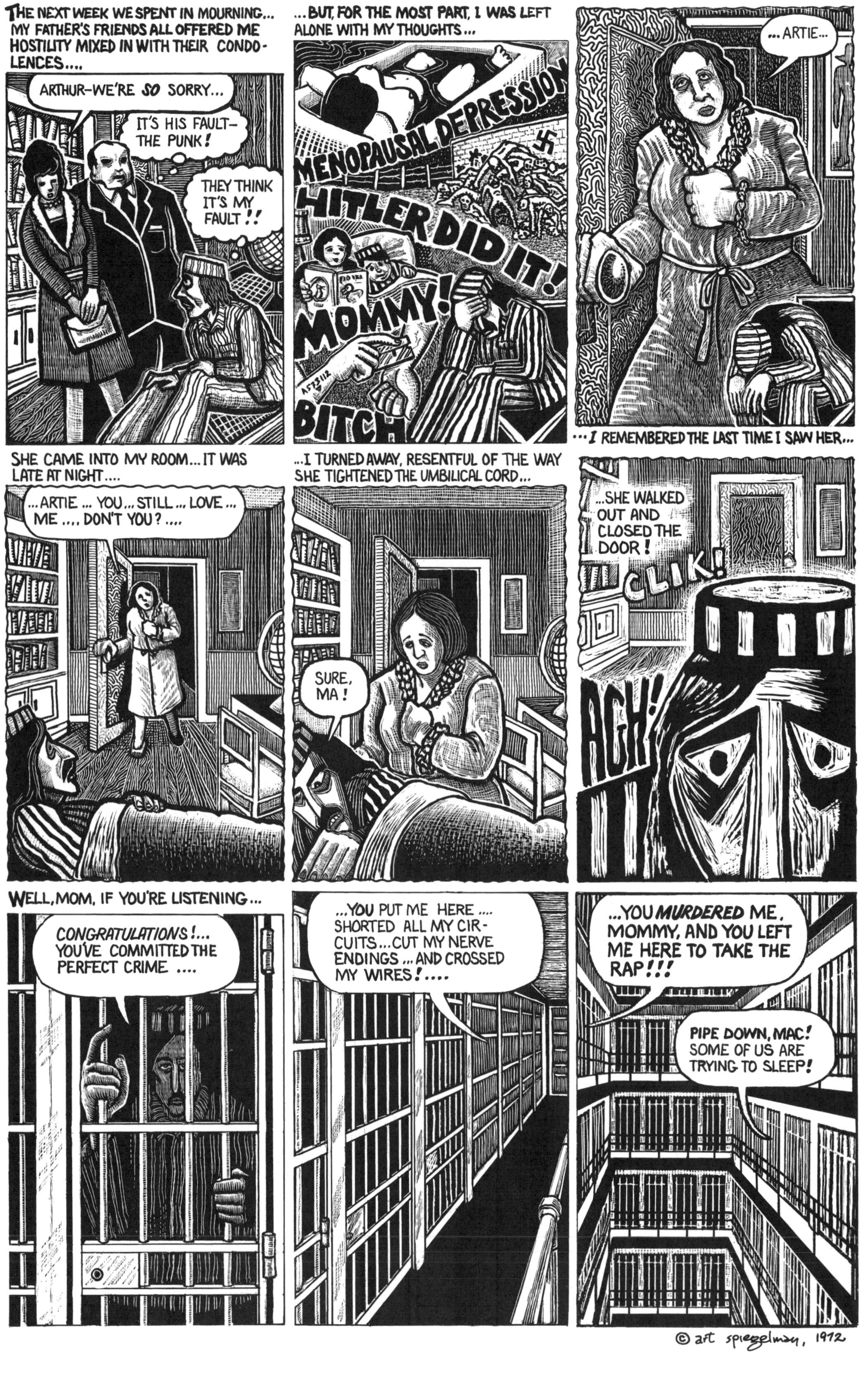
THE NEXT WEEK WE SPENT IN MOURNING... MY FATHER'S FRIENDS ALL OFFERED ME HOSTILITY MIXED IN WITH THEIR CONDO-LENCES....
ARTHUR-WE'RE SO SORRY...
IT'S HIS FAULT-THE PUNK!
THEY THINK IT'S MY FAULT!!
...BUT, FOR THE MOST PART, I WAS LEFT ALONE WITH MY THOUGHTS...
MENOPAUSAL DEPRESSION
HITLER DID IT!
MOMMY!
BITCH
...ARTIE...
...I REMEMBERED THE LAST TIME I SAW HER...
SHE CAME INTO MY ROOM... IT WAS LATE AT NIGHT....
...ARTIE ... YOU... STILL... LOVE... ME .... DON'T YOU? ....
...I TURNED AWAY, RESENTFUL OF THE WAY SHE TIGHTENED THE UMBILICAL CORD...
SURE, MA!
...SHE WALKED OUT AND CLOSED THE DOOR!
CLIK!
AGH!
WELL, MOM, IF YOU'RE LISTENING...
CONGRATULATIONS!... YOU'VE COMMITTED THE PERFECT CRIME ....
...YOU PUT ME HERE .... SHORTED ALL MY CIR-CUITS...CUT MY NERVE ENDINGS ... AND CROSSED MY WIRES!....
...YOU MURDERED ME, MOMMY, AND YOU LEFT ME HERE TO TAKE THE RAP!!!
PIPE DOWN, MAC! SOME OF US ARE TRYING TO SLEEP!
© art spiegelman, 1972

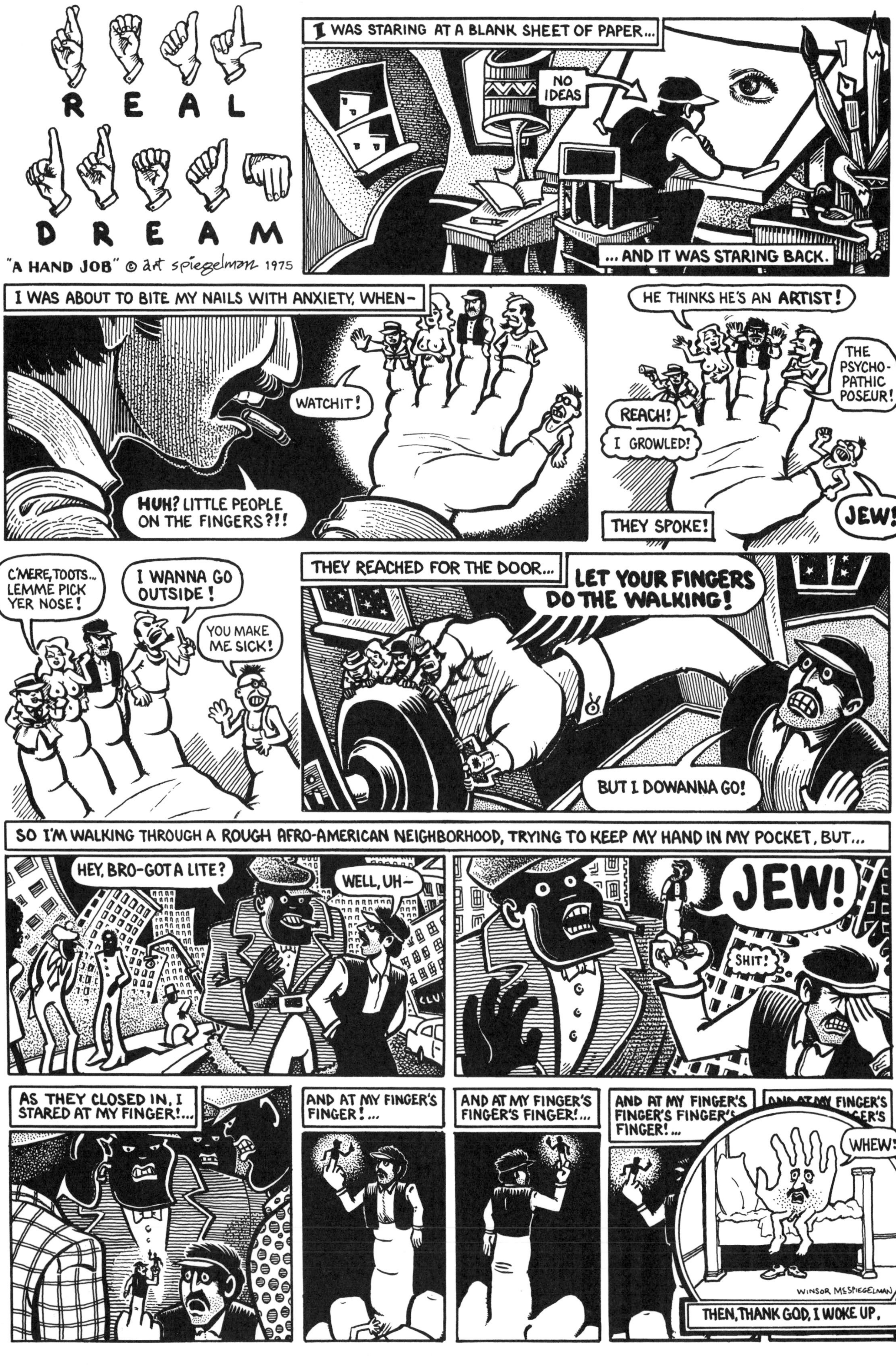

REAL
DREAM
"A HAND JOB" © art spiegelman 1975
I WAS STARING AT A BLANK SHEET OF PAPER...
NO IDEAS
...AND IT WAS STARING BACK.
I WAS ABOUT TO BITE MY NAILS WITH ANXIETY, WHEN–
WATCHIT!
HUH? LITTLE PEOPLE ON THE FINGERS?!!
HE THINKS HE'S AN ARTIST!
THE PSYCHO-PATHIC POSEUR!
REACH!
I GROWLED!
THEY SPOKE!
JEW!
C'MERE, TOOTS... LEMME PICK YER NOSE!
I WANNA GO OUTSIDE!
YOU MAKE ME SICK!
THEY REACHED FOR THE DOOR...
LET YOUR FINGERS DO THE WALKING!
BUT I DOWANNA GO!
SO I'M WALKING THROUGH A ROUGH AFRO-AMERICAN NEIGHBORHOOD, TRYING TO KEEP MY HAND IN MY POCKET, BUT...
HEY, BRO–GOT A LITE?
WELL, UH–
JEW!
SHIT!
AS THEY CLOSED IN, I STARED AT MY FINGER!...
AND AT MY FINGER'S FINGER!...
AND AT MY FINGER'S FINGER'S FINGER!...
AND AT MY FINGER'S FINGER'S FINGER'S FINGER!...
WHEW!
WINSOR McSPIEGELMAN
THEN, THANK GOD, I WOKE UP.

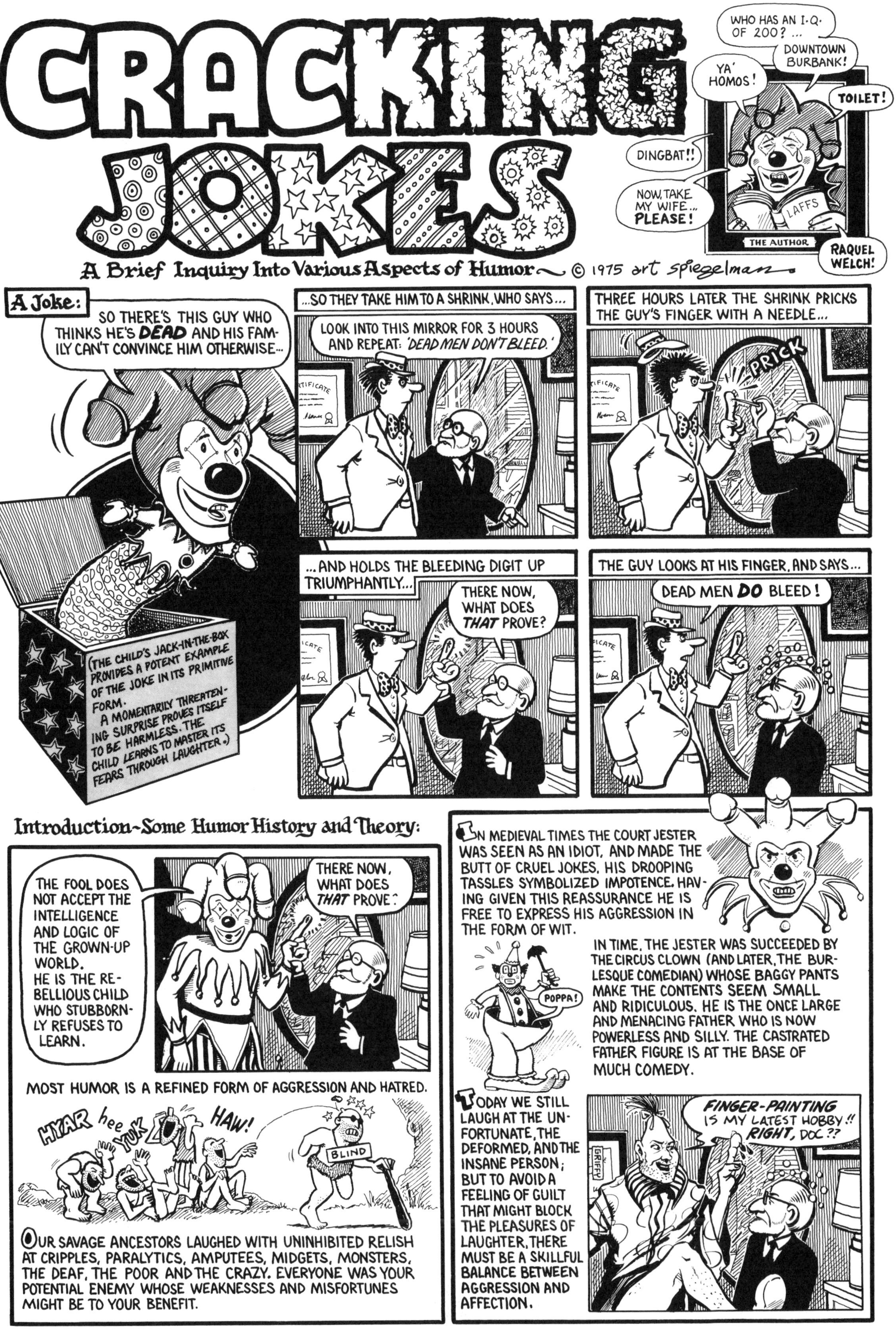
CRACKING JOKES
WHO HAS AN I.Q. OF 200? ...
DOWNTOWN BURBANK!
YA' HOMOS!
TOILET!
DINGBAT!!
NOW, TAKE MY WIFE... PLEASE!
LAFFS
THE AUTHOR
RAQUEL WELCH!
A Brief Inquiry Into Various Aspects of Humor ~ © 1975 art spiegelman
A Joke:
SO THERE'S THIS GUY WHO THINKS HE'S DEAD AND HIS FAMILY CAN'T CONVINCE HIM OTHERWISE...
(THE CHILD'S JACK-IN-THE-BOX PROVIDES A POTENT EXAMPLE OF THE JOKE IN ITS PRIMITIVE FORM. A MOMENTARILY THREATENING SURPRISE PROVES ITSELF TO BE HARMLESS. THE CHILD LEARNS TO MASTER ITS FEARS THROUGH LAUGHTER.)
...SO THEY TAKE HIM TO A SHRINK, WHO SAYS...
LOOK INTO THIS MIRROR FOR 3 HOURS AND REPEAT: 'DEAD MEN DON'T BLEED.'
THREE HOURS LATER THE SHRINK PRICKS THE GUY'S FINGER WITH A NEEDLE...
PRICK
...AND HOLDS THE BLEEDING DIGIT UP TRIUMPHANTLY...
THERE NOW, WHAT DOES THAT PROVE?
THE GUY LOOKS AT HIS FINGER, AND SAYS...
DEAD MEN DO BLEED!
Introduction~Some Humor History and Theory:
THE FOOL DOES NOT ACCEPT THE INTELLIGENCE AND LOGIC OF THE GROWN-UP WORLD. HE IS THE REBELLIOUS CHILD WHO STUBBORNLY REFUSES TO LEARN.
THERE NOW, WHAT DOES THAT PROVE?
MOST HUMOR IS A REFINED FORM OF AGGRESSION AND HATRED.
HYAR hee YUK HAW!
BLIND
OUR SAVAGE ANCESTORS LAUGHED WITH UNINHIBITED RELISH AT CRIPPLES, PARALYTICS, AMPUTEES, MIDGETS, MONSTERS, THE DEAF, THE POOR AND THE CRAZY. EVERYONE WAS YOUR POTENTIAL ENEMY WHOSE WEAKNESSES AND MISFORTUNES MIGHT BE TO YOUR BENEFIT.
IN MEDIEVAL TIMES THE COURT JESTER WAS SEEN AS AN IDIOT, AND MADE THE BUTT OF CRUEL JOKES. HIS DROOPING TASSLES SYMBOLIZED IMPOTENCE. HAVING GIVEN THIS REASSURANCE HE IS FREE TO EXPRESS HIS AGGRESSION IN THE FORM OF WIT.
POPPA!
IN TIME, THE JESTER WAS SUCCEEDED BY THE CIRCUS CLOWN (AND LATER, THE BURLESQUE COMEDIAN) WHOSE BAGGY PANTS MAKE THE CONTENTS SEEM SMALL AND RIDICULOUS. HE IS THE ONCE LARGE AND MENACING FATHER WHO IS NOW POWERLESS AND SILLY. THE CASTRATED FATHER FIGURE IS AT THE BASE OF MUCH COMEDY.
TODAY WE STILL LAUGH AT THE UNFORTUNATE, THE DEFORMED, AND THE INSANE PERSON; BUT TO AVOID A FEELING OF GUILT THAT MIGHT BLOCK THE PLEASURES OF LAUGHTER, THERE MUST BE A SKILLFUL BALANCE BETWEEN AGGRESSION AND AFFECTION.
FINGER-PAINTING IS MY LATEST HOBBY!! RIGHT, DOC??
GRIFFY

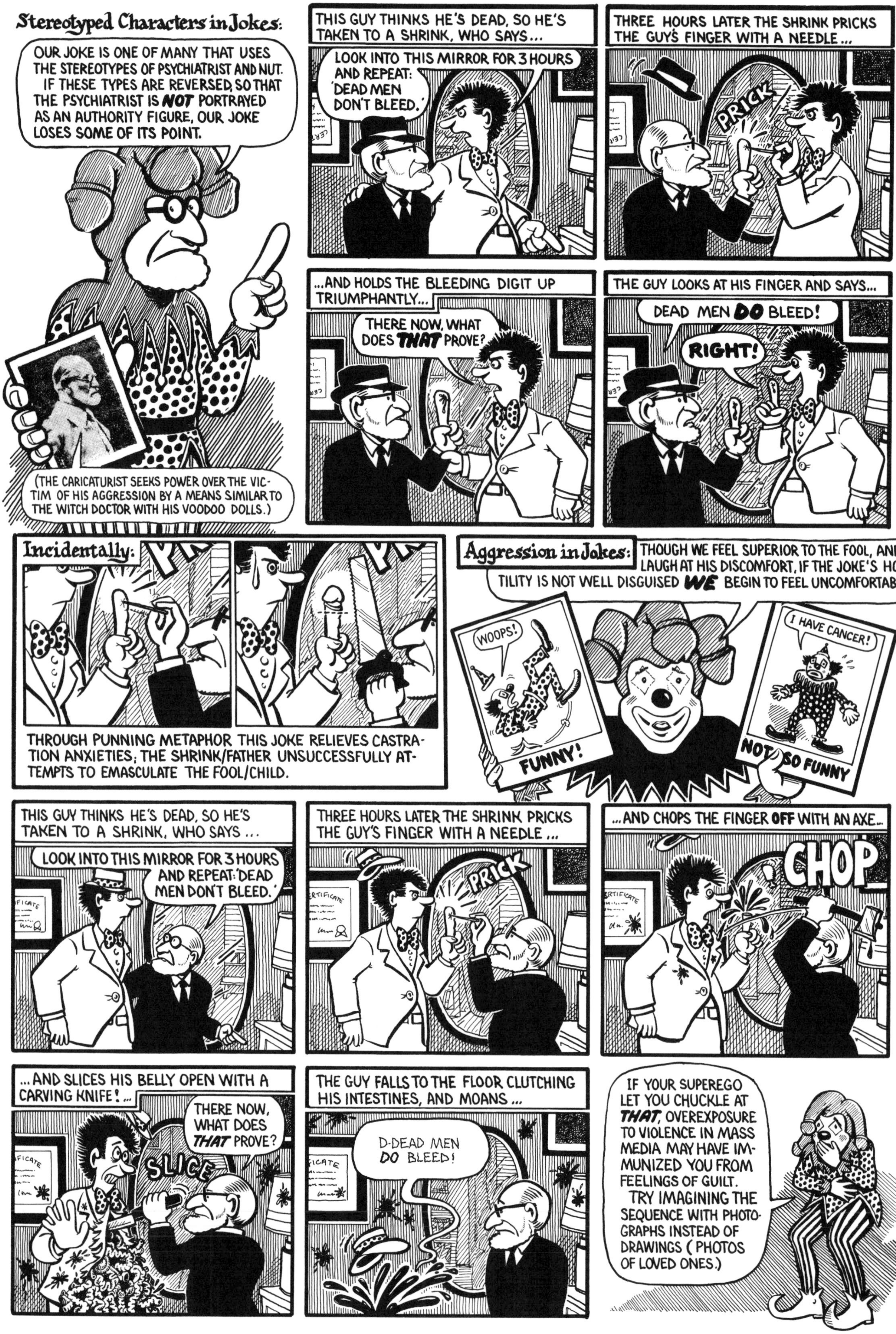
Stereotyped Characters in Jokes:
OUR JOKE IS ONE OF MANY THAT USES THE STEREOTYPES OF PSYCHIATRIST AND NUT. IF THESE TYPES ARE REVERSED, SO THAT THE PSYCHIATRIST IS NOT PORTRAYED AS AN AUTHORITY FIGURE, OUR JOKE LOSES SOME OF ITS POINT.
(THE CARICATURIST SEEKS POWER OVER THE VICTIM OF HIS AGGRESSION BY A MEANS SIMILAR TO THE WITCH DOCTOR WITH HIS VOODOO DOLLS.)
THIS GUY THINKS HE'S DEAD, SO HE'S TAKEN TO A SHRINK, WHO SAYS...
LOOK INTO THIS MIRROR FOR 3 HOURS AND REPEAT: 'DEAD MEN DON'T BLEED.'
THREE HOURS LATER THE SHRINK PRICKS THE GUY'S FINGER WITH A NEEDLE...
PRICK
...AND HOLDS THE BLEEDING DIGIT UP TRIUMPHANTLY...
THERE NOW, WHAT DOES THAT PROVE?
THE GUY LOOKS AT HIS FINGER AND SAYS...
DEAD MEN DO BLEED!
RIGHT!
Incidentally:
THROUGH PUNNING METAPHOR THIS JOKE RELIEVES CASTRATION ANXIETIES; THE SHRINK/FATHER UNSUCCESSFULLY ATTEMPTS TO EMASCULATE THE FOOL/CHILD.
Aggression in Jokes:
THOUGH WE FEEL SUPERIOR TO THE FOOL, AND LAUGH AT HIS DISCOMFORT, IF THE JOKE'S HOSTILITY IS NOT WELL DISGUISED WE BEGIN TO FEEL UNCOMFORTABLE.
WOOPS!
FUNNY!
I HAVE CANCER!
NOT SO FUNNY
THIS GUY THINKS HE'S DEAD, SO HE'S TAKEN TO A SHRINK, WHO SAYS...
LOOK INTO THIS MIRROR FOR 3 HOURS AND REPEAT: 'DEAD MEN DON'T BLEED.'
THREE HOURS LATER THE SHRINK PRICKS THE GUY'S FINGER WITH A NEEDLE...
PRICK
...AND CHOPS THE FINGER OFF WITH AN AXE...
CHOP
...AND SLICES HIS BELLY OPEN WITH A CARVING KNIFE!...
THERE NOW, WHAT DOES THAT PROVE?
SLICE
THE GUY FALLS TO THE FLOOR CLUTCHING HIS INTESTINES, AND MOANS...
D-DEAD MEN DO BLEED!
IF YOUR SUPEREGO LET YOU CHUCKLE AT THAT, OVEREXPOSURE TO VIOLENCE IN MASS MEDIA MAY HAVE IMMUNIZED YOU FROM FEELINGS OF GUILT. TRY IMAGINING THE SEQUENCE WITH PHOTOGRAPHS INSTEAD OF DRAWINGS (PHOTOS OF LOVED ONES.)

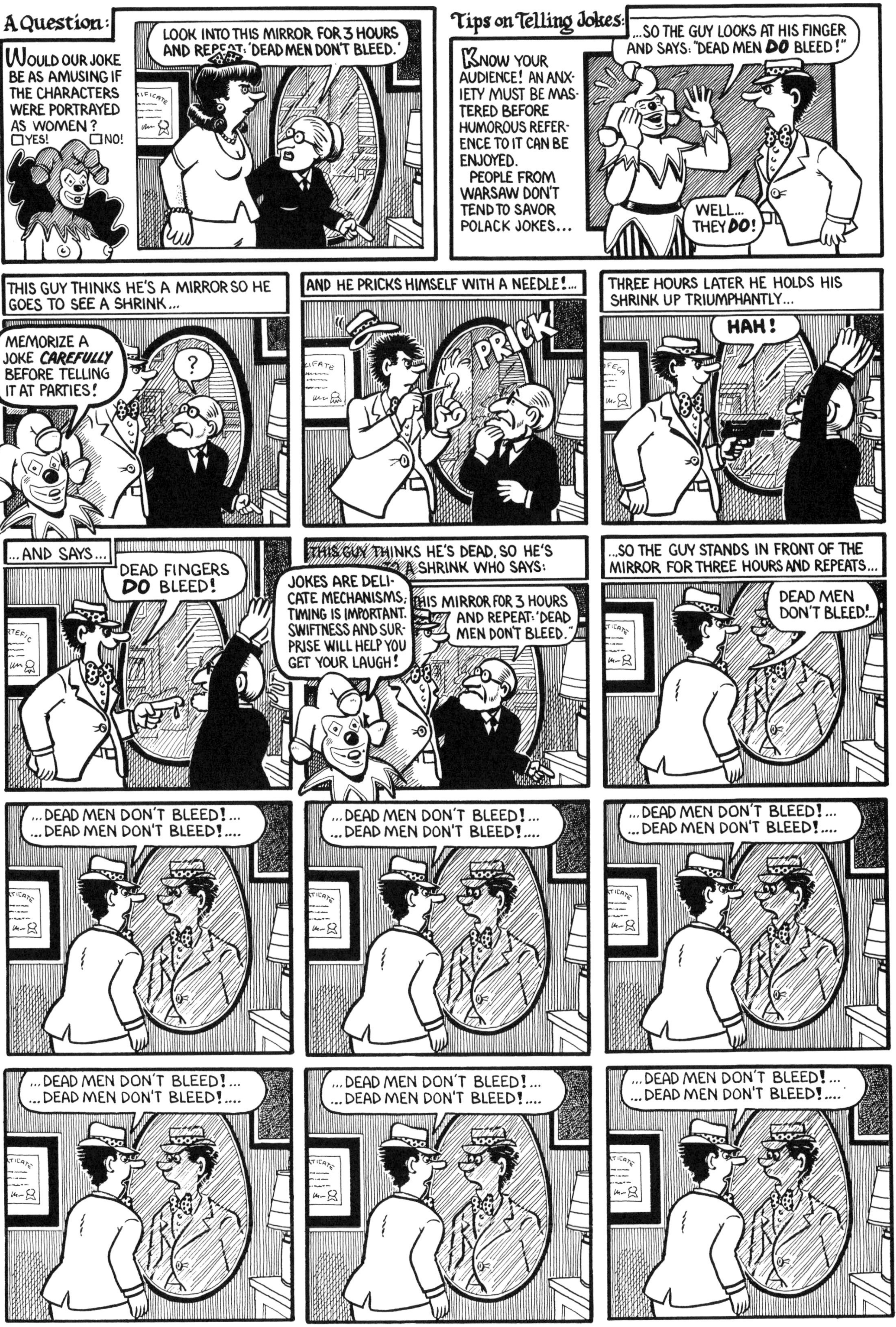
A Question:
WOULD OUR JOKE BE AS AMUSING IF THE CHARACTERS WERE PORTRAYED AS WOMEN?
☐YES! ☐NO!
LOOK INTO THIS MIRROR FOR 3 HOURS AND REPEAT: 'DEAD MEN DON'T BLEED.'
Tips on Telling Jokes:
KNOW YOUR AUDIENCE! AN ANXIETY MUST BE MASTERED BEFORE HUMOROUS REFERENCE TO IT CAN BE ENJOYED.
PEOPLE FROM WARSAW DON'T TEND TO SAVOR POLACK JOKES...
...SO THE GUY LOOKS AT HIS FINGER AND SAYS: "DEAD MEN DO BLEED!"
WELL... THEY DO!
THIS GUY THINKS HE'S A MIRROR SO HE GOES TO SEE A SHRINK...
MEMORIZE A JOKE CAREFULLY BEFORE TELLING IT AT PARTIES!
?
AND HE PRICKS HIMSELF WITH A NEEDLE!...
PRICK
THREE HOURS LATER HE HOLDS HIS SHRINK UP TRIUMPHANTLY...
HAH!
...AND SAYS...
DEAD FINGERS DO BLEED!
THIS GUY THINKS HE'S DEAD, SO HE'S
A SHRINK WHO SAYS:
JOKES ARE DELICATE MECHANISMS; TIMING IS IMPORTANT. SWIFTNESS AND SURPRISE WILL HELP YOU GET YOUR LAUGH!
THIS MIRROR FOR 3 HOURS AND REPEAT: 'DEAD MEN DON'T BLEED.'
...SO THE GUY STANDS IN FRONT OF THE MIRROR FOR THREE HOURS AND REPEATS...
DEAD MEN DON'T BLEED!...
...DEAD MEN DON'T BLEED!... ...DEAD MEN DON'T BLEED!....
...DEAD MEN DON'T BLEED!... ...DEAD MEN DON'T BLEED!....
...DEAD MEN DON'T BLEED!... ...DEAD MEN DON'T BLEED!....
...DEAD MEN DON'T BLEED!... ...DEAD MEN DON'T BLEED!....
...DEAD MEN DON'T BLEED!... ...DEAD MEN DON'T BLEED!....
...DEAD MEN DON'T BLEED!... ...DEAD MEN DON'T BLEED!...'

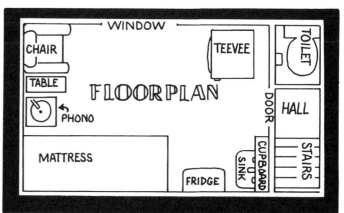

FLOORPLAN

WINDOW · CHAIR · TABLE · PHONO · MATTRESS · TEEVEE · TOILET · DOOR · HALL · STAIRS · CUPBOARD · SINK · FRIDGE

DON'T GET AROUND MUCH ANYMORE

TO BE READ TO THE ACCOMPANIMENT OF A DRIPPING FAUCET, SLOWLY.

copyright © 1973 ~ art spiegelman

MY CABLE BILL IS PAID UP FOR THE NEXT THREE MONTHS ....

...I HAVE A ROOM WITH A VIEW....

...AND WHOEVER LIVED HERE BEFORE LEFT A STACK OF LIFE MAGAZINES.

THE SOUND DOESN'T WORK ON THE TEEVEE...

...BUT I DON'T CARE. I OWN A RECORD!

THE REFRIGERATOR IS EMPTY.

THERE ARE SOME CRACKERS IN THE CUPBOARD, AND ...

...ALL THE WATER I CAN USE POURS OUT OF THE FAUCET WITH A FLICK OF THE WRIST.

...I DON'T GET AROUND MUCH ANYMORE...

THE CRACKERS AND WATER SHOULD KEEP ME GOING.

SEE THAT KID OUTSIDE?...

HE'S BEEN BOUNCING THAT BALL FOR HOURS ... YOU'D THINK HE'D GET TIRED!

I READ IN LIFE THAT ANN MARGRET IS MAKING A COMEBACK...

AT LAST A STAR? — SHE STILL HAS DOUBTS!

put more flavor in your life

AT LAST A STAR? — SHE STILL HAS DOUBTS!

put more flavor in your life

...AND MELVIN MADDOCKS DIDN'T CARE FOR HERMAN WOUK'S NEW BOOK!

THE RECORD SKIPS. IT HAS A SCRATCH.

-DID I TELL YOU THE REFRIGERATOR IS EMPTY?

3-12-73

WELL THERE IS MARSHA AND SHE IS A MIDGET AND SHE SITS IN THE GLASS BOOTH OF THE ROXIE AND SELLS TICKETS.

AND WELL THERE IS AUGIE AND HE PAINTS SIGNS IN A SHOP UP THE STREET. AND AUGIE IS A DWARF.

AND THAT IS ALL THERE IS TO IT EXCEPT FOR FOUL BERNIE THE GIMP. HE IS FOUL WHEN HE IS DRUNK AND HE IS ALWAYS DRUNK. SO HE IS CALLED FOUL BERNIE.

MARSHA

AUGIE

FOUL BERNIE

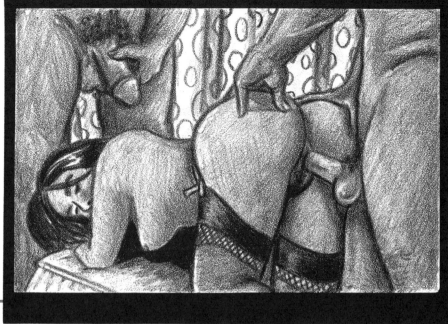

LITTLE SIGNS OF PASSION

WELL THERE WAS MARSHA AND SHE WAS A MIDGET...

...AND SHE SAT IN THE GLASS BOOTH OF THE ROXIE AND SOLD TICKETS.

BOTTOMS UP! CLUB

HARD-CORE FEATURE plus FULL COLOR ACTION SHORTS

BAR

AND WELL THERE WAS AUGIE AND HE PAINTED SIGNS IN A SHOP UP THE STREET.

SHOE REPAIR

Coca-Cola

LIQUORS FRUIT

FOR RENT COLONIAL REALTY

FROZEN FO

AND AUGIE WAS A DWARF.

RKET

Augie's SIGNS

HIC

FOR RENT COLONIAL REALTY

FROZEN

TERMITE CONTROL

LIQUORS 7¢

AND THAT WAS ALL THERE WAS TO IT EXCEPT FOR FOUL BERNIE THE GIMP.

WHAT TH—

HE WAS FOUL WHEN HE WAS DRUNK AND HE WAS ALWAYS DRUNK.

SO HE WAS CALLED FOUL BERNIE.

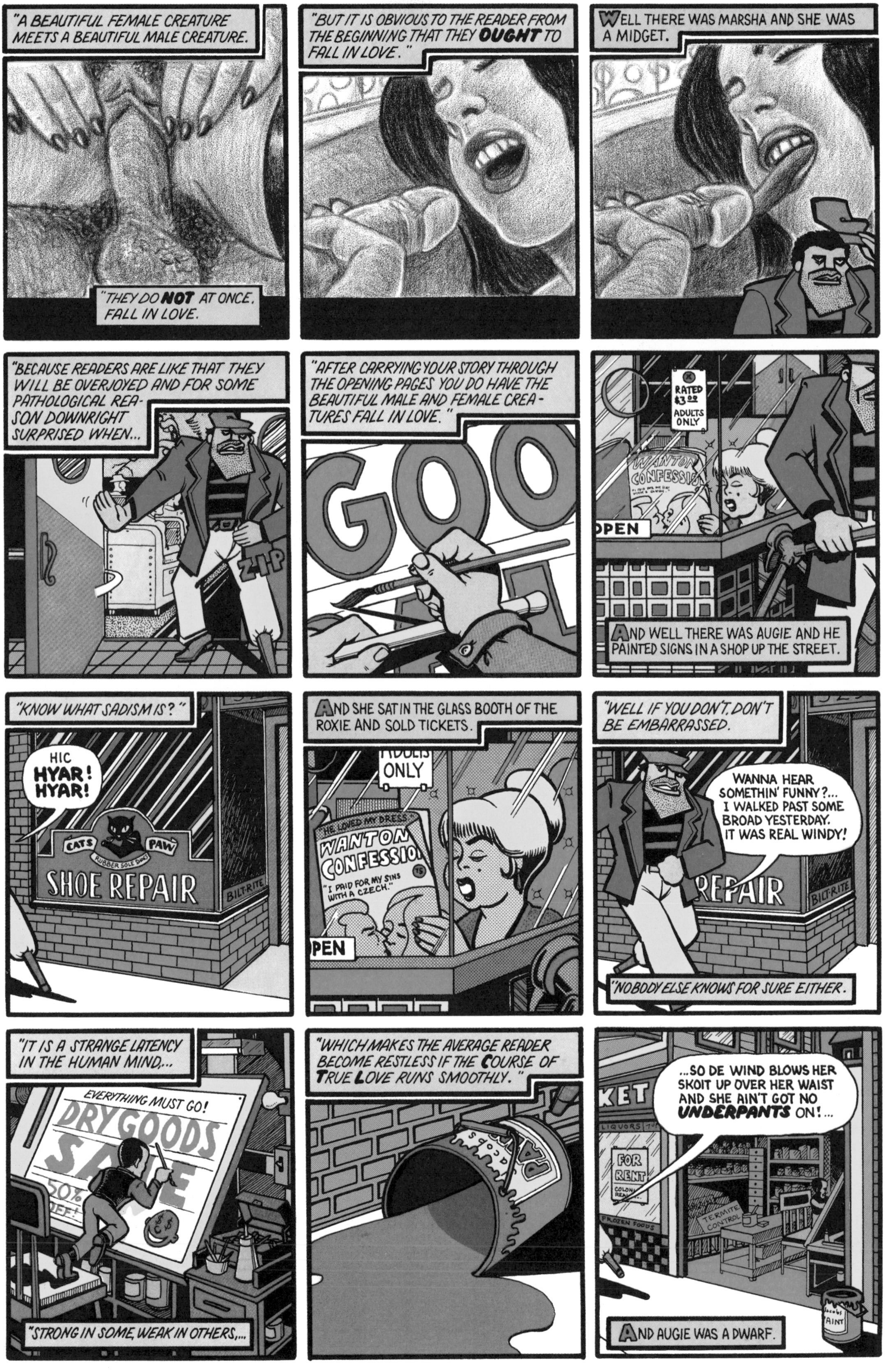
"A BEAUTIFUL FEMALE CREATURE MEETS A BEAUTIFUL MALE CREATURE.
"THEY DO NOT AT ONCE, FALL IN LOVE.
"BUT IT IS OBVIOUS TO THE READER FROM THE BEGINNING THAT THEY OUGHT TO FALL IN LOVE."
WELL THERE WAS MARSHA AND SHE WAS A MIDGET.
"BECAUSE READERS ARE LIKE THAT THEY WILL BE OVERJOYED AND FOR SOME PATHOLOGICAL REA-SON DOWNRIGHT SURPRISED WHEN...
ZIP
"AFTER CARRYING YOUR STORY THROUGH THE OPENING PAGES YOU DO HAVE THE BEAUTIFUL MALE AND FEMALE CREA-TURES FALL IN LOVE."
GOO
RATED $3.00 ADULTS ONLY
WANTON CONFESSIONS
OPEN
AND WELL THERE WAS AUGIE AND HE PAINTED SIGNS IN A SHOP UP THE STREET.
"KNOW WHAT SADISM IS?"
HIC HYAR! HYAR!
CATS PAW
SHOE REPAIR
BILT-RITE
AND SHE SAT IN THE GLASS BOOTH OF THE ROXIE AND SOLD TICKETS.
ONLY
HE LOVED MY DRESS
WANTON CONFESSIONS
"I PAID FOR MY SINS WITH A CZECH."
OPEN
"WELL IF YOU DON'T, DON'T BE EMBARRASSED.
WANNA HEAR SOMETHIN' FUNNY?... I WALKED PAST SOME BROAD YESTERDAY. IT WAS REAL WINDY!
REPAIR
BILT-RITE
"NOBODY ELSE KNOWS FOR SURE EITHER.
"IT IS A STRANGE LATENCY IN THE HUMAN MIND,...
EVERYTHING MUST GO!
DRY GOODS
50%
"STRONG IN SOME, WEAK IN OTHERS,...
"WHICH MAKES THE AVERAGE READER BECOME RESTLESS IF THE COURSE OF TRUE LOVE RUNS SMOOTHLY."
...SO DE WIND BLOWS HER SKOIT UP OVER HER WAIST AND SHE AIN'T GOT NO UNDERPANTS ON!...
KET
LIQUORS
FOR RENT
FROZEN FOODS
TERMITE CONTROL
PAINT
AND AUGIE WAS A DWARF.

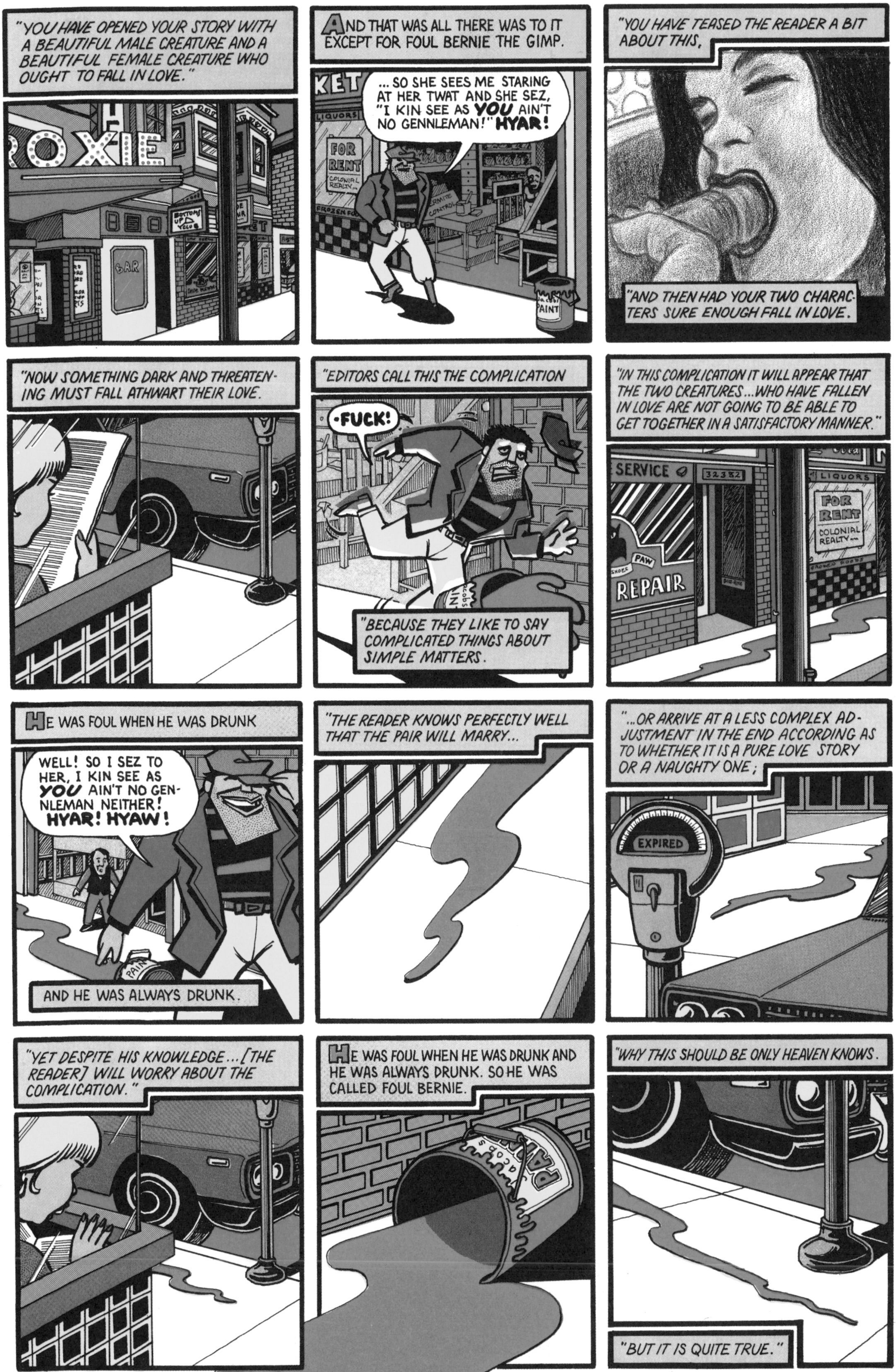
"YOU HAVE OPENED YOUR STORY WITH A BEAUTIFUL MALE CREATURE AND A BEAUTIFUL FEMALE CREATURE WHO OUGHT TO FALL IN LOVE."
ROXIE
BAR
AND THAT WAS ALL THERE WAS TO IT EXCEPT FOR FOUL BERNIE THE GIMP.
... SO SHE SEES ME STARING AT HER TWAT AND SHE SEZ, "I KIN SEE AS YOU AIN'T NO GENNLEMAN!" HYAR!
FOR RENT
COLONIAL REALTY
PAINT
"YOU HAVE TEASED THE READER A BIT ABOUT THIS,
"AND THEN HAD YOUR TWO CHARACTERS SURE ENOUGH FALL IN LOVE.
"NOW SOMETHING DARK AND THREATENING MUST FALL ATHWART THEIR LOVE.
"EDITORS CALL THIS THE COMPLICATION
·FUCK!
"BECAUSE THEY LIKE TO SAY COMPLICATED THINGS ABOUT SIMPLE MATTERS.
"IN THIS COMPLICATION IT WILL APPEAR THAT THE TWO CREATURES... WHO HAVE FALLEN IN LOVE ARE NOT GOING TO BE ABLE TO GET TOGETHER IN A SATISFACTORY MANNER."
SERVICE
32382
LIQUORS
FOR RENT
COLONIAL REALTY
SHOE REPAIR
HE WAS FOUL WHEN HE WAS DRUNK
WELL! SO I SEZ TO HER, I KIN SEE AS YOU AIN'T NO GENNLEMAN NEITHER! HYAR! HYAW!
AND HE WAS ALWAYS DRUNK.
"THE READER KNOWS PERFECTLY WELL THAT THE PAIR WILL MARRY...
"...OR ARRIVE AT A LESS COMPLEX ADJUSTMENT IN THE END ACCORDING AS TO WHETHER IT IS A PURE LOVE STORY OR A NAUGHTY ONE;
EXPIRED
"YET DESPITE HIS KNOWLEDGE ... [THE READER] WILL WORRY ABOUT THE COMPLICATION."
HE WAS FOUL WHEN HE WAS DRUNK AND HE WAS ALWAYS DRUNK. SO HE WAS CALLED FOUL BERNIE.
PAINT
"WHY THIS SHOULD BE ONLY HEAVEN KNOWS.
"BUT IT IS QUITE TRUE."

Quotation from *TRIAL AND ERROR, A KEY TO THE SECRET OF WRITING AND SELLING* by Jack Woodford; Garden City Pub. N.Y. 1933. Pages 22-23.

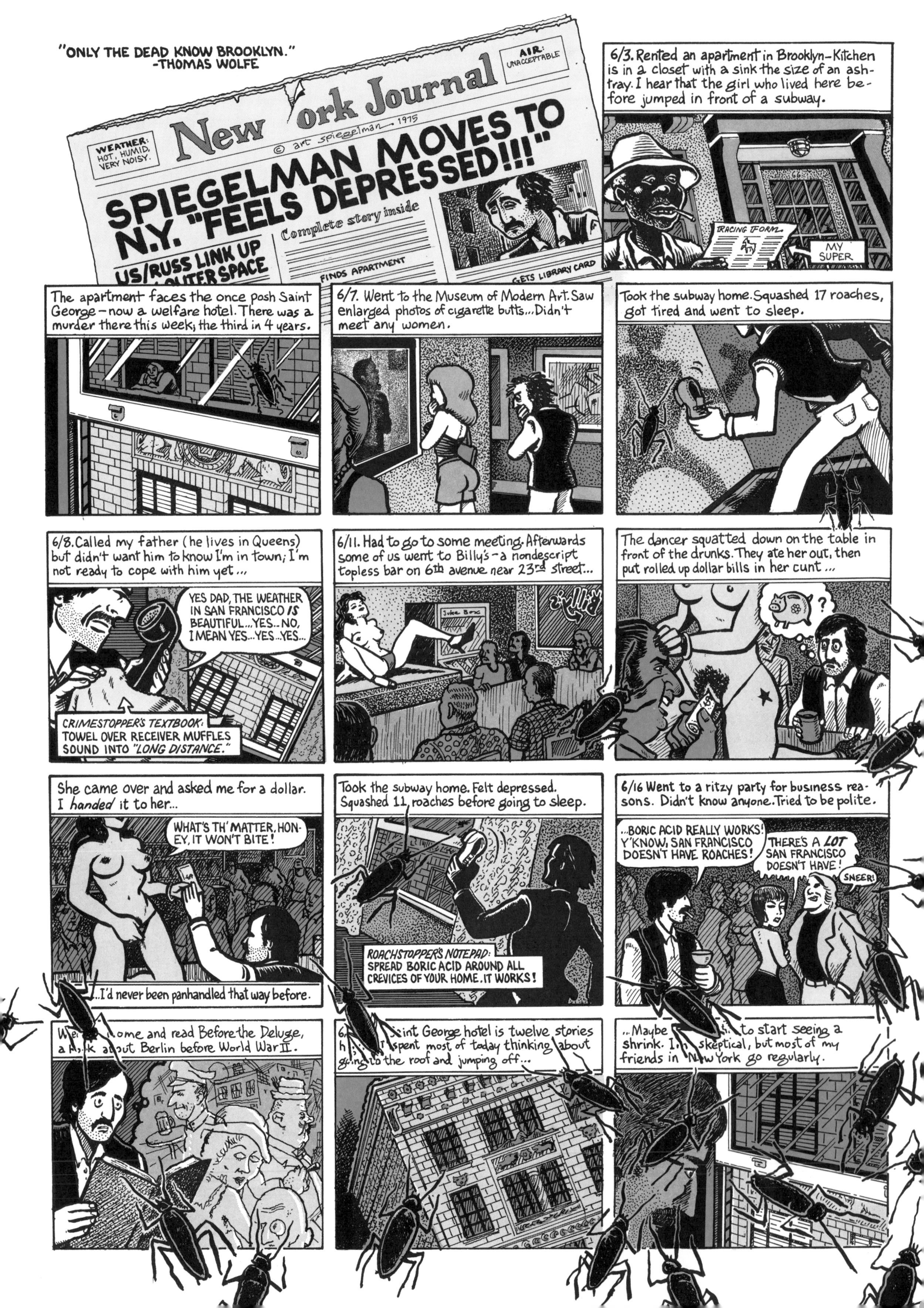
"ONLY THE DEAD KNOW BROOKLYN."
-THOMAS WOLFE
New York Journal
AIR: UNACCEPTABLE
WEATHER: HOT, HUMID, VERY NOISY.
© art spiegelman 1975
SPIEGELMAN MOVES TO N.Y. "FEELS DEPRESSED!!!"
Complete story inside
US/RUSS LINK UP IN OUTER SPACE
FINDS APARTMENT
GETS LIBRARY CARD
6/3. Rented an apartment in Brooklyn–Kitchen is in a closet with a sink the size of an ash-tray. I hear that the girl who lived here before jumped in front of a subway.
RACING FORM
MY SUPER
The apartment faces the once posh Saint George–now a welfare hotel. There was a murder there this week; the third in 4 years.
6/7. Went to the Museum of Modern Art. Saw enlarged photos of cigarette butts... Didn't meet any women.
Took the subway home. Squashed 17 roaches, got tired and went to sleep.
6/8. Called my father (he lives in Queens) but didn't want him to know I'm in town; I'm not ready to cope with him yet...
YES DAD, THE WEATHER IN SAN FRANCISCO IS BEAUTIFUL... YES... NO, I MEAN YES... YES... YES...
CRIMESTOPPER'S TEXTBOOK: TOWEL OVER RECEIVER MUFFLES SOUND INTO "LONG DISTANCE."
6/11. Had to go to some meeting. Afterwards some of us went to Billy's–a nondescript topless bar on 6th avenue near 23rd street...
Juke Box
Billy's
The dancer squatted down on the table in front of the drunks. They ate her out, then put rolled up dollar bills in her cunt...
?
She came over and asked me for a dollar. I handed it to her...
WHAT'S TH' MATTER, HONEY, IT WON'T BITE!
...I'd never been panhandled that way before.
Took the subway home. Felt depressed. Squashed 11 roaches before going to sleep.
ROACHSTOPPER'S NOTEPAD: SPREAD BORIC ACID AROUND ALL CREVICES OF YOUR HOME. IT WORKS!
6/16 Went to a ritzy party for business reasons. Didn't know anyone. Tried to be polite.
...BORIC ACID REALLY WORKS! Y'KNOW, SAN FRANCISCO DOESN'T HAVE ROACHES!
THERE'S A LOT SAN FRANCISCO DOESN'T HAVE!
SNEER!
ome and read Before the Deluge, about Berlin before World War II.
int George hotel is twelve stories spent most of today thinking about to the roof and jumping off...
...Maybe to start seeing a shrink. skeptical, but most of my friends in York go regularly.

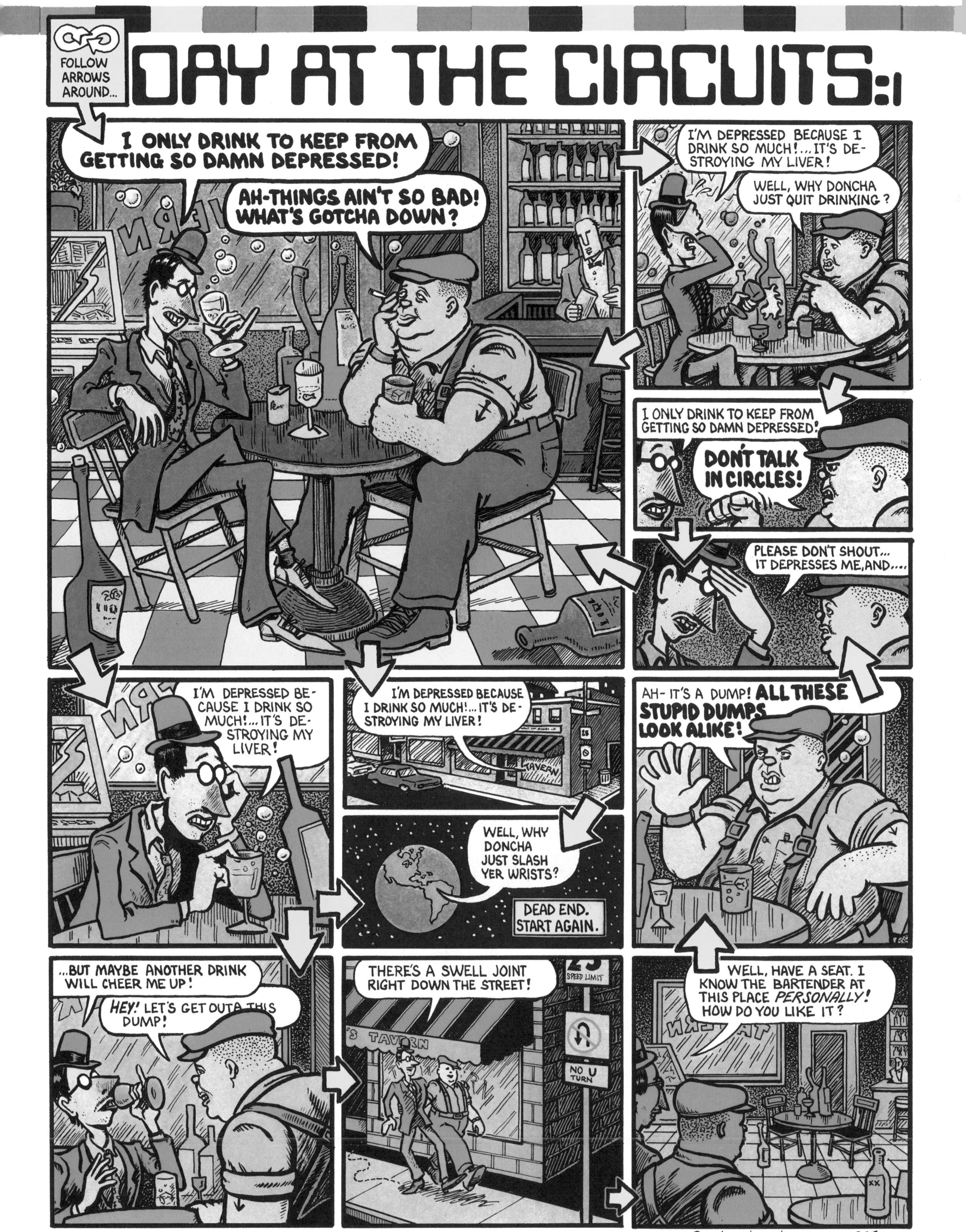

FOLLOW ARROWS AROUND...
DAY AT THE CIRCUITS:1
I ONLY DRINK TO KEEP FROM GETTING SO DAMN DEPRESSED!
AH-THINGS AIN'T SO BAD! WHAT'S GOTCHA DOWN?
I'M DEPRESSED BECAUSE I DRINK SO MUCH!... IT'S DESTROYING MY LIVER!
WELL, WHY DONCHA JUST QUIT DRINKING?
I ONLY DRINK TO KEEP FROM GETTING SO DAMN DEPRESSED!
DON'T TALK IN CIRCLES!
PLEASE DON'T SHOUT... IT DEPRESSES ME, AND....
I'M DEPRESSED BECAUSE I DRINK SO MUCH!... IT'S DESTROYING MY LIVER!
I'M DEPRESSED BECAUSE I DRINK SO MUCH!... IT'S DESTROYING MY LIVER!
TAVERN
AH- IT'S A DUMP! ALL THESE STUPID DUMPS LOOK ALIKE!
WELL, WHY DONCHA JUST SLASH YER WRISTS?
DEAD END. START AGAIN.
...BUT MAYBE ANOTHER DRINK WILL CHEER ME UP!
HEY! LET'S GET OUTA THIS DUMP!
THERE'S A SWELL JOINT RIGHT DOWN THE STREET!
25
SPEED LIMIT
'S TAVERN
NO U TURN
WELL, HAVE A SEAT. I KNOW THE BARTENDER AT THIS PLACE PERSONALLY! HOW DO YOU LIKE IT?

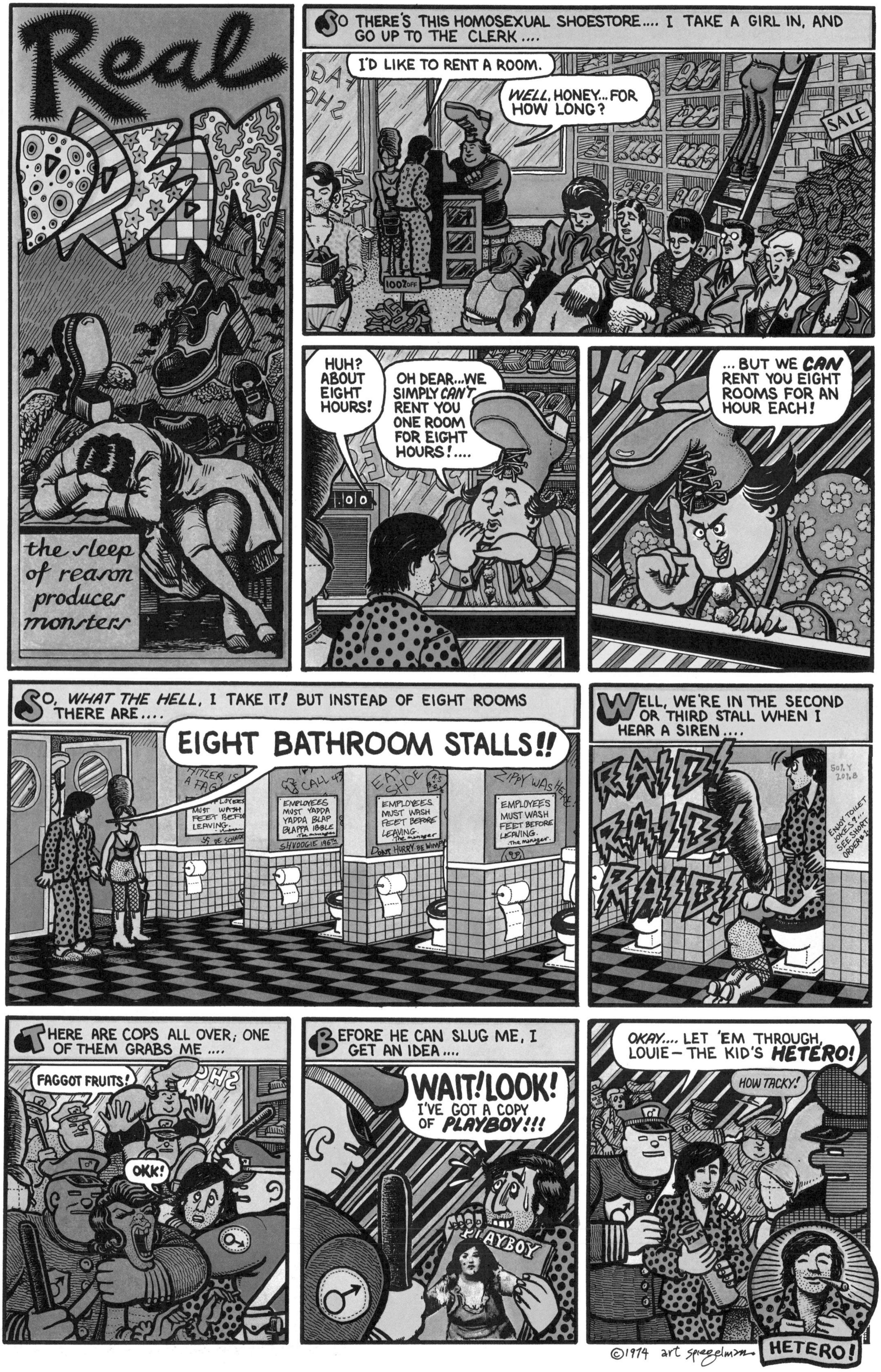
Real Dream
the sleep of reason produces monsters
SO THERE'S THIS HOMOSEXUAL SHOESTORE.... I TAKE A GIRL IN, AND GO UP TO THE CLERK....
I'D LIKE TO RENT A ROOM.
WELL, HONEY... FOR HOW LONG?
SALE
100% OFF
HUH? ABOUT EIGHT HOURS!
OH DEAR...WE SIMPLY CAN'T RENT YOU ONE ROOM FOR EIGHT HOURS!....
... BUT WE CAN RENT YOU EIGHT ROOMS FOR AN HOUR EACH!
SO, WHAT THE HELL, I TAKE IT! BUT INSTEAD OF EIGHT ROOMS THERE ARE....
EIGHT BATHROOM STALLS!!
EMPLOYEES MUST YADDA YADDA BLAP BLAPPA IBBLE
EMPLOYEES MUST WASH FEET BEFORE LEAVING. The manager
ZIPPY WAS HERE!
WELL, WE'RE IN THE SECOND OR THIRD STALL WHEN I HEAR A SIREN....
RAID! RAID! RAID!
ENJOY TOILET JOKES?... SEE SHORT ORDER #1
THERE ARE COPS ALL OVER; ONE OF THEM GRABS ME....
FAGGOT FRUITS!
OKK!
BEFORE HE CAN SLUG ME, I GET AN IDEA....
WAIT! LOOK! I'VE GOT A COPY OF PLAYBOY!!!
PLAYBOY
OKAY.... LET 'EM THROUGH, LOUIE – THE KID'S HETERO!
HOW TACKY!
HETERO!

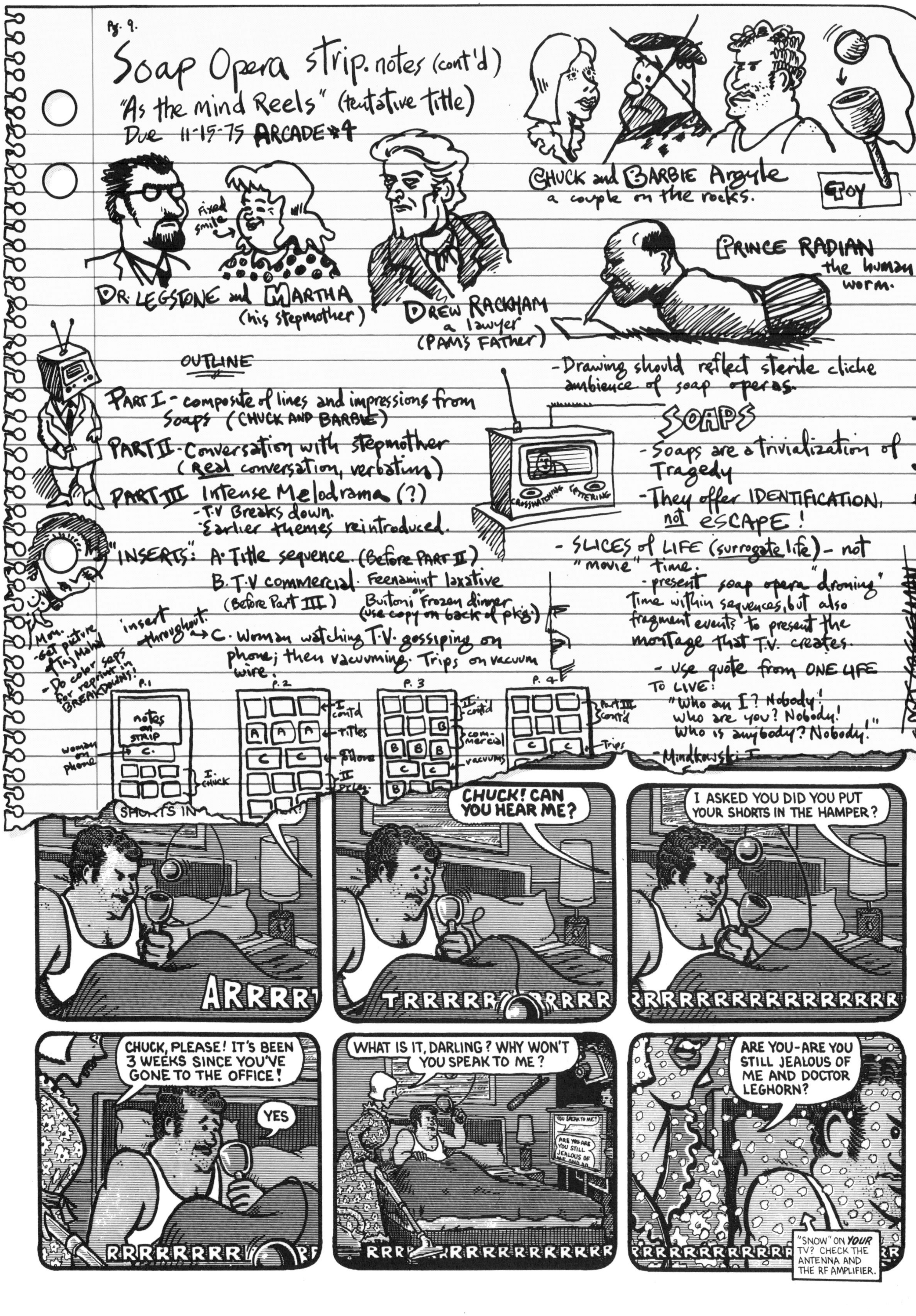

Pg. 9.
Soap Opera strip. notes (cont'd)
"As the mind Reels" (tentative title)
Due 11-15-75 ARCADE #4
CHUCK and BARBIE Argyle
a couple on the rocks.
TOY
Fixed smile
DR. LEGSTONE and MARTHA
(his stepmother)
DREW RACKHAM
a lawyer
(PAM'S FATHER)
PRINCE RADIAN
the human worm.
OUTLINE
PART I - composite of lines and impressions from Soaps (CHUCK AND BARBIE)
PART II - Conversation with stepmother (Real conversation, verbatim)
PART III Intense Melodrama (?)
-T.V Breaks down.
-Earlier themes reintroduced.
"INSERTS": A. Title sequence. (Before PART II)
B. T.V commercial. Feenamint laxative or Buitoni Frozen dinner (use copy on back of pkg.)
(Before Part III)
insert throughout → C. Woman watching T.V. gossiping on phone; then vacuuming. Trips on vacuum wire.
Mom. -Get picture of Taj Mahal
-Do color seps for reprint in BREAKDOWNS!
-Drawing should reflect sterile cliche ambience of soap operas.
CROSSWATCHING LETTERING
SOAPS
-Soaps are a trivialization of Tragedy
-They offer IDENTIFICATION, not ESCAPE!
- SLICES of LIFE (surrogate life) - not "movie" time.
- present soap opera "droning" Time within sequences, but also fragment events to present the montage that T.V. creates.
- use quote from ONE LIFE TO LIVE:
"Who am I? Nobody! Who are you? Nobody! Who is anybody? Nobody!"
-Mindkowski I.
© art spiegelman 1975
P. 1
notes on STRIP
woman on phone
C.
I. CHUCK
P. 2
I cont'd
A A A
titles
C C
II
P. 3
II cont'd
B
com-mercial
B B B
C C
vacuums
P. 4
Part III cont'd
C C
Trips
SHORTS IN
ARRRRRT
CHUCK! CAN YOU HEAR ME?
TRRRRRRRRRRRR
I ASKED YOU DID YOU PUT YOUR SHORTS IN THE HAMPER?
RRRRRRRRRRRRRRRRRR
CHUCK, PLEASE! IT'S BEEN 3 WEEKS SINCE YOU'VE GONE TO THE OFFICE!
YES
RRRRRRRRR
WHAT IS IT, DARLING? WHY WON'T YOU SPEAK TO ME?
YOU SPEAK TO ME?
ARE YOU-ARE YOU STILL JEALOUS OF
RRRRRRRRRRRRRRRR
ARE YOU-ARE YOU STILL JEALOUS OF ME AND DOCTOR LEGHORN?
"SNOW" ON YOUR TV? CHECK THE ANTENNA AND THE RF AMPLIFIER.
RRRRRRRRRR

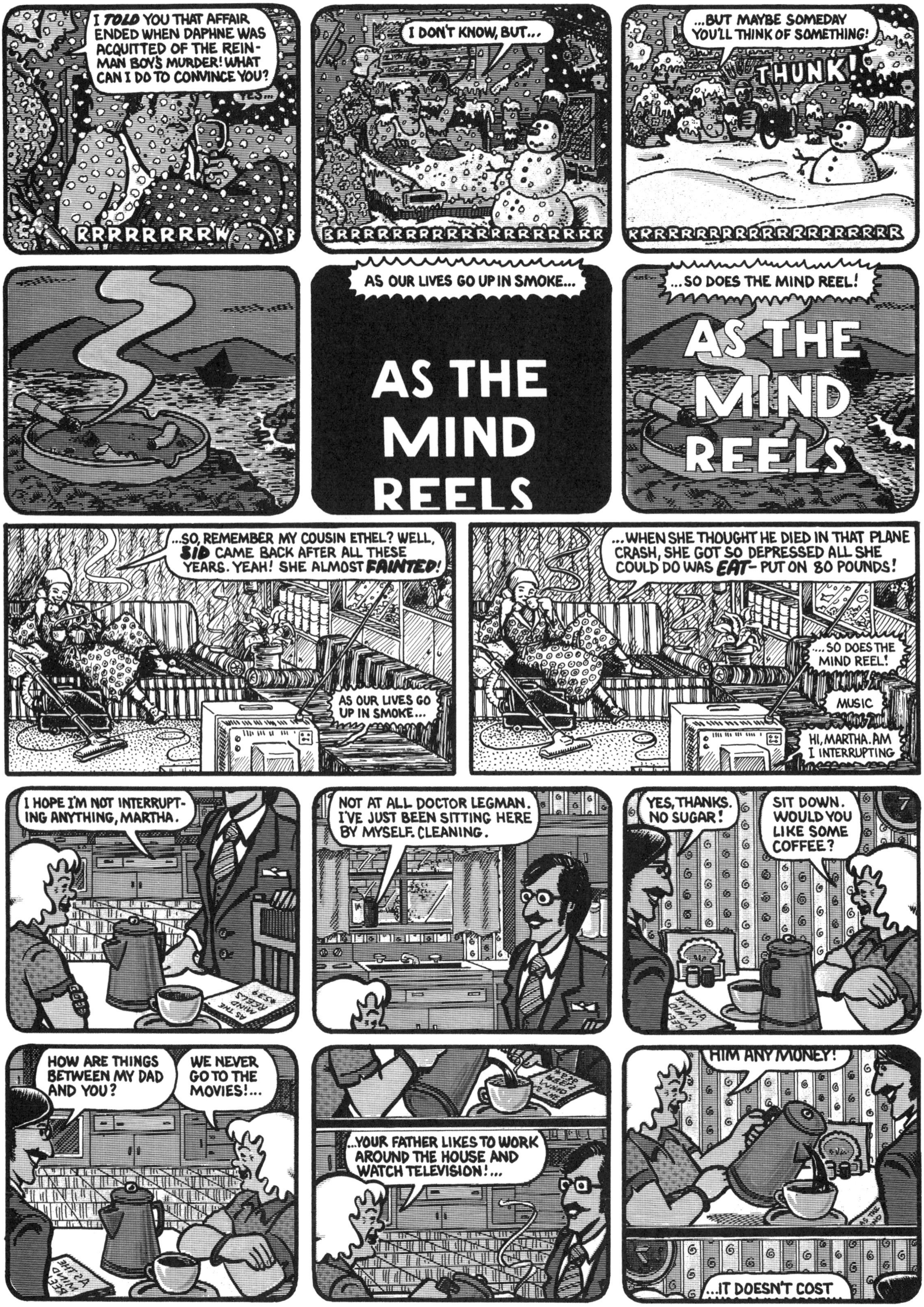I TOLD YOU THAT AFFAIR ENDED WHEN DAPHNE WAS ACQUITTED OF THE REIN-MAN BOY'S MURDER! WHAT CAN I DO TO CONVINCE YOU?
YES...
RRRRRRRRRW
I DON'T KNOW, BUT...
...BUT MAYBE SOMEDAY YOU'LL THINK OF SOMETHING!
THUNK!
AS OUR LIVES GO UP IN SMOKE...
AS THE MIND REELS
...SO DOES THE MIND REEL!
AS THE MIND REELS
...SO, REMEMBER MY COUSIN ETHEL? WELL, SID CAME BACK AFTER ALL THESE YEARS. YEAH! SHE ALMOST FAINTED!
AS OUR LIVES GO UP IN SMOKE...
...WHEN SHE THOUGHT HE DIED IN THAT PLANE CRASH, SHE GOT SO DEPRESSED ALL SHE COULD DO WAS EAT- PUT ON 80 POUNDS!
...SO DOES THE MIND REEL!
MUSIC
HI, MARTHA. AM I INTERRUPTING
I HOPE I'M NOT INTERRUPT-ING ANYTHING, MARTHA.
NOT AT ALL DOCTOR LEGMAN. I'VE JUST BEEN SITTING HERE BY MYSELF. CLEANING.
SIT DOWN. WOULD YOU LIKE SOME COFFEE?
YES, THANKS. NO SUGAR!
HOW ARE THINGS BETWEEN MY DAD AND YOU?
WE NEVER GO TO THE MOVIES!...
...YOUR FATHER LIKES TO WORK AROUND THE HOUSE AND WATCH TELEVISION!...
...IT DOESN'T COST
HIM ANY MONEY!

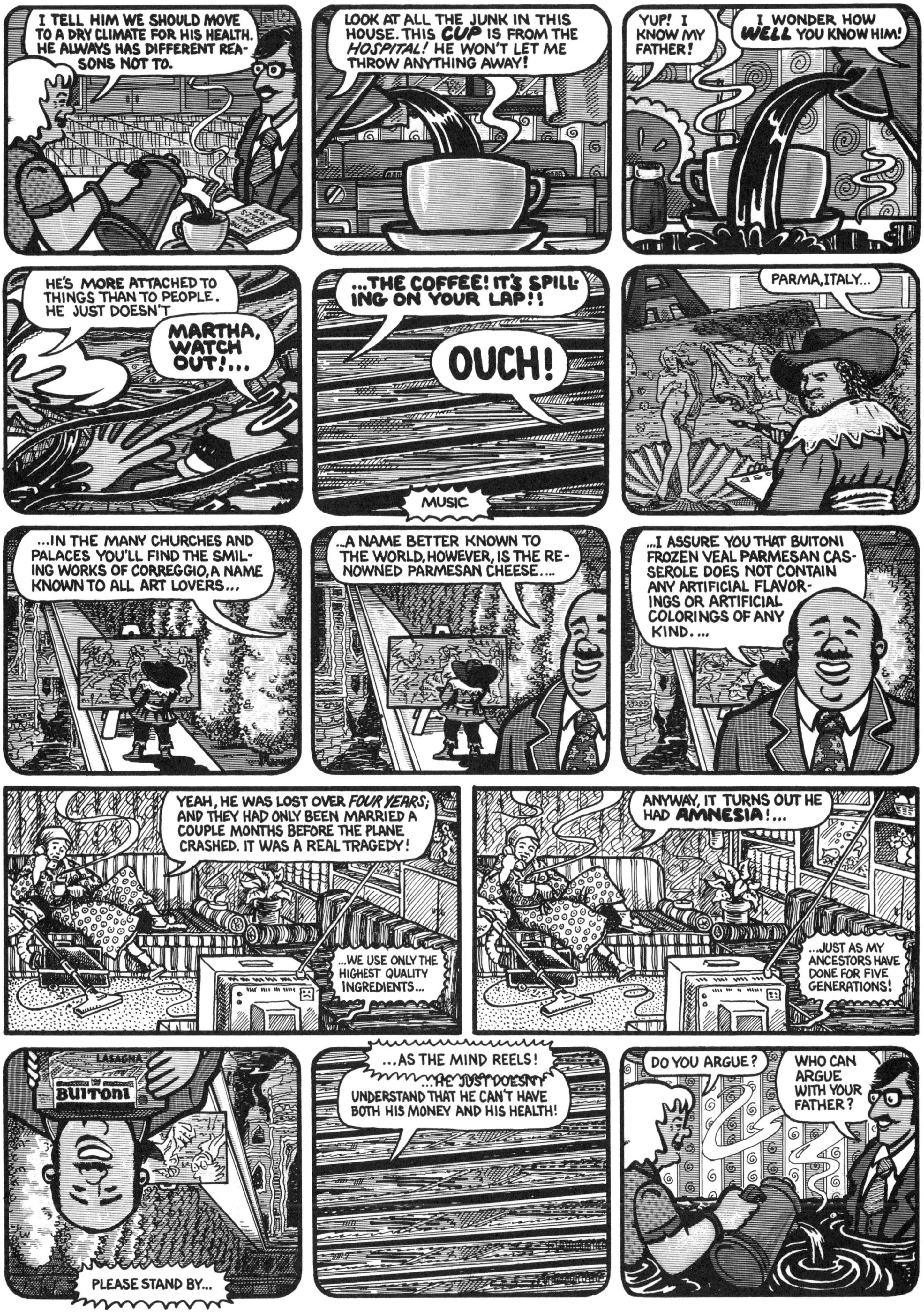
I TELL HIM WE SHOULD MOVE TO A DRY CLIMATE FOR HIS HEALTH. HE ALWAYS HAS DIFFERENT REASONS NOT TO.
LOOK AT ALL THE JUNK IN THIS HOUSE. THIS CUP IS FROM THE HOSPITAL! HE WON'T LET ME THROW ANYTHING AWAY!
YUP! I KNOW MY FATHER!
I WONDER HOW WELL YOU KNOW HIM!
HE'S MORE ATTACHED TO THINGS THAN TO PEOPLE. HE JUST DOESN'T
MARTHA, WATCH OUT!...
...THE COFFEE! IT'S SPILLING ON YOUR LAP!!
OUCH!
MUSIC
PARMA, ITALY...
...IN THE MANY CHURCHES AND PALACES YOU'LL FIND THE SMILING WORKS OF CORREGGIO, A NAME KNOWN TO ALL ART LOVERS...
...A NAME BETTER KNOWN TO THE WORLD, HOWEVER, IS THE RENOWNED PARMESAN CHEESE....
...I ASSURE YOU THAT BUITONI FROZEN VEAL PARMESAN CASSEROLE DOES NOT CONTAIN ANY ARTIFICIAL FLAVORINGS OR ARTIFICIAL COLORINGS OF ANY KIND....
YEAH, HE WAS LOST OVER FOUR YEARS; AND THEY HAD ONLY BEEN MARRIED A COUPLE MONTHS BEFORE THE PLANE CRASHED. IT WAS A REAL TRAGEDY!
...WE USE ONLY THE HIGHEST QUALITY INGREDIENTS...
ANYWAY, IT TURNS OUT HE HAD AMNESIA!...
...JUST AS MY ANCESTORS HAVE DONE FOR FIVE GENERATIONS!
LASAGNA
BUITONI
PLEASE STAND BY...
...AS THE MIND REELS!
...HE JUST DOESN'T UNDERSTAND THAT HE CAN'T HAVE BOTH HIS MONEY AND HIS HEALTH!
DO YOU ARGUE?
WHO CAN ARGUE WITH YOUR FATHER?

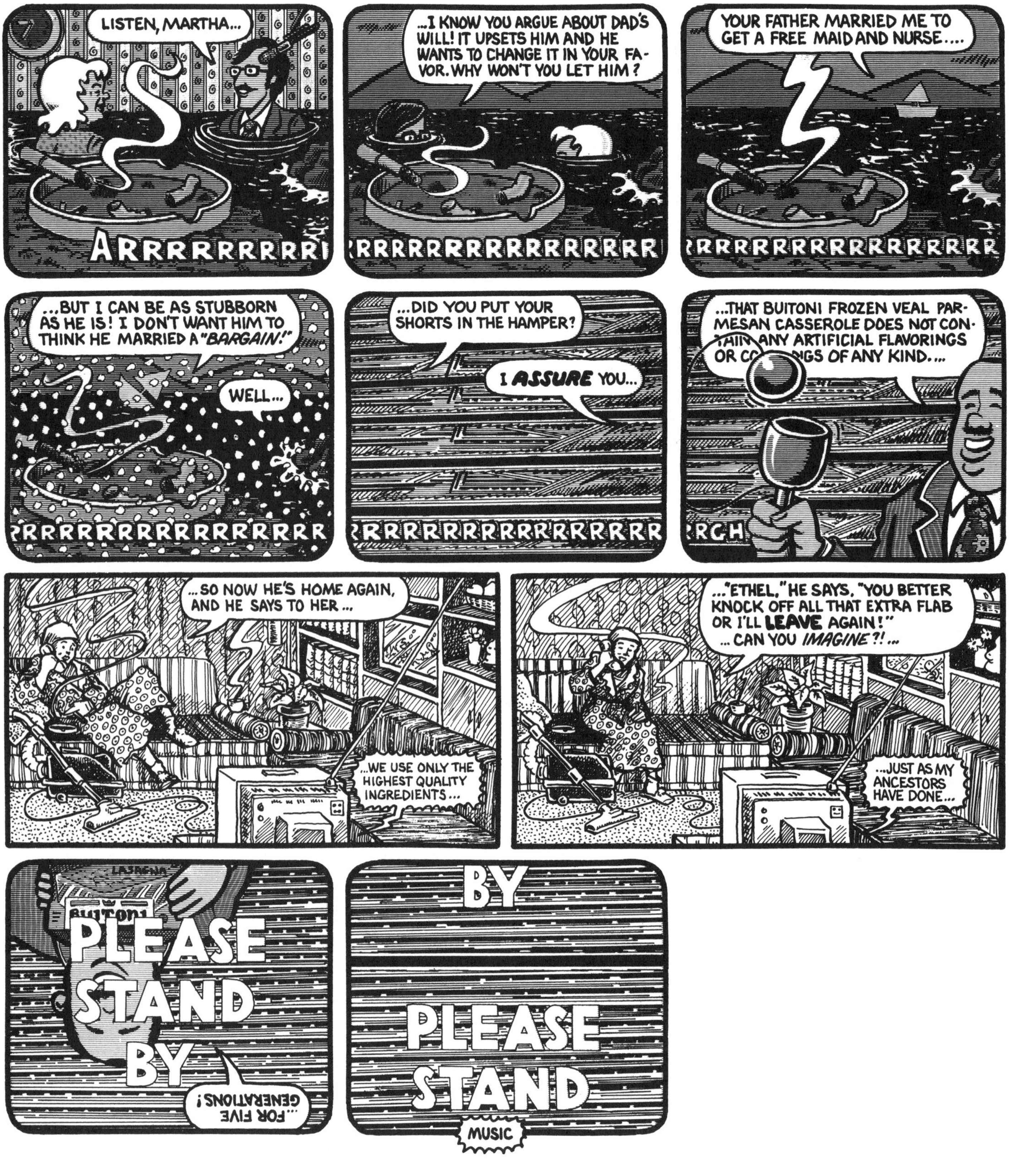

LISTEN, MARTHA...
ARRRRRRRRRR
...I KNOW YOU ARGUE ABOUT DAD'S WILL! IT UPSETS HIM AND HE WANTS TO CHANGE IT IN YOUR FA-VOR. WHY WON'T YOU LET HIM?
RRRRRRRRRRRRRRRRR
YOUR FATHER MARRIED ME TO GET A FREE MAID AND NURSE....
RRRRRRRRRRRRRRRRRR
...BUT I CAN BE AS STUBBORN AS HE IS! I DON'T WANT HIM TO THINK HE MARRIED A "BARGAIN!"
WELL...
RRRRRRRRRRRRRRRRR
...DID YOU PUT YOUR SHORTS IN THE HAMPER?
I ASSURE YOU...
RRRRRRRRRRRRRRRRR
...THAT BUITONI FROZEN VEAL PAR-MESAN CASSEROLE DOES NOT CON-TAIN ANY ARTIFICIAL FLAVORINGS OR CO NGS OF ANY KIND....
RGH
...SO NOW HE'S HOME AGAIN, AND HE SAYS TO HER...
...WE USE ONLY THE HIGHEST QUALITY INGREDIENTS...
..."ETHEL," HE SAYS, "YOU BETTER KNOCK OFF ALL THAT EXTRA FLAB OR I'LL LEAVE AGAIN!" ...CAN YOU IMAGINE?!...
...JUST AS MY ANCESTORS HAVE DONE...
BUITONI
PLEASE STAND BY
...FOR FIVE GENERATIONS!
BY
PLEASE STAND
MUSIC

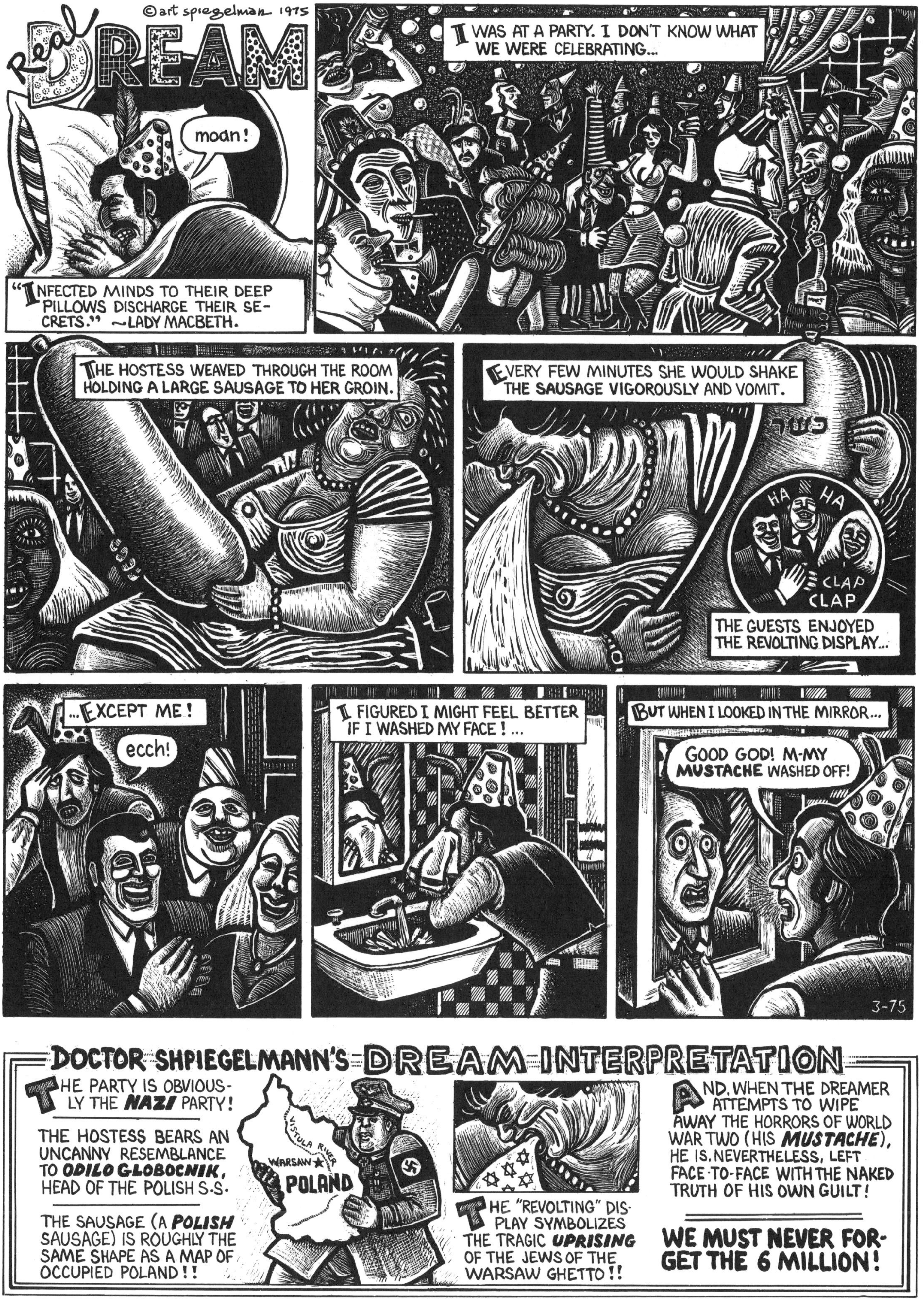

©art spiegelman 1975
Real DREAM
moan!
"INFECTED MINDS TO THEIR DEEP PILLOWS DISCHARGE THEIR SECRETS." ~LADY MACBETH.
I WAS AT A PARTY. I DON'T KNOW WHAT WE WERE CELEBRATING...
THE HOSTESS WEAVED THROUGH THE ROOM HOLDING A LARGE SAUSAGE TO HER GROIN.
EVERY FEW MINUTES SHE WOULD SHAKE THE SAUSAGE VIGOROUSLY AND VOMIT.
כשר
HA HA
CLAP CLAP
THE GUESTS ENJOYED THE REVOLTING DISPLAY...
...EXCEPT ME!
ecch!
I FIGURED I MIGHT FEEL BETTER IF I WASHED MY FACE! ...
BUT WHEN I LOOKED IN THE MIRROR...
GOOD GOD! M-MY MUSTACHE WASHED OFF!
3-75
DOCTOR SHPIEGELMANN'S DREAM INTERPRETATION
THE PARTY IS OBVIOUSLY THE NAZI PARTY!
THE HOSTESS BEARS AN UNCANNY RESEMBLANCE TO ODILO GLOBOCNIK, HEAD OF THE POLISH S.S.
THE SAUSAGE (A POLISH SAUSAGE) IS ROUGHLY THE SAME SHAPE AS A MAP OF OCCUPIED POLAND!!
VISTULA RIVER
WARSAW
POLAND
THE "REVOLTING" DISPLAY SYMBOLIZES THE TRAGIC UPRISING OF THE JEWS OF THE WARSAW GHETTO!!
AND, WHEN THE DREAMER ATTEMPTS TO WIPE AWAY THE HORRORS OF WORLD WAR TWO (HIS MUSTACHE), HE IS, NEVERTHELESS, LEFT FACE-TO-FACE WITH THE NAKED TRUTH OF HIS OWN GUILT!
WE MUST NEVER FORGET THE 6 MILLION!

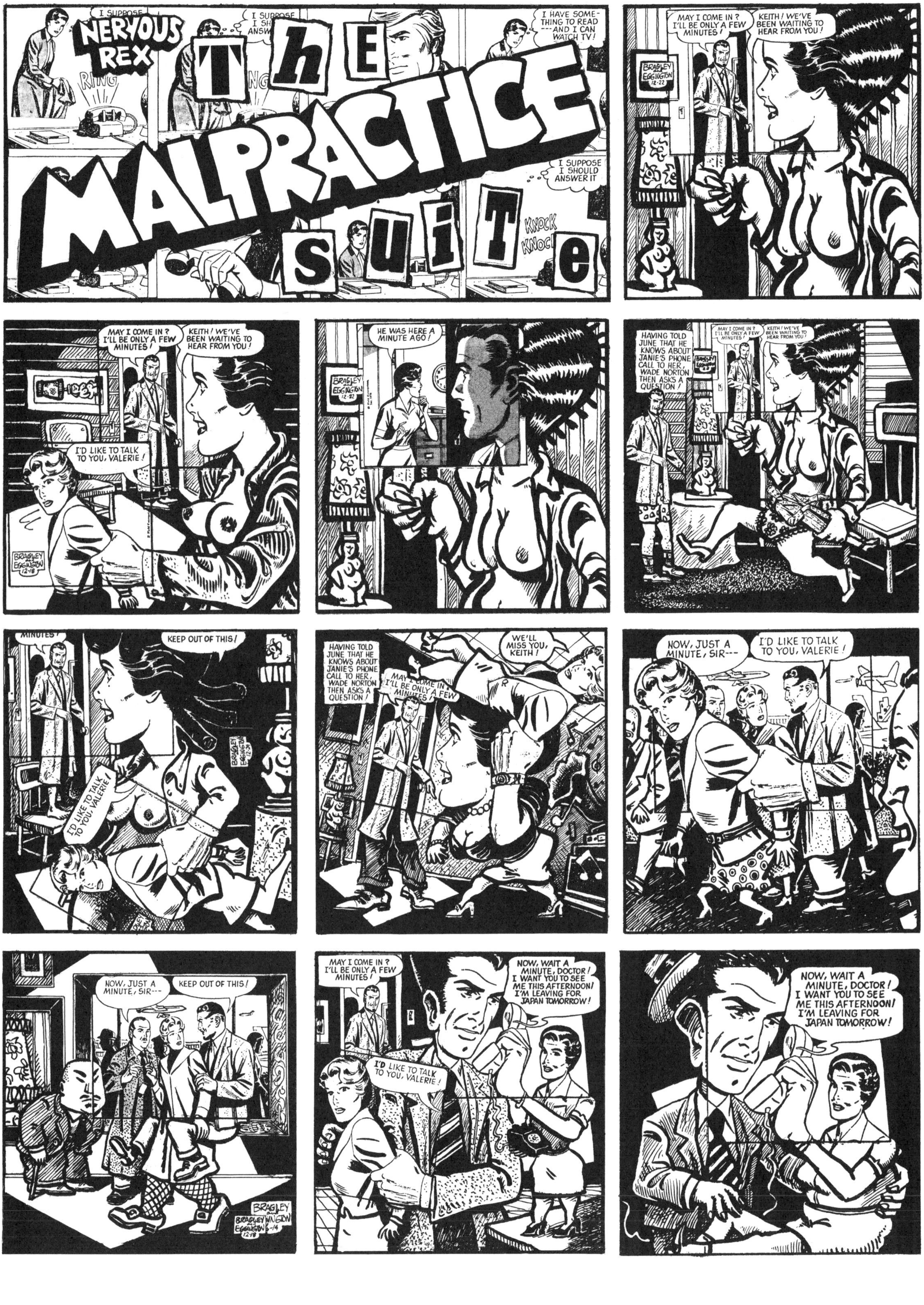
I SUPPOSE
NERVOUS REX
RING
The MALPRACTICE suite
I HAVE SOME-THING TO READ ---AND I CAN WATCH TV!
I SUPPOSE I SHOULD ANSWER IT
KNOCK
MAY I COME IN? I'LL BE ONLY A FEW MINUTES!
KEITH! WE'VE BEEN WAITING TO HEAR FROM YOU!
BRAGLEY EGGINGTON 12-22
MAY I COME IN? I'LL BE ONLY A FEW MINUTES!
KEITH! WE'VE BEEN WAITING TO HEAR FROM YOU!
I'D LIKE TO TALK TO YOU, VALERIE!
BRAGLEY EGGINGTON 12-18
HE WAS HERE A MINUTE AGO!
BRAGLEY EGGINGTON 12-22
HAVING TOLD JUNE THAT HE KNOWS ABOUT JANIE'S PHONE CALL TO HER, WADE NORTON THEN ASKS A QUESTION!
MAY I COME IN? I'LL BE ONLY A FEW MINUTES!
KEITH! WE'VE BEEN WAITING TO HEAR FROM YOU!
MINUTES!
KEEP OUT OF THIS!
I'D LIKE TO TALK TO YOU, VALERIE!
HAVING TOLD JUNE THAT HE KNOWS ABOUT JANIE'S PHONE CALL TO HER, WADE NORTON THEN ASKS A QUESTION!
MAY I COME IN? I'LL BE ONLY A FEW MINUTES!
WE'LL MISS YOU, KEITH!
NOW, JUST A MINUTE, SIR---
I'D LIKE TO TALK TO YOU, VALERIE!
NOW, JUST A MINUTE, SIR---
KEEP OUT OF THIS!
BRAGLEY EGGINGTON 12-18
MAY I COME IN? I'LL BE ONLY A FEW MINUTES!
NOW, WAIT A MINUTE, DOCTOR! I WANT YOU TO SEE ME THIS AFTERNOON! I'M LEAVING FOR JAPAN TOMORROW!
I'D LIKE TO TALK TO YOU, VALERIE!
NOW, WAIT A MINUTE, DOCTOR! I WANT YOU TO SEE ME THIS AFTERNOON! I'M LEAVING FOR JAPAN TOMORROW!

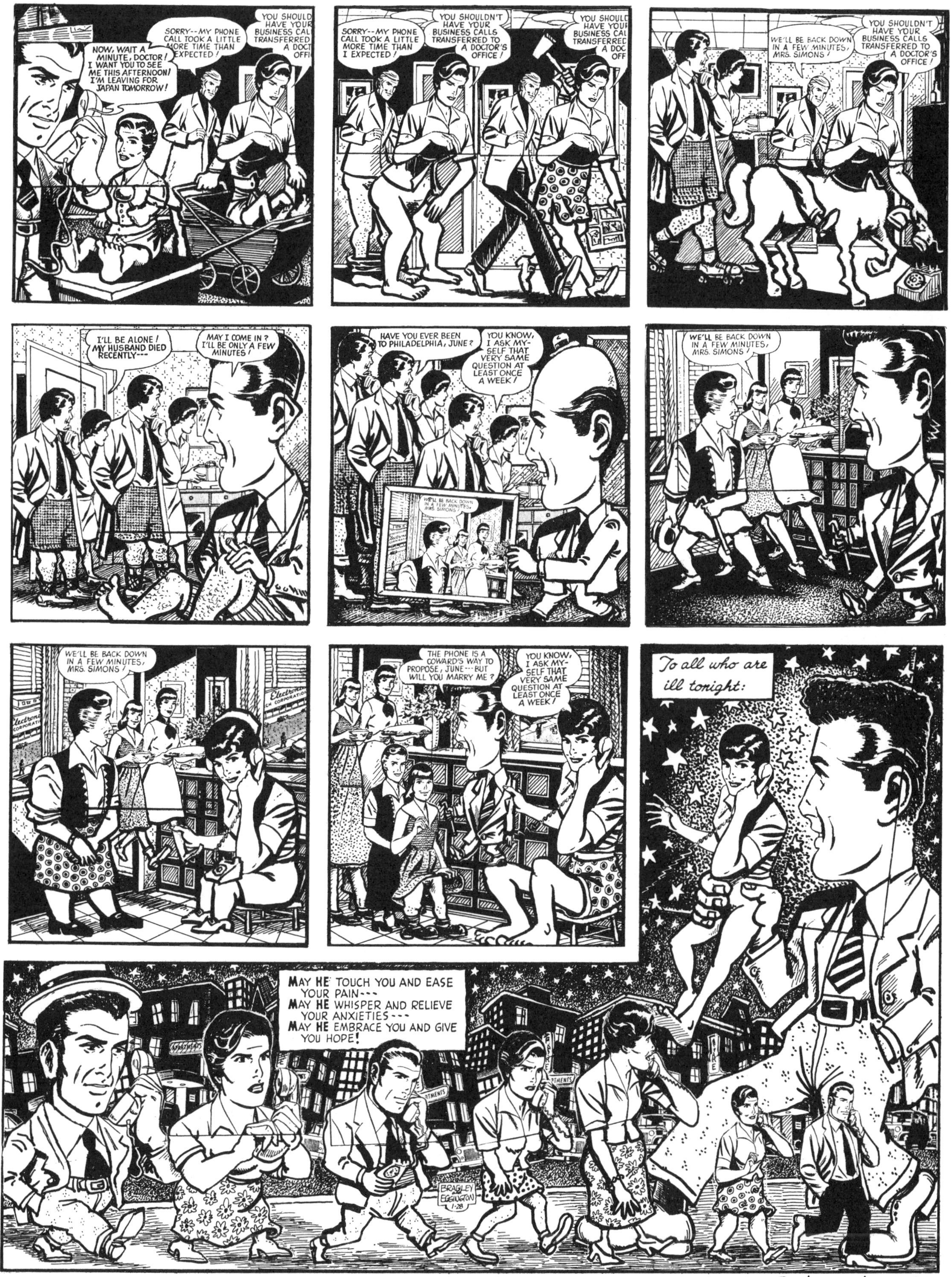

NOW, WAIT A MINUTE, DOCTOR! I WANT YOU TO SEE ME THIS AFTERNOON! I'M LEAVING FOR JAPAN TOMORROW!
SORRY--MY PHONE CALL TOOK A LITTLE MORE TIME THAN EXPECTED!
YOU SHOULD HAVE YOUR BUSINESS CALL TRANSFERRED A DOCT OFFI
SORRY--MY PHONE CALL TOOK A LITTLE MORE TIME THAN I EXPECTED!
YOU SHOULDN'T HAVE YOUR BUSINESS CALLS TRANSFERRED TO A DOCTOR'S OFFICE!
YOU SHOULD HAVE YOUR BUSINESS CAL TRANSFERRED A DOC OFF
WE'LL BE BACK DOWN IN A FEW MINUTES, MRS. SIMONS!
YOU SHOULDN'T HAVE YOUR BUSINESS CALLS TRANSFERRED TO A DOCTOR'S OFFICE!
I'LL BE ALONE! MY HUSBAND DIED RECENTLY---
MAY I COME IN? I'LL BE ONLY A FEW MINUTES!
HAVE YOU EVER BEEN TO PHILADELPHIA, JUNE?
YOU KNOW, I ASK MY-SELF THAT VERY SAME QUESTION AT LEAST ONCE A WEEK!
WE'LL BE BACK DOWN IN A FEW MINUTES, MRS. SIMONS!
WE'LL BE BACK DOWN IN A FEW MINUTES, MRS. SIMONS!
WE'LL BE BACK DOWN IN A FEW MINUTES, MRS. SIMONS!
THE PHONE IS A COWARD'S WAY TO PROPOSE, JUNE---BUT WILL YOU MARRY ME?
YOU KNOW, I ASK MY-SELF THAT VERY SAME QUESTION AT LEAST ONCE A WEEK!
To all who are ill tonight:
MAY HE TOUCH YOU AND EASE YOUR PAIN---
MAY HE WHISPER AND RELIEVE YOUR ANXIETIES---
MAY HE EMBRACE YOU AND GIVE YOU HOPE!
BRADLEY EGGINGTON 1-28

"AS THEY STARTED OUT THE DOOR, GERTRUDE HANDED PICASSO...THE COMICS SECTION FROM ONE OF THE AMERICAN SUNDAY PAPERS: THE PAINTER WAS AN AVID FOLLOWER OF THE KATZENJAMMER KIDS AND OF LITTLE JIMMY. PICASSO BEAMED AND THANKED HER."

Chapter One: THE SHORT GOODBYE!
ACE HOLE
MIDGET DETECTI
ACE HOLE
GRETA
POTATO-HEAD
I DIDN'T REALLY WANT THE JOB – BUT I NEEDED THE DOUGH... 25 DUCATS POST HASTE OR THEY'D REPOSSESS MY HAT – AND WITHOUT IT WHAT WOULD I USE FOR AN OFFICE ?!!
©art spiegelman • 1974
IT WAS A MEAN AND VICIOUS CAPER IN A MEAN AND VICIOUS CITY... LAURENCE POTATO-HEAD, THE ART DEALER, HIRED ME...
...I WAS TO DIG UP ONE AL FLOOGLEMAN, A BIRD WHO'D PASSED HIM SOME BUM PICASSOS!
I DIDN'T WANT THE JOB, BUT... DOWN THESE MEAN STREETS A MIDGET MUST GO!
IT WAS TOUGH SCARING UP A LINE ON FLOOGLEMAN... I LEARNED HE'D BEEN A SMALL-CHANGE UNDERGROUND CARTOONIST!
WHEN TOUGH PORNO LAWS PUT HIM OUT OF BUSINESS, I GUESS HE STEPPED UP INTO THE FORGERY RACKET!
?
...A GOOD LOOKING FRAIL CRUISED PAST ME.... CALL IT A HUNCH, BUT I DECIDED TO TAIL HER!
SHIT!...
...I'M BEING SHADOWED!
MY OPTICS CHEERFULLY CRUISED HER FANCY CURVES DOWN THE BLOCK. SHE WHEELED THE CORNER BEFORE I DID...
AIEEEEEEKKK!
BANG
A SHOT AND A SCREAM! MY BLOOD FROZE INTO POPSICLES!... I TURNED THE CORNER FAST, LIKE SOME CLOWN TURNING THE PAGES OF A GOOD FUNNY-BOOK!
ZOOM

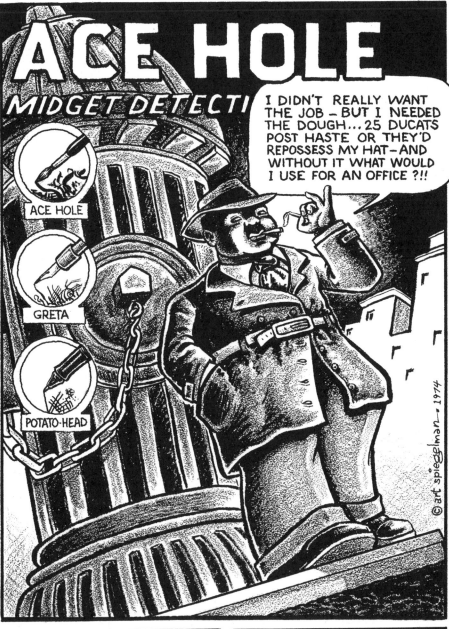

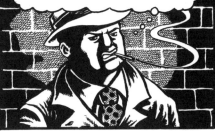

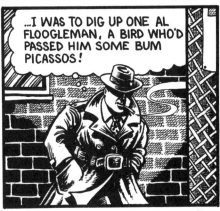

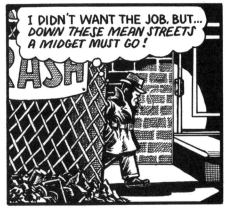

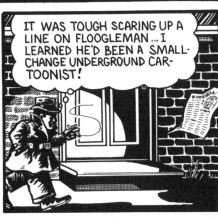

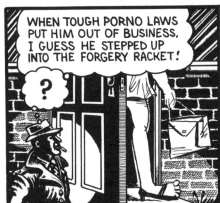

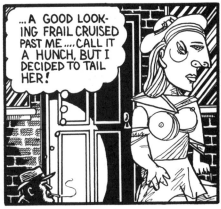

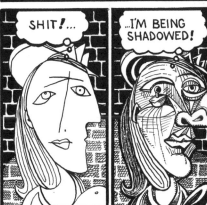

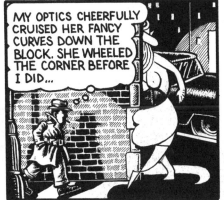

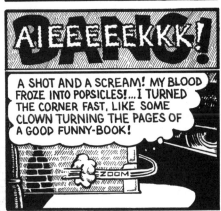

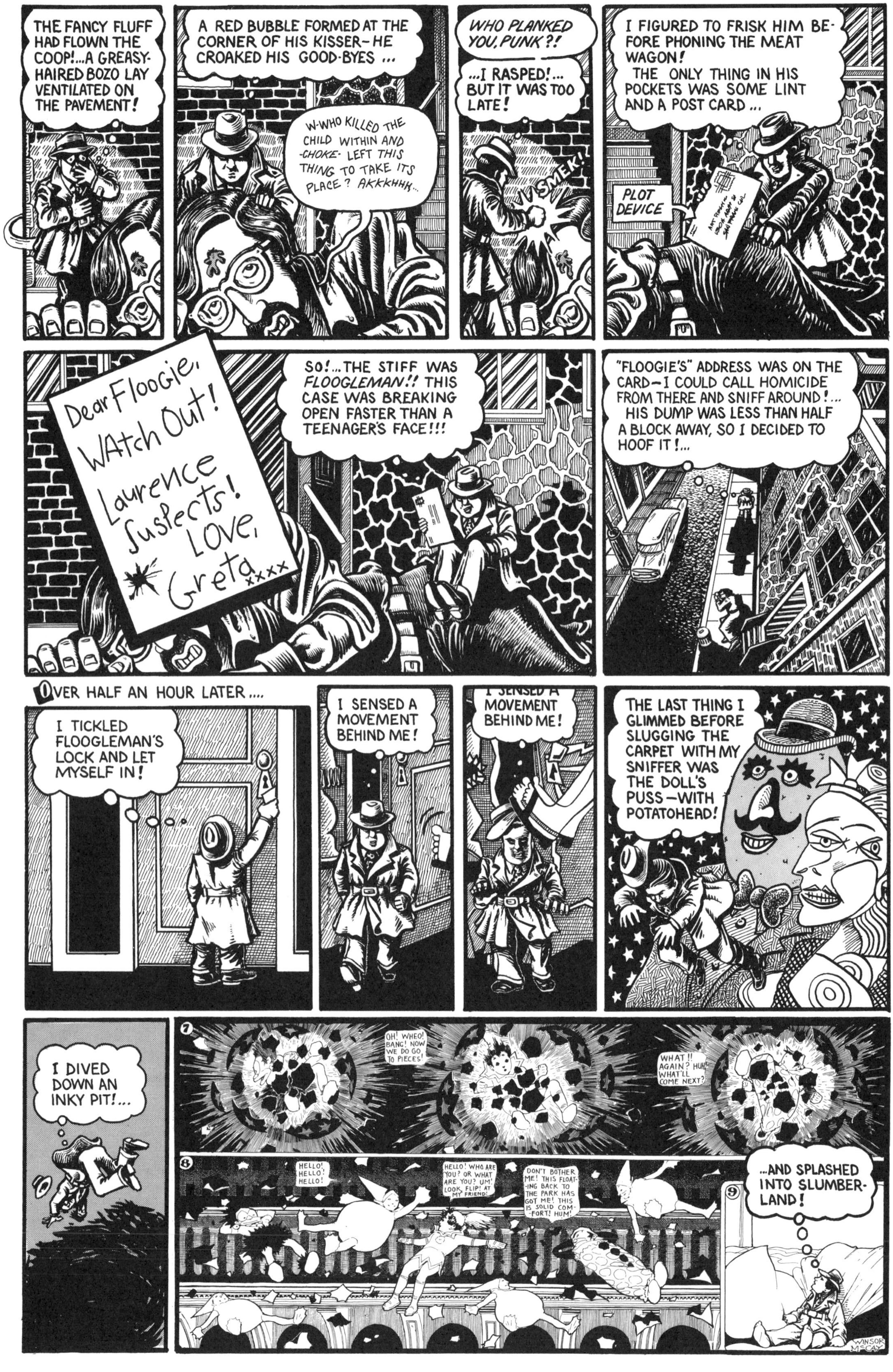
THE FANCY FLUFF HAD FLOWN THE COOP!...A GREASY-HAIRED BOZO LAY VENTILATED ON THE PAVEMENT!
A RED BUBBLE FORMED AT THE CORNER OF HIS KISSER–HE CROAKED HIS GOOD-BYES ...
W-WHO KILLED THE CHILD WITHIN AND -CHOKE- LEFT THIS THING TO TAKE ITS PLACE? AKKKHHH...
WHO PLANKED YOU, PUNK?!
...I RASPED!... BUT IT WAS TOO LATE!
SMEK!
I FIGURED TO FRISK HIM BEFORE PHONING THE MEAT WAGON!
THE ONLY THING IN HIS POCKETS WAS SOME LINT AND A POST CARD ...
PLOT DEVICE
Dear Floogie, WAtch Out! Laurence Suspects! LOve, Greta xxxx
SO!...THE STIFF WAS FLOOGLEMAN!! THIS CASE WAS BREAKING OPEN FASTER THAN A TEENAGER'S FACE!!!
"FLOOGIE'S" ADDRESS WAS ON THE CARD–I COULD CALL HOMICIDE FROM THERE AND SNIFF AROUND!...
HIS DUMP WAS LESS THAN HALF A BLOCK AWAY, SO I DECIDED TO HOOF IT!...
OVER HALF AN HOUR LATER....
I TICKLED FLOOGLEMAN'S LOCK AND LET MYSELF IN!
I SENSED A MOVEMENT BEHIND ME!
I SENSED A MOVEMENT BEHIND ME!
THE LAST THING I GLIMMED BEFORE SLUGGING THE CARPET WITH MY SNIFFER WAS THE DOLL'S PUSS–WITH POTATOHEAD!
I DIVED DOWN AN INKY PIT!...
7
OH! WHEO! BANG! NOW WE DO GO TO PIECES!
WHAT!! AGAIN? HUH! WHAT'LL COME NEXT?
8
HELLO! HELLO! HELLO!
HELLO! WHO ARE YOU? OR WHAT ARE YOU? UM! LOOK, FLIP! AT MY FRIEND!
DON'T BOTHER ME! THIS FLOAT-ING BACK TO THE PARK HAS GOT ME! THIS IS SOLID COM-FORT! HUM!
9
...AND SPLASHED INTO SLUMBER-LAND!
WINSOR McCAY

Chapter Two: NO POCKETS IN A MIDGET, DON'T THEY?

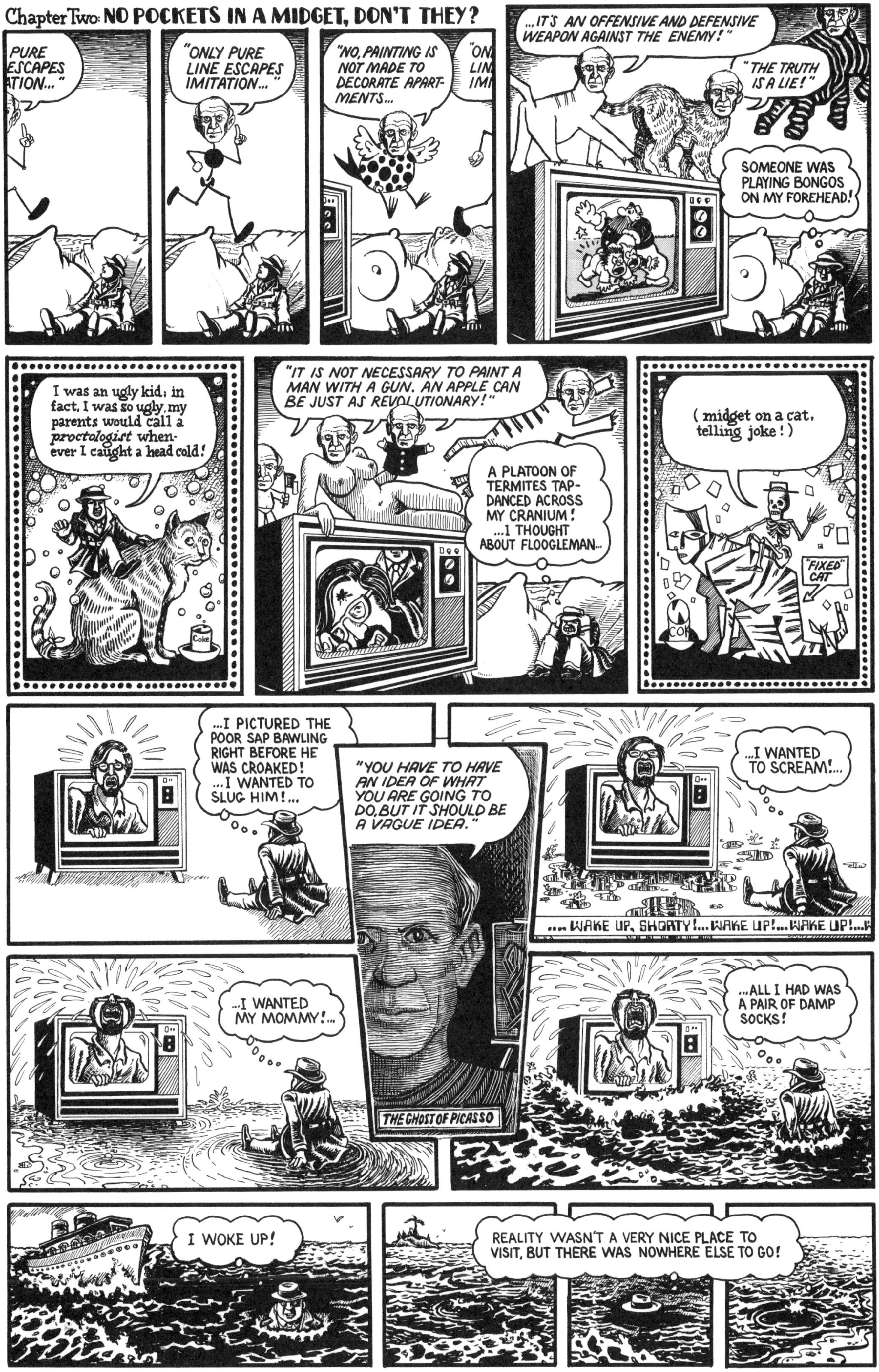

PURE ESCAPES ATION..."
"ONLY PURE LINE ESCAPES IMITATION..."
"NO, PAINTING IS NOT MADE TO DECORATE APARTMENTS...
...IT'S AN OFFENSIVE AND DEFENSIVE WEAPON AGAINST THE ENEMY!"
"THE TRUTH IS A LIE!"
SOMEONE WAS PLAYING BONGOS ON MY FOREHEAD!
I was an ugly kid; in fact, I was so ugly, my parents would call a *proctologist* whenever I caught a head cold!
Coke
"IT IS NOT NECESSARY TO PAINT A MAN WITH A GUN. AN APPLE CAN BE JUST AS REVOLUTIONARY!"
A PLATOON OF TERMITES TAP-DANCED ACROSS MY CRANIUM! ...I THOUGHT ABOUT FLOOGLEMAN...
(midget on a cat, telling joke!)
"FIXED" CAT
...I PICTURED THE POOR SAP BAWLING RIGHT BEFORE HE WAS CROAKED! ...I WANTED TO SLUG HIM!...
"YOU HAVE TO HAVE AN IDEA OF WHAT YOU ARE GOING TO DO, BUT IT SHOULD BE A VAGUE IDEA."
THE GHOST OF PICASSO
...I WANTED TO SCREAM!...
....WAKE UP, SHORTY!...WAKE UP!...WAKE UP!...
...I WANTED MY MOMMY!...
...ALL I HAD WAS A PAIR OF DAMP SOCKS!
I WOKE UP!
REALITY WASN'T A VERY NICE PLACE TO VISIT, BUT THERE WAS NOWHERE ELSE TO GO!

Chapter Three: ACE DEFECTIVE, MIDGET HOLE.

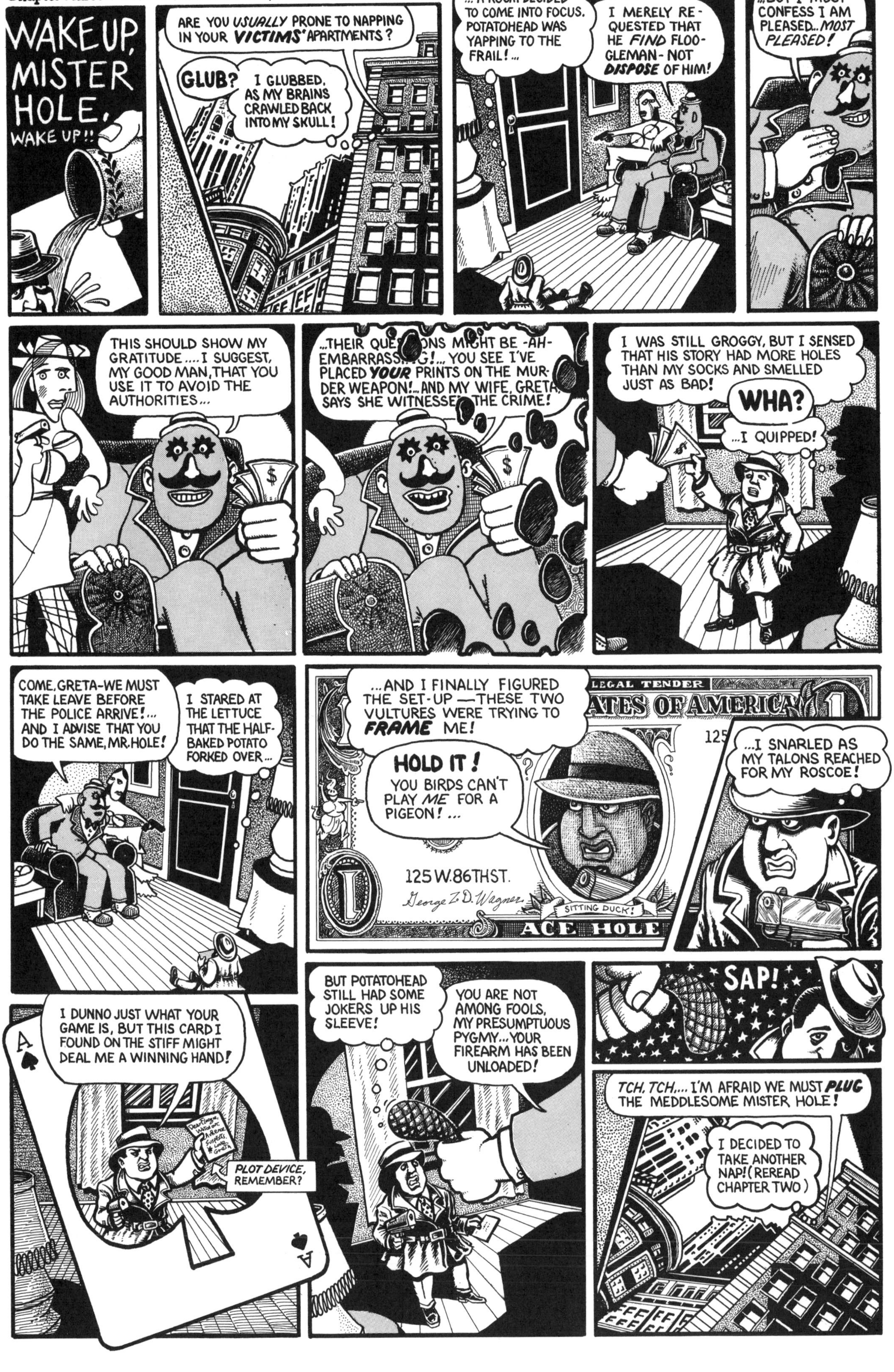

WAKE UP, MISTER HOLE, WAKE UP!!
ARE YOU USUALLY PRONE TO NAPPING IN YOUR VICTIMS' APARTMENTS?
GLUB?
I GLUBBED, AS MY BRAINS CRAWLED BACK INTO MY SKULL!
... A ROOM DECIDED TO COME INTO FOCUS. POTATOHEAD WAS YAPPING TO THE FRAIL! ...
I MERELY REQUESTED THAT HE FIND FLOOGLEMAN - NOT DISPOSE OF HIM!
... BUT I MUST CONFESS I AM PLEASED... MOST PLEASED!
THIS SHOULD SHOW MY GRATITUDE .... I SUGGEST, MY GOOD MAN, THAT YOU USE IT TO AVOID THE AUTHORITIES ...
... THEIR QUESTIONS MIGHT BE -AH- EMBARRASSING! ... YOU SEE I'VE PLACED YOUR PRINTS ON THE MURDER WEAPON! ... AND MY WIFE, GRETA, SAYS SHE WITNESSED THE CRIME!
I WAS STILL GROGGY, BUT I SENSED THAT HIS STORY HAD MORE HOLES THAN MY SOCKS AND SMELLED JUST AS BAD!
WHA?
... I QUIPPED!
COME, GRETA - WE MUST TAKE LEAVE BEFORE THE POLICE ARRIVE! ... AND I ADVISE THAT YOU DO THE SAME, MR. HOLE!
I STARED AT THE LETTUCE THAT THE HALF-BAKED POTATO FORKED OVER ...
... AND I FINALLY FIGURED THE SET-UP — THESE TWO VULTURES WERE TRYING TO FRAME ME!
LEGAL TENDER
ATES OF AMERICA
125
HOLD IT! YOU BIRDS CAN'T PLAY ME FOR A PIGEON! ...
125 W. 86TH ST.
George Z. D. Wagner
SITTING DUCK!
ACE HOLE
... I SNARLED AS MY TALONS REACHED FOR MY ROSCOE!
I DUNNO JUST WHAT YOUR GAME IS, BUT THIS CARD I FOUND ON THE STIFF MIGHT DEAL ME A WINNING HAND!
PLOT DEVICE, REMEMBER?
BUT POTATOHEAD STILL HAD SOME JOKERS UP HIS SLEEVE!
YOU ARE NOT AMONG FOOLS, MY PRESUMPTUOUS PYGMY ... YOUR FIREARM HAS BEEN UNLOADED!
SAP!
TCH, TCH, ... I'M AFRAID WE MUST PLUG THE MEDDLESOME MISTER HOLE!
I DECIDED TO TAKE ANOTHER NAP! (REREAD CHAPTER TWO)

"WE ARTISTS ARE INDESTRUCTABLE ....

"..EVEN IN A PRISON OR IN A CONCENTRATION CAMP, I WOULD BE ALMIGHTY IN MY OWN WORLD OF ART. ...

"...EVEN IF I HAD TO PAINT MY PICTURES WITH MY WET TONGUE ON THE DUSTY FLOOR OF MY CELL."

REALITY WASN'T A VERY NICE PLACE TO VISIT....

Hurry Ace Wake Up

..I WOKE UP - MY GRAY MATTER FELT LIKE SHATTERED SILLY PUTTY!

IF THIS KIND OF TREATMENT KEPT UP, I **WOULD** NEED A PROCTOLOGIST FOR MY HEADACHES!

THE SCENERY HAD CHANGED WHILE I SNOOZED. I WAS IN POTATOHEAD'S APARTMENT AND HIS MOLL WAS STROKING MY BROW... THINGS WERE LOOKING UP A LITTLE!

We Must Hurry !!!...

My Husband Went out for some Tobacco. He Left me here to keep an Eye on you!

THIS DAME...

He'll Kill You! *Kill You!!* But... I... don't... want you... Dead!

...WAS DYNAMITE! SHE HAD MORE SIDES THAN A REVOLVING DOOR!

HER KISSES MADE MY TOENAILS QUIVER, BUT BUSINESS HAD TO COME BEFORE I COULD

GET ME MY GUN!

I GROWLED!

SHE HANDED IT OVER. I DIDN'T KNOW MUCH ABOUT ART, BUT THIS BABE WAS JAKE WITH ME! I GRINNED AND SAID...

FILL IN THE *DE-TAILS* TOOTSIE... I DON'T GET THE PICTURE!

Well... Laurence and FlooGleman Were Partners....

FlooGleman forged the Paintings; Laurence was the fence...

Now he was and said...

FILL IN THE *DE-TAILS* TOOTSIE I DON'T

All went well until I fell for Floogie...

Laurence found out. He went crazy and **m-murdered** him!...

THE TOOTSIE I DON'T GET THE PICTURE!

He tried to set you up as the fall guy, but you knew too much!

"IT FIT LIKE A GLOVE!..."

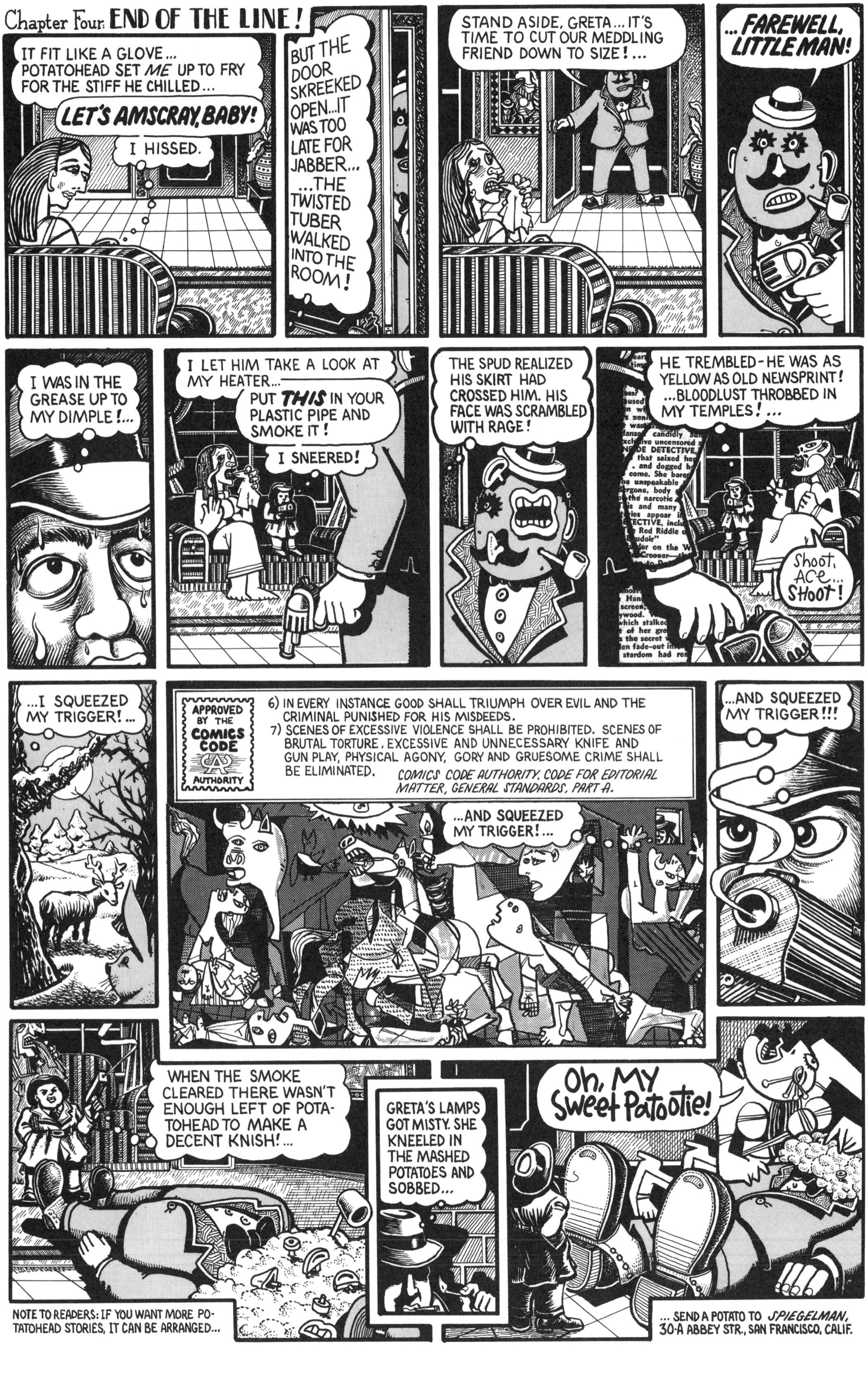

Chapter Four: END OF THE LINE!
IT FIT LIKE A GLOVE... POTATOHEAD SET *ME* UP TO FRY FOR THE STIFF HE CHILLED...
LET'S AMSCRAY, BABY!
I HISSED.
BUT THE DOOR SKREEKED OPEN...IT WAS TOO LATE FOR JABBER... ...THE TWISTED TUBER WALKED INTO THE ROOM!
STAND ASIDE, GRETA... IT'S TIME TO CUT OUR MEDDLING FRIEND DOWN TO SIZE!...
...FAREWELL, LITTLE MAN!
I WAS IN THE GREASE UP TO MY DIMPLE!...
I LET HIM TAKE A LOOK AT MY HEATER...
PUT **THIS** IN YOUR PLASTIC PIPE AND SMOKE IT!
I SNEERED!
THE SPUD REALIZED HIS SKIRT HAD CROSSED HIM. HIS FACE WAS SCRAMBLED WITH RAGE!
HE TREMBLED-HE WAS AS YELLOW AS OLD NEWSPRINT! ...BLOODLUST THROBBED IN MY TEMPLES!...
Shoot, Ace... Shoot!
...I SQUEEZED MY TRIGGER!...
APPROVED BY THE COMICS CODE AUTHORITY
6) IN EVERY INSTANCE GOOD SHALL TRIUMPH OVER EVIL AND THE CRIMINAL PUNISHED FOR HIS MISDEEDS.
7) SCENES OF EXCESSIVE VIOLENCE SHALL BE PROHIBITED. SCENES OF BRUTAL TORTURE, EXCESSIVE AND UNNECESSARY KNIFE AND GUN PLAY, PHYSICAL AGONY, GORY AND GRUESOME CRIME SHALL BE ELIMINATED.
COMICS CODE AUTHORITY, CODE FOR EDITORIAL MATTER, GENERAL STANDARDS, PART A.
...AND SQUEEZED MY TRIGGER!...
...AND SQUEEZED MY TRIGGER!!!
WHEN THE SMOKE CLEARED THERE WASN'T ENOUGH LEFT OF POTATOHEAD TO MAKE A DECENT KNISH!...
GRETA'S LAMPS GOT MISTY. SHE KNEELED IN THE MASHED POTATOES AND SOBBED...
Oh, MY Sweet Patootie!
NOTE TO READERS: IF YOU WANT MORE POTATOHEAD STORIES, IT CAN BE ARRANGED...
... SEND A POTATO TO *SPIEGELMAN*, 30-A ABBEY STR., SAN FRANCISCO, CALIF.

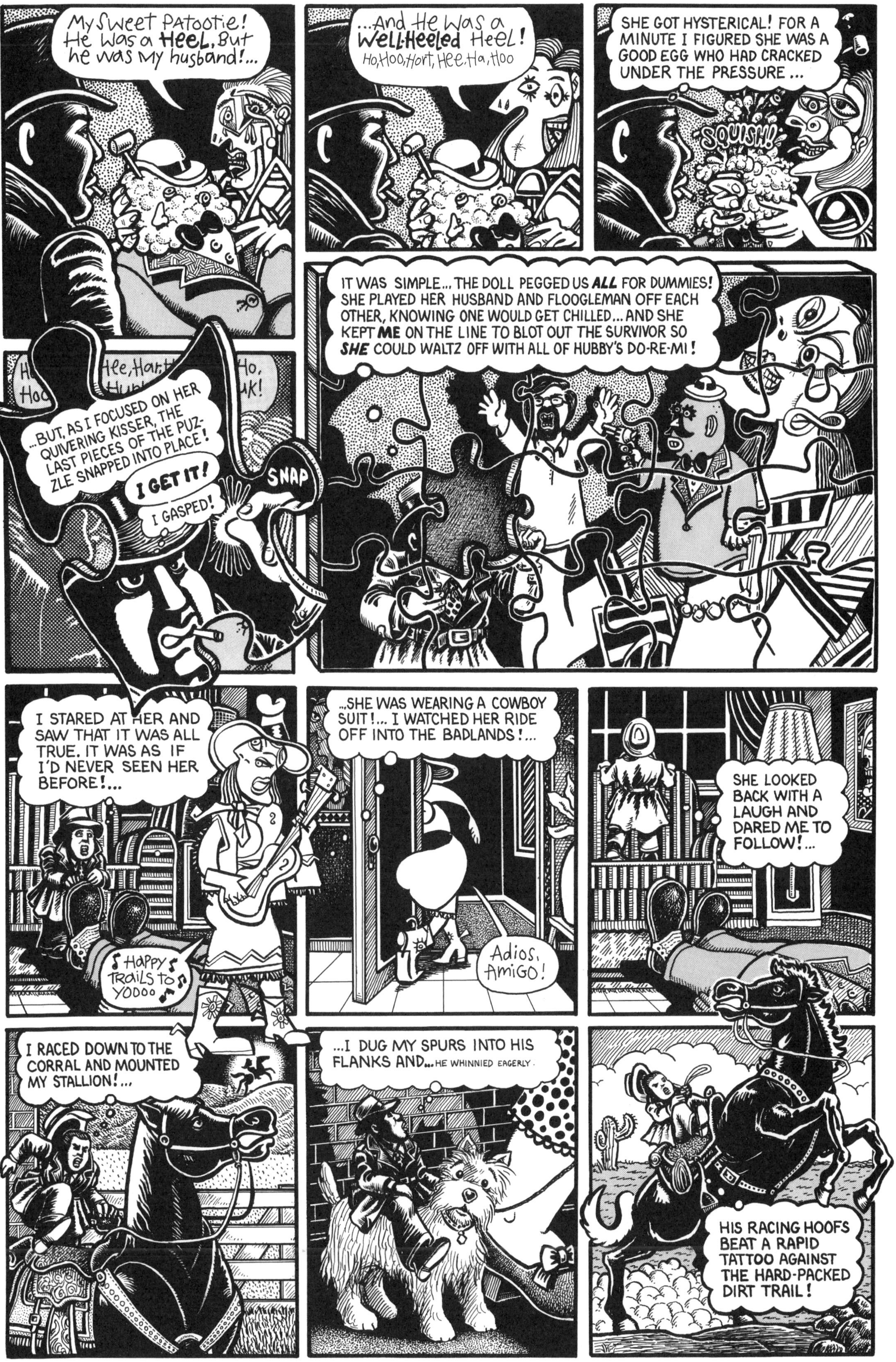

My Sweet Patootie! He Was a Heel, But he was My husband!...
...And He Was a Well-Heeled Heel!
Ho, Hoo, Hort, Hee, Ha, Hoo
SHE GOT HYSTERICAL! FOR A MINUTE I FIGURED SHE WAS A GOOD EGG WHO HAD CRACKED UNDER THE PRESSURE ...
SQUISH!
...BUT, AS I FOCUSED ON HER QUIVERING KISSER, THE LAST PIECES OF THE PUZZLE SNAPPED INTO PLACE!
I GET IT!
I GASPED!
SNAP
IT WAS SIMPLE... THE DOLL PEGGED US ALL FOR DUMMIES! SHE PLAYED HER HUSBAND AND FLOOGLEMAN OFF EACH OTHER, KNOWING ONE WOULD GET CHILLED... AND SHE KEPT ME ON THE LINE TO BLOT OUT THE SURVIVOR SO SHE COULD WALTZ OFF WITH ALL OF HUBBY'S DO-RE-MI!
I STARED AT HER AND SAW THAT IT WAS ALL TRUE. IT WAS AS IF I'D NEVER SEEN HER BEFORE!...
Happy Trails to Yoooo
...SHE WAS WEARING A COWBOY SUIT!... I WATCHED HER RIDE OFF INTO THE BADLANDS!...
Adios, Amigo!
SHE LOOKED BACK WITH A LAUGH AND DARED ME TO FOLLOW!...
I RACED DOWN TO THE CORRAL AND MOUNTED MY STALLION!...
...I DUG MY SPURS INTO HIS FLANKS AND... HE WHINNIED EAGERLY.
HIS RACING HOOFS BEAT A RAPID TATTOO AGAINST THE HARD-PACKED DIRT TRAIL!

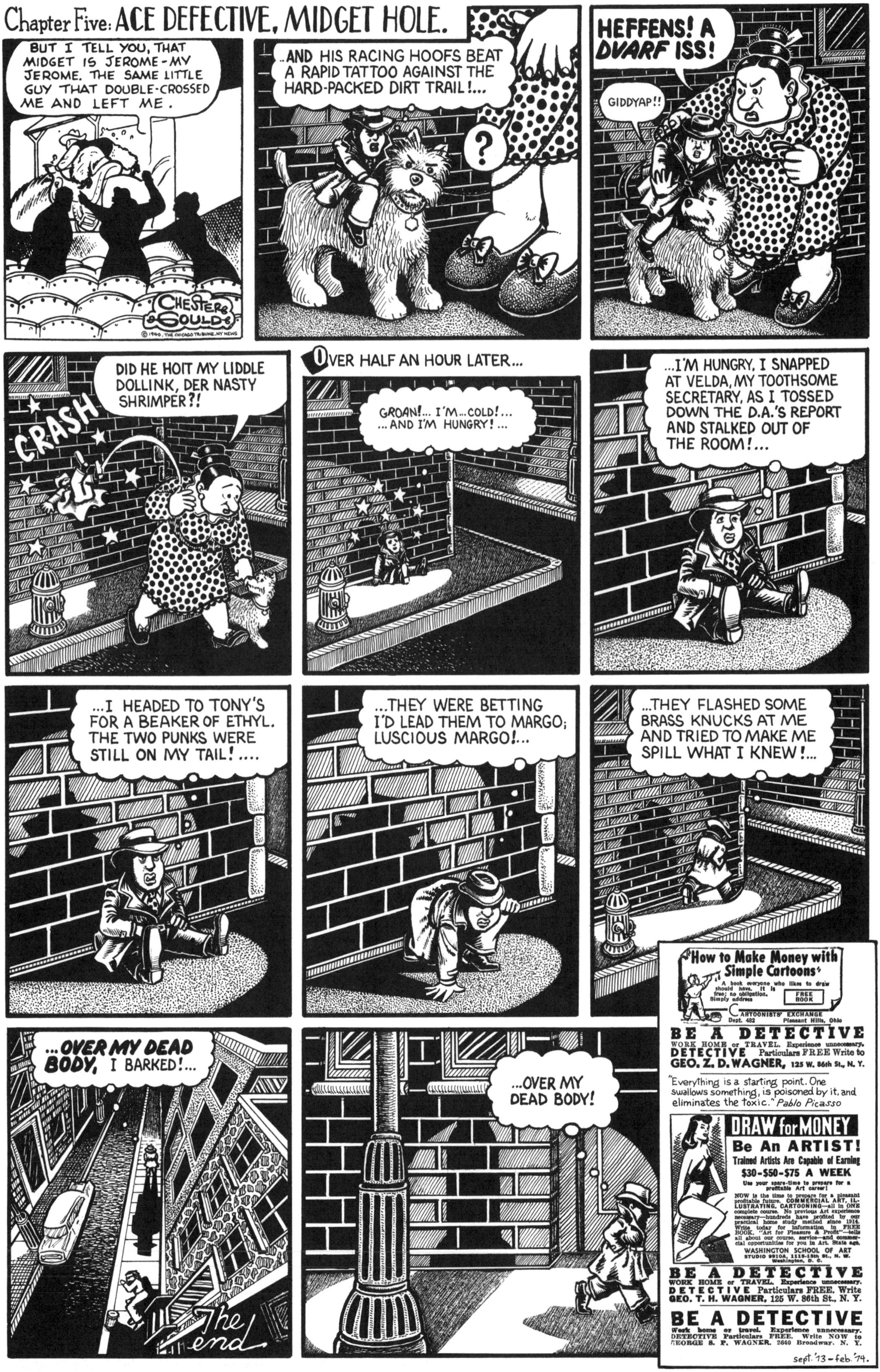

Chapter Five: ACE DEFECTIVE, MIDGET HOLE.
BUT I TELL YOU, THAT MIDGET IS JEROME - MY JEROME. THE SAME LITTLE GUY THAT DOUBLE-CROSSED ME AND LEFT ME.
CHESTER GOULD
© 1940, THE CHICAGO TRIBUNE-NY NEWS
...AND HIS RACING HOOFS BEAT A RAPID TATTOO AGAINST THE HARD-PACKED DIRT TRAIL!...
?
HEFFENS! A DVARF ISS!
GIDDYAP!!
DID HE HOIT MY LIDDLE DOLLINK, DER NASTY SHRIMPER?!
CRASH
OVER HALF AN HOUR LATER...
GROAN!... I'M...COLD!... ...AND I'M HUNGRY!...
...I'M HUNGRY, I SNAPPED AT VELDA, MY TOOTHSOME SECRETARY, AS I TOSSED DOWN THE D.A.'S REPORT AND STALKED OUT OF THE ROOM!...
...I HEADED TO TONY'S FOR A BEAKER OF ETHYL. THE TWO PUNKS WERE STILL ON MY TAIL!....
...THEY WERE BETTING I'D LEAD THEM TO MARGO; LUSCIOUS MARGO!...
...THEY FLASHED SOME BRASS KNUCKS AT ME AND TRIED TO MAKE ME SPILL WHAT I KNEW!...
...OVER MY DEAD BODY, I BARKED!...
The end
...OVER MY DEAD BODY!
"How to Make Money with Simple Cartoons"
A book everyone who likes to draw should have. It is free; no obligation. Simply address
FREE BOOK
CARTOONISTS' EXCHANGE Dept. 482 Pleasant Hills, Ohio
BE A DETECTIVE
WORK HOME or TRAVEL. Experience unnecessary. DETECTIVE Particulars FREE Write to GEO. Z. D. WAGNER, 125 W. 86th St., N. Y.
"Everything is a starting point. One swallows something, is poisoned by it, and eliminates the toxic." Pablo Picasso
DRAW for MONEY
Be An ARTIST!
Trained Artists Are Capable of Earning
$30-$50-$75 A WEEK
Use your spare-time to prepare for a profitable Art career!
NOW is the time to prepare for a pleasant profitable future. COMMERCIAL ART, ILLUSTRATING, CARTOONING—all in ONE complete course. No previous Art experience necessary—hundreds have profited by our practical home study method since 1914. Write today for information in FREE BOOK, "Art for Pleasure & Profit"—tells all about our course, service—and commercial opportunities for you in Art. State age.
WASHINGTON SCHOOL OF ART
STUDIO 9910A, 1115-15th St., N. W. Washington, D. C.
BE A DETECTIVE
WORK HOME or TRAVEL. Experience unnecessary. DETECTIVE Particulars FREE. Write GEO. T. H. WAGNER, 125 W. 86th St., N. Y.
BE A DETECTIVE
Work home or travel. Experience unnecessary. DETECTIVE Particulars FREE. Write NOW to GEORGE S. P. WAGNER. 2640 Broadway. N. Y.
sept. '73 - feb. '74.

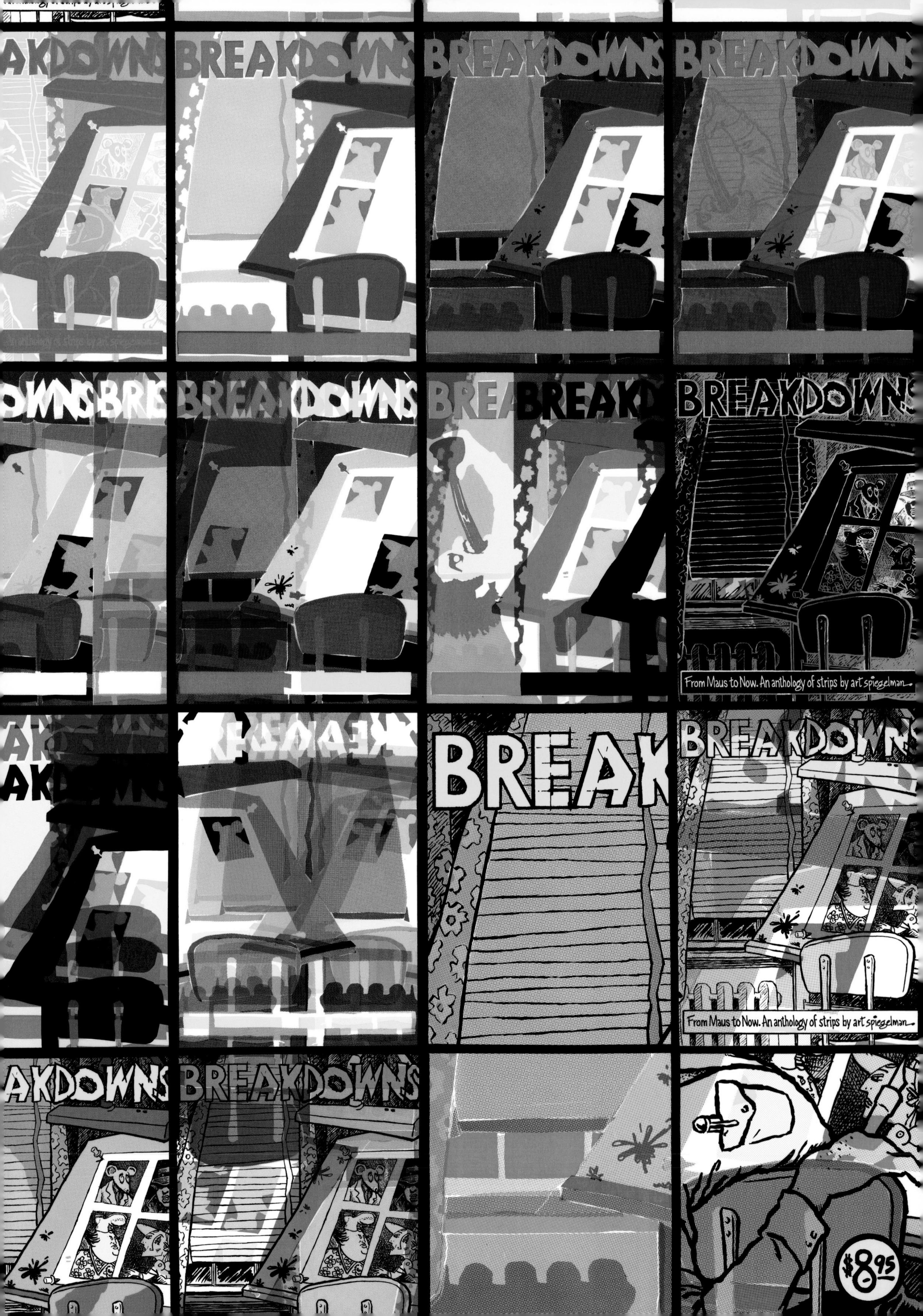
BREAKDOWNS
From Maus to Now. An anthology of strips by art spiegelman.
From Maus to Now. An anthology of strips by art spiegelman.
$8.95

%@₉★!!

AN AFTERWORD

Breakdowns was published in 1978 against all odds. There was no demand for a deluxe large-format album that collected the scattered handful of short autobiographical and structurally "experimental" comics I'd made between 1972 and 1977—except by me. I had finally found my voice as a cartoonist, and needed to see my strips in a setting separate from the underground comix they had been born in, to understand what I had articulated.

Breakdowns' now confusing subtitle, "From Maus to Now," referred to a three-page strip that I had done in 1972, not the three-hundred-page book in two volumes that grew from that seed years later. The "Now" in the subtitle refers to "Then," as it *always* does once it's uttered. The three-

page "Maus" I did back then is the earliest piece included in Breakdowns. It followed a stumbling apprenticeship that started before I could read.

In the claustrophobic confines of my refugee parents' home, comics were my picture window onto American culture. The first fresh air from the outside world came from Carl Barks' Donald Duck, John Stanley's Little Lulu, and, most penetratingly, from the strong blast of Harvey Kurtzman's MAD. As soon as I found out that cartoons weren't exactly natural phenomena—like trees—but were actually made by people, I desperately wanted to be one of the people who made them. The only thing that changed over the years was the kind of cartoons I wanted to make.

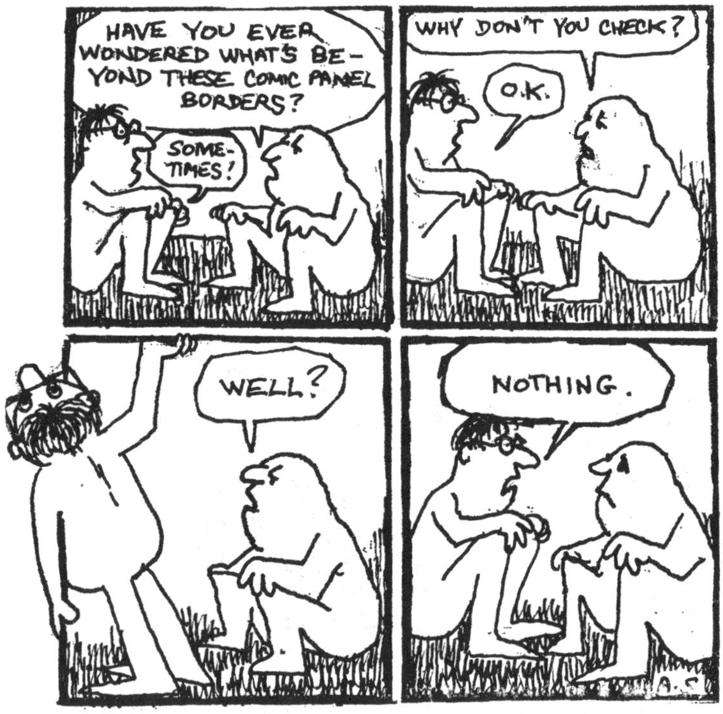
HAVE YOU EVER WONDERED WHAT'S BEYOND THESE COMIC PANEL BORDERS?
SOMETIMES!
WHY DON'T YOU CHECK?
O.K.
WELL?
NOTHING.
A.S.

ABOVE: **From *Pipe Dreams*, Harpur College's weekly newspaper in 1965**

I had my first drawing published in 1961, when I was thirteen. I had taken a sheaf of cartoons to a small weekly newspaper in Queens, looking for a gig. Instead, they ran a small feature about me, accompanied by my drawing of Frankenstein, under the humiliating headline: "BUDDING ARTIST WANTS ATTENTION!" I got a better reception a few years later, when I was a student at the High School of Art and Design—a vocational school for commercial art in midtown Manhattan—and the same paper hired me as a regular freelancer. In high school I started making strange, surreal and decidedly uncommercial comics between homework assignments. In 1965, I took some of these to the just-launched *East Village Other*, one of the first of the underground weekly papers that helped define what we now call the Sixties. The comics in their first few issues really sucked, so I was sure my work would fit right in. The editor, Walter Bowart, looked my pages over with sympathy if not comprehension, and asked if I could do some strips about sex and drugs. I knew little about either, so I enrolled at Harpur College in Binghamton, NY, and set out to find out about both while dodging the Vietnam War–era draft as a student.

By 1967, my virginity and mind were both long gone, and I began a hazy period of bouncing from Binghamton to the East Village, San Francisco and back, with pit stops at a psychedelicized commune in Vermont. I drew leaflets printed in runs of a hundred or so at a time, passing them out on street corners and in parks when I wasn't passing out myself. Sometimes in comics format, sometimes in imitation of Fillmore concert posters, they extolled LSD, protested the war and, as often as not, had no discernible message at all.

That year—before Underground Comix were quite definable as such—I first met R. Crumb, visiting him in his Haight-Ashbury apartment as a fellow protégé of Woody Gelman. (Woody was my mentor back in New York, giving me a summer job as an idea man at Topps Chewing Gum, Inc. as soon as I turned eighteen, a position that ended up lasting twenty years and helped subsidize my "career" as an underground cartoonist.) Crumb showed me the unpublished pages he'd recently made, the results of his LSD experiences. To put it as I did then: they totally, like, blew my mind. The work served up a parodic reinvention of lost lowbrow cartoon art styles, rubbery, hairy and convoluted, at a moment when cartoon art was still striving toward the streamlined and

BELOW: **"A Flash of Insight..."**
Drawn in 1965 or 1966, and eventually published in 1967 by revered comic book artist Wally Wood in the second issue of his experimental proto-underground comics magazine, *Witzend*

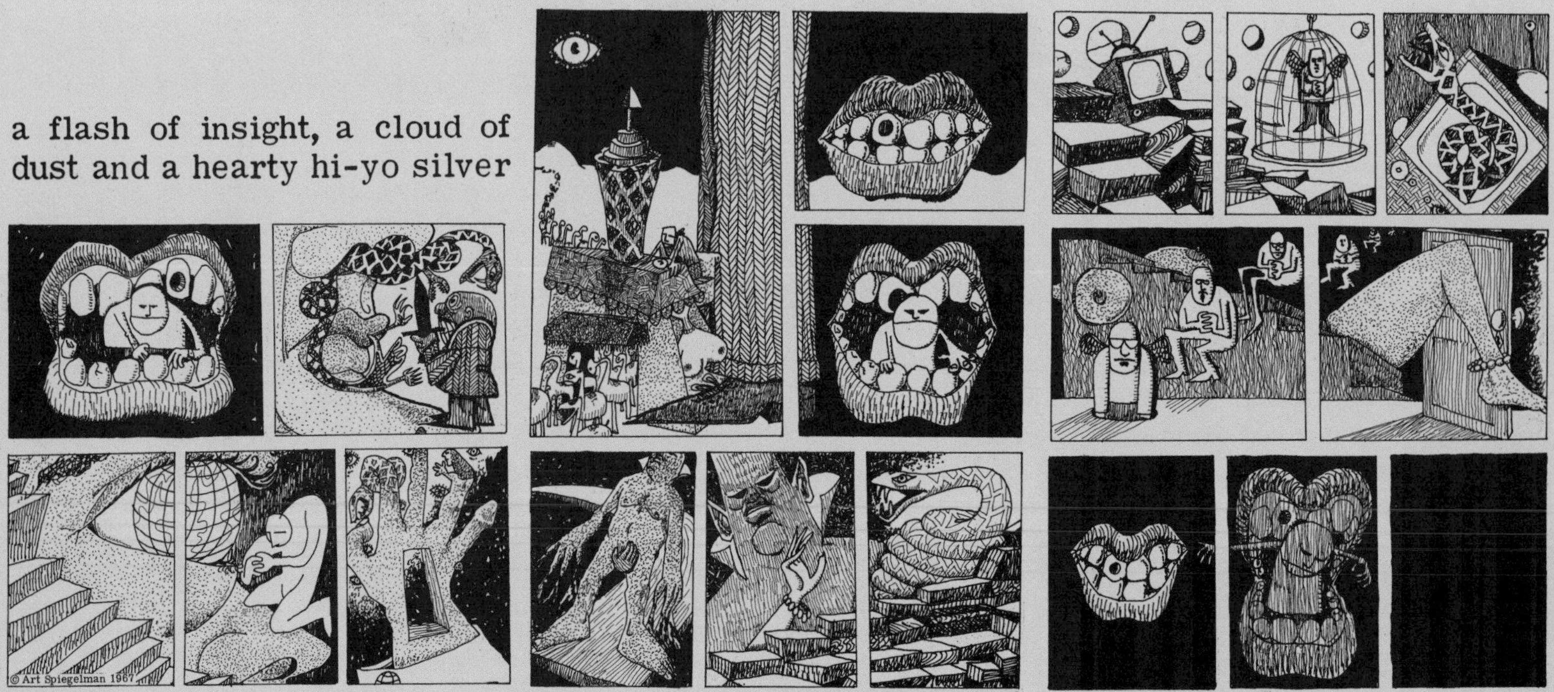
a flash of insight, a cloud of dust and a hearty hi-yo silver
© Art Spiegelman 1967

minimalist. These pages seemed to be dredged directly from the subconscious, but couldn't glibly be labeled surreal. They were all-too-real, urgent, existential, scary and hilarious, though often without anything as conventional as a punch line.

My own experiments with mind-altering drugs at the time had more banally shifted my ambitions toward becoming At One With the Universe and Achieving Egoless Buddhahood; the ambition to make Strange Comics that had gripped me in high school came in second. Seeing Crumb's radically new work in 1967 was a relief. I could leave this comics stuff in his uniquely capable hands and pursue Enlightenment unencumbered, since it would take several lifetimes—reincarnation was then part of my mixed-up mix!—to get anywhere near his achievements. I remember babbling to him about my incipient ideas of what comics might do ("Panels can be inset into bigger panels to show different points in space simultaneously! Repeating panels can freeze the flow of time! Time is an illusion that can be shattered in comics! Showing the same scene from different angles freezes it in time by turning the page into a diagram—an orthographic projection!") and wandering off to nearby Golden Gate Park to drop acid.

As I crash-landed back on Earth over the next couple of years, I tried to absorb what Crumb and other underground cartoonists I admired were up to by badly imitating them all. It made for some very embarrassing work: substandard stabs at erotica and transgressive humor, as well as grotesque exercises in taboo breaking that featured patricide, necrophilia and other misguided eruptions of violence on paper. One of these strips "climaxed" with a character of mine, The Viper, fucking a young boy's severed head in the neck. Oh God! I wanted to draw the most disturbing images I could think up...and they at least disturbed Crumb's then wife, Dana, enough to bar me from ever visiting her home. I was an enterprising junior member of an exhilarating scene but, man, was I lost.

Several significant encounters helped me find myself as the Sixties blurred into the Seventies. In 1969 (after an eventful year that included a breakdown of the mental hospital variety, being booted out of college, my mother's suicide and a particularly disastrous attempt at communal living) I returned to Binghamton to convalesce. There I met Ken Jacobs, an avant-garde filmmaker and cinema professor who was enthusiastic about an art history paper I'd once written, a panel-by-panel analysis of Bernard Krigstein's "Master Race" (a then obscure, formally complex 1955 comic book story that alluded to the Nazi death camps). Ken took me under his wing and taught me the value of Art that didn't have speech balloons. When I moved to San Francisco in 1970, Bill Griffith, who was just settling there as well, became my closest colleague and confidant. Our friendship gave me needed stability in the land of lotus-eaters. Virtually all the pieces in *Breakdowns* were first published in projects we co-edited, most notably *Short Order Comix* and *Arcade, The Comix Revue.*

In 1971, I got to know Justin Green, who was then making the masterpiece that opened up confessional autobiography as subject matter for comix. Strung on a long clothesline in his Mission-district cottage were the pages that would become *Binky Brown Meets the Holy Virgin Mary.* Unlike Crumb, who transmuted his personal obsessions into a universal cartoon language, Justin used the psychosexual and Catholic guilt of his personal life as subject matter to be intimately reported

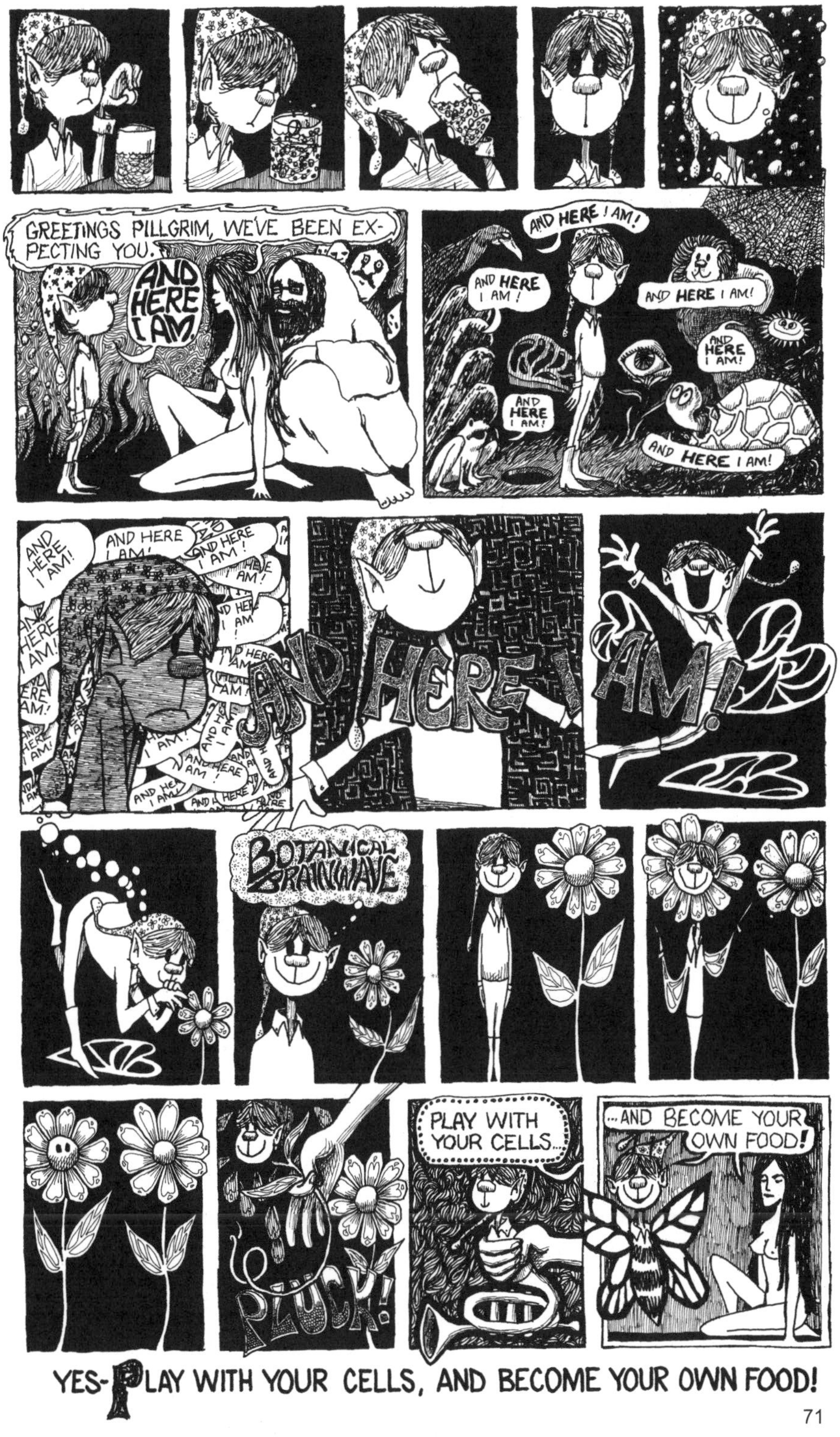
GREETINGS PILLGRIM, WE'VE BEEN EXPECTING YOU.
AND HERE I AM.
AND HERE I AM!
AND HERE I AM!
AND HERE I AM!
AND HERE I AM!
AND HERE I AM!
AND HERE I AM!
AND HERE I AM!
AND HERE I AM!
BOTANICAL BRAINWAVE
PLUCK!
PLAY WITH YOUR CELLS...
...AND BECOME YOUR OWN FOOD!
YES-PLAY WITH YOUR CELLS, AND BECOME YOUR OWN FOOD!

RIGHT: **Leaflet, 1967. Reprinted in various underground newspapers and in *Witzend* #3, 1967**

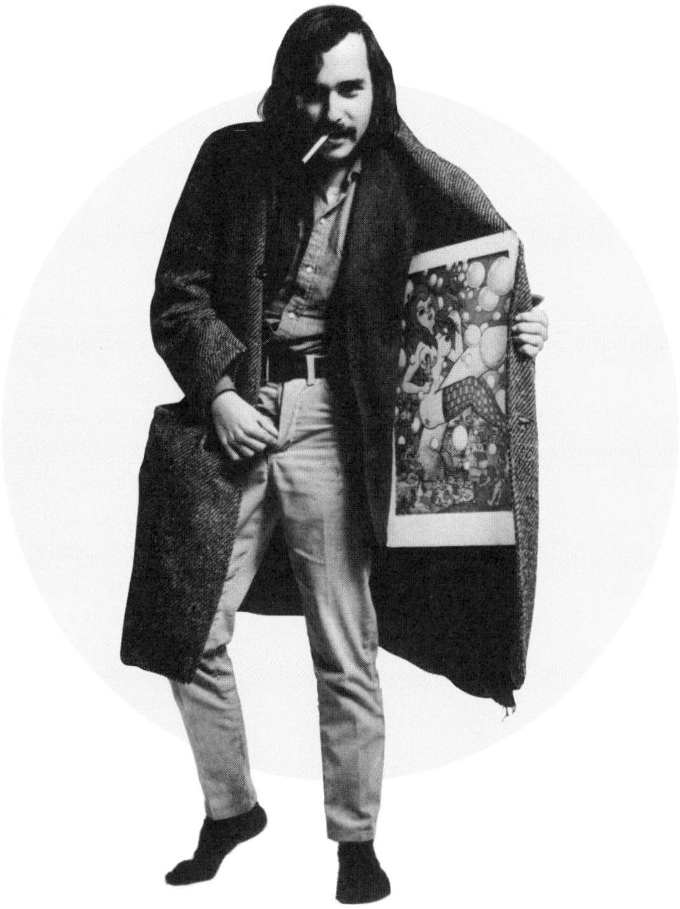

in quirkily drawn, tightly composed pages. It let me finally connect the dots in my own psyche: instead of drawing the most appallingly lurid violence I could dream up, I could now locate the atrocities present in the real world that my parents had survived and brought me into.

The 1972 "Maus" strip that came from this eye-opener was drawn in a somewhat more sober style than my earlier comics, but was radical mainly in its content. "Prisoner on the Hell Planet" came later that year, drawn in Justin's cottage, in fact. (Justin had moved out after helpfully warning me not to face my drawing table north, since rays from the nearby Mission Dolores church could interfere with my work.) "Hell Planet" was more complex in its form and style than anything I'd made before, strengthened by its emotional charge and deepened by my new appetite for the "High" arts on the other side of the High-Low class divide. When "Hell Planet" was published, reduced to standard 7" x 10" underground comix format and printed on newsprint, the detailed scratchboard drawings, inspired by Expressionist woodcuts, looked clotted and congested. I began to want better paper and the larger scale that the oversized *Breakdowns* would eventually allow. (Ironically, most readers were exposed to "Hell Planet" in a terminally cramped incarnation when it was later "entered into the deposition" of the small-size *Maus* book.)

ABOVE: **Portrait of the Artist... Photo by Raeanne Rubenstein, 1969**

BELOW LEFT: **Leaflet, 1967**

BELOW RIGHT: **"LSD Did This to Me!"** *East Village Other*, circa 1968

FACING PAGE: **Cover, *East Village Other*, volume 4, no. 44, 1969**

My interests began to diverge from an underground comix scene still dominated by sex, dope and transgressive genre stories. I became consumed with finding out how narrative comics had to be to be comics at all, infatuated with the cross-pollination of High and Low. It was actually a very short walk from Chester Gould's *Dick Tracy* to German Expressionism and only a slightly longer stretch to get immersed in Cézanne, via Cubism and the entire convulsion that painting went through when photography threatened all of painting's previous premises.

Painters had then begun to poke at how things were represented in painting—paint and canvas became subject matter. Experimental filmmakers around me were looking

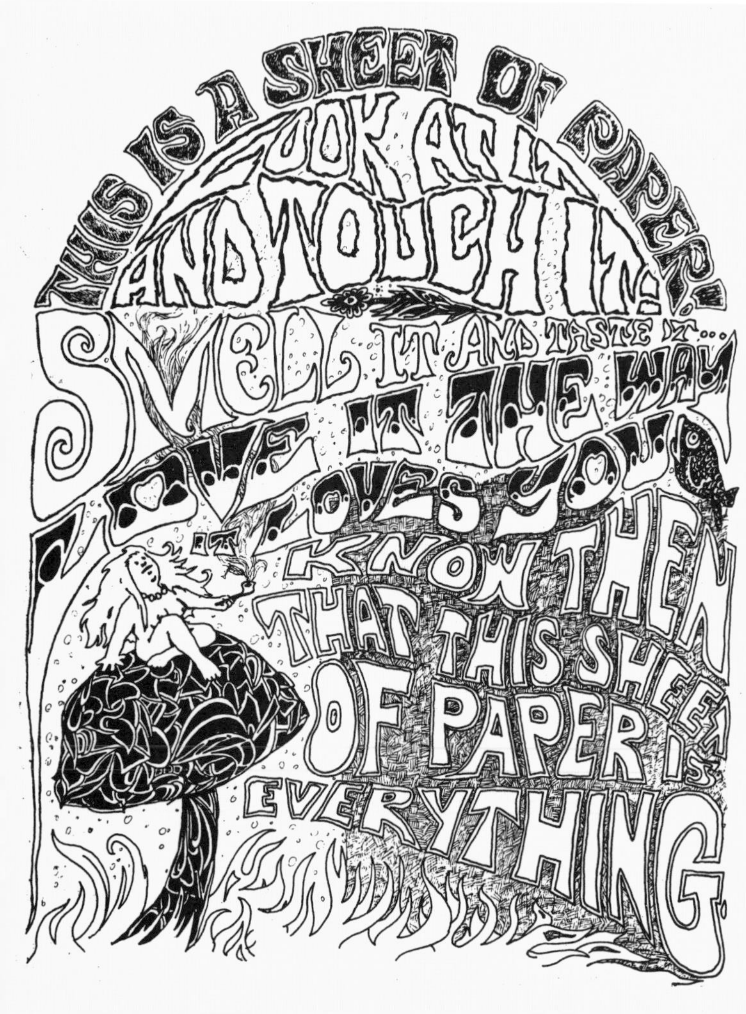
THIS IS A SHEET OF PAPER!
LOOK AT IT
AND TOUCH IT...
SMELL IT AND TASTE IT...
LOVE IT THE WAY
IT LOVES YOU
KNOW THEN
THAT THIS SHEET
OF PAPER IS
EVERYTHING

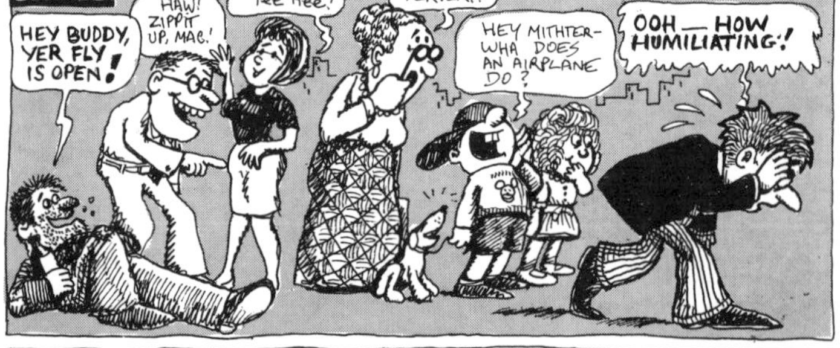
LSD DID THIS TO ME!
CASE HISTORY NUMBER 4,317.
BEFORE
HEY BUDDY, YER FLY IS OPEN!
HAW! ZIPPIT UP, MAC!
Tee Hee!
PERVERT!
HEY MITHTER- WHA DOES AN AIRPLANE DO?
OOH — HOW HUMILIATING!
AFTER
(ITS HIS FLY- IT'S OPEN!)
SIGH!
HYUK! HYUK! I'M SUCH A FREAK!
WOTTA MAN!
art spiegelman

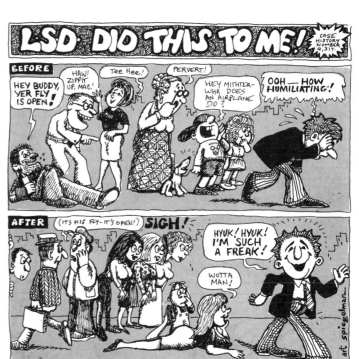

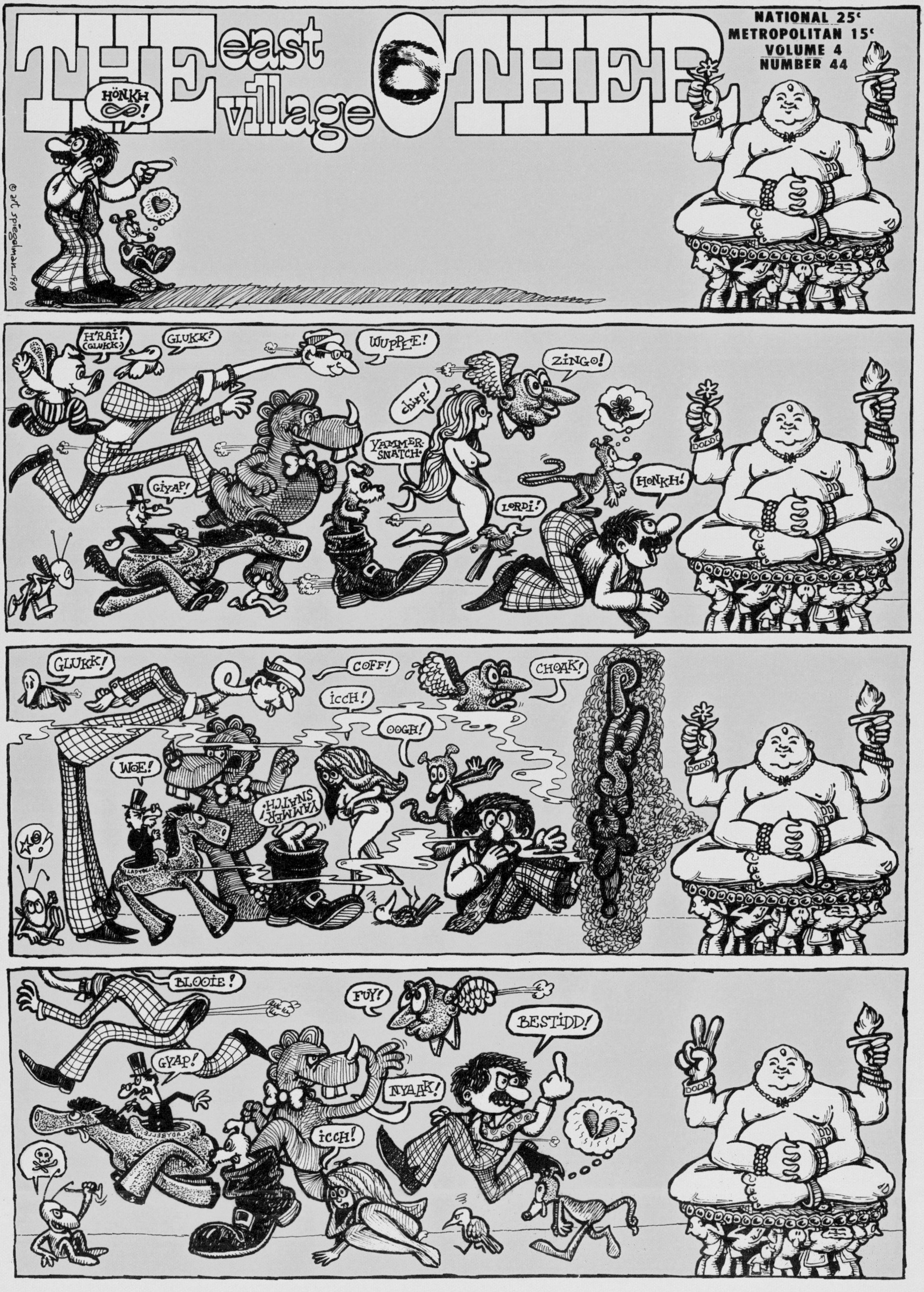
THE east village OTHER
NATIONAL 25¢
METROPOLITAN 15¢
VOLUME 4
NUMBER 44
HÖNKH ∞!
© art spiegelman
H'RAI! (GLUKK)
GLUKK?
WUPPEE!
ZINGO!
chirp!
YAMMER-SNATCH
GIYAP!
LORDI!
HONKH!
GLUKK!
COFF!
CHOAK!
ICCH!
OOGH!
WOE!
YAMMER-SNATCH
BLOOIE!
FUY!
BESTIDD!
GYAP!
NYAAK!
ICCH!

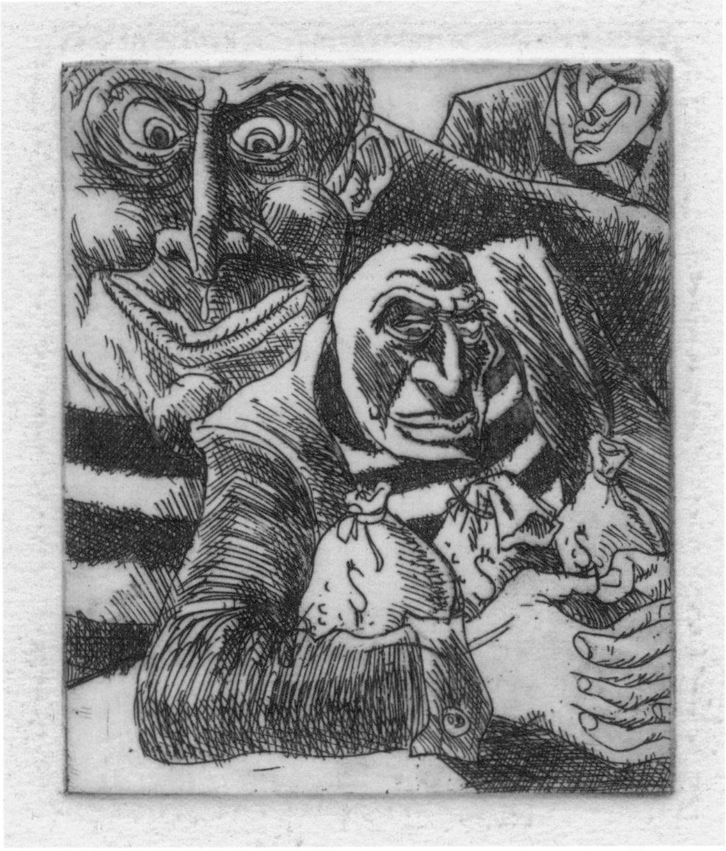

ABOVE: "Greed," Un-editioned etching, circa 1974

BELOW LEFT: Cover, *Bijou Funnies* #7, 1972
The Viper (with cameos by Skip Williamson and Jay Lynch)

BELOW RIGHT: The Viper, "Pop Goes the Poppa"
in *Real Pulp Comics* #2, 1971

into film as light passing through celluloid at 24 frames per second. Some of this self-reflexive thinking had been deployed to satirical effect in Harvey Kurtzman's 1950s *MAD* and served as a point of departure for me as a cartoonist looking at the "stuff" of his own medium. I looked at how the illusion of time that is created by juxtaposing images on a page might best be ruptured, at how words and pictures interact and—goofily enough—at Zipatone.

Those self-adhesive sheets of pre-printed dot-screens that simulate a gray tone were still a common part of the cartoonist's tool kit in the pre-digital world, and essential for creating color comix covers. (These color separations involved an esoteric, unlamentably lost craft, difficult to explain to the uninitiated, and far removed from the sensual act of painting. One tediously cut and placed the black dot-screen tints on overlays—one overlay for each of the four color printing inks: cyan, magenta, yellow and black. When the tints were placed at the wrong angle, the result was a dreaded, rippled "moiré" pattern.) Anyway, contemplating this process while plucking tiny stray pieces of Zipatone off my clothes led to "Zip-a-tunes and Moiré Melodies," first published as a small 16-page booklet designed to look vaguely like a Thirties "Tijuana Bible" porno comic. This later steered me toward the complex covers and endpapers of *Breakdowns*. The fact that comix were printed objects had become part of my subject matter.

"Don't Get Around Much Anymore," drawn over several months in 1973, and physically as well as conceptually at the

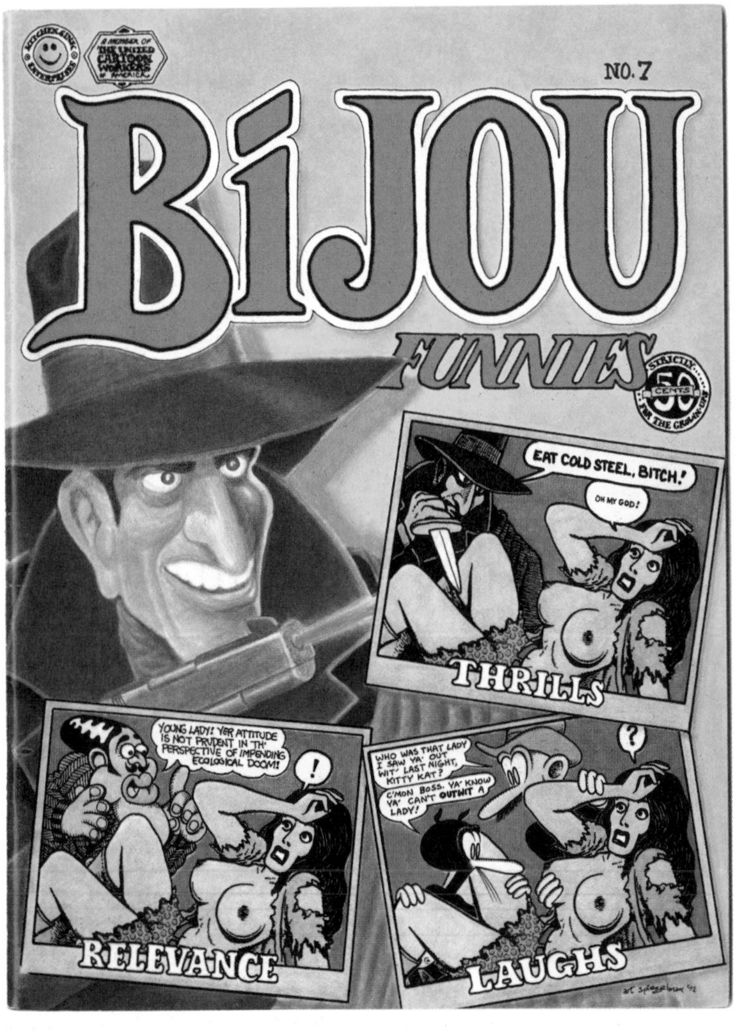
NO.7
BiJOU
FUNNIES
EAT COLD STEEL, BITCH!
OH MY GOD!
THRILLS
YOUNG LADY! YER ATTITUDE IS NOT PRUDENT IN TH' PERSPECTIVE OF IMPENDING ECOLOGICAL DOOM!
!
WHO WAS THAT LADY I SAW YA' OUT WIT' LAST NIGHT, KITTY KAT?
C'MON BOSS. YA' KNOW YA' CAN'T OUTWIT A LADY!
?
RELEVANCE
LAUGHS

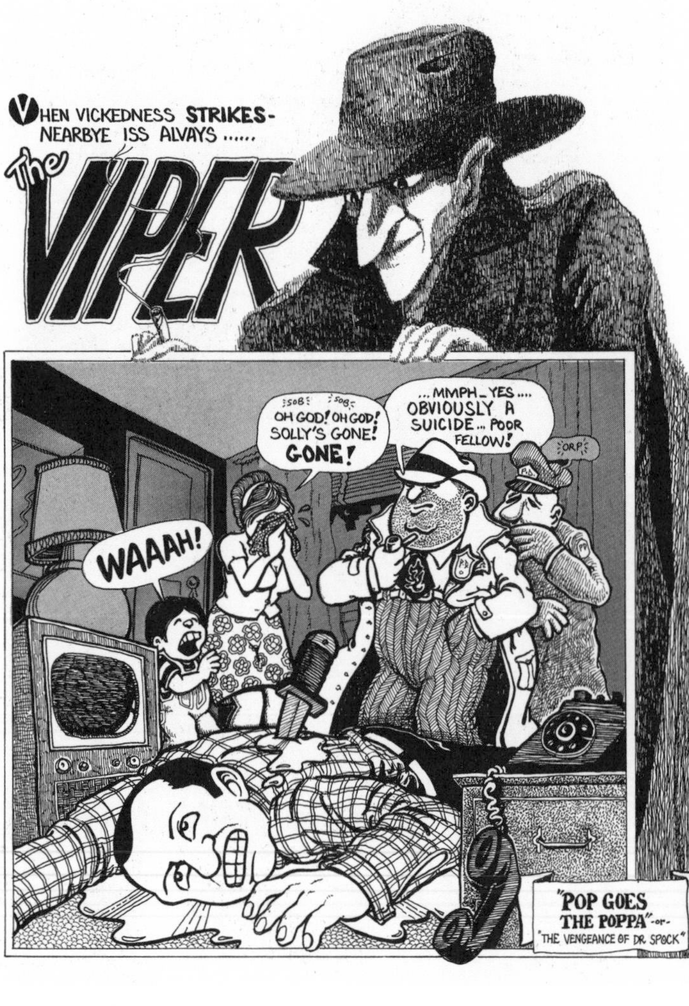
VHEN VICKEDNESS STRIKES- NEARBYE ISS ALVAYS ......
The VIPER
OH GOD! OH GOD! SOLLY'S GONE! GONE!
... MMPH_YES.... OBVIOUSLY A SUICIDE... POOR FELLOW!
WAAAH!
"POP GOES THE POPPA" -or- "THE VENGEANCE OF DR. SPOCK"

center of *Breakdowns*, was the result of my wrestling match with Cubism. (Only when it was done did I realize that the graphic style I'd distilled for this page looked something like Art Deco, a style that itself owed a lot to Cubism.) Many of my cartooning cronies greeted the page with indifference, and encouraged me to pursue things more like *Sleazy Scandals of the Silver Screen*, a comic I was working on at about the same time, or the "Real Dream" pages I did after. I had smashed into the wall that separated cartoonists from Artists. Arteests get to be shamans; us cartoonists are mere "communicators." As Chris Ware succinctly put it years later: "When you don't understand a painting, you assume you're stupid. When you don't understand a comic strip, you assume the cartoonist is stupid."

Yet I continued to peer over the High-Low fence with "Ace Hole, Midget Detective." Though I kept derailing its soft-boiled narrative, at least it seemed to have one. The two-faced femmes fatales that Picasso had painted in the Twenties and Thirties seemed like perfect analogs to the dames Hammett, Chandler and Cain were writing about in the pulps of the same period. The density of ideas compacted into Ace Hole's eight pages resulted from the economic downturn that

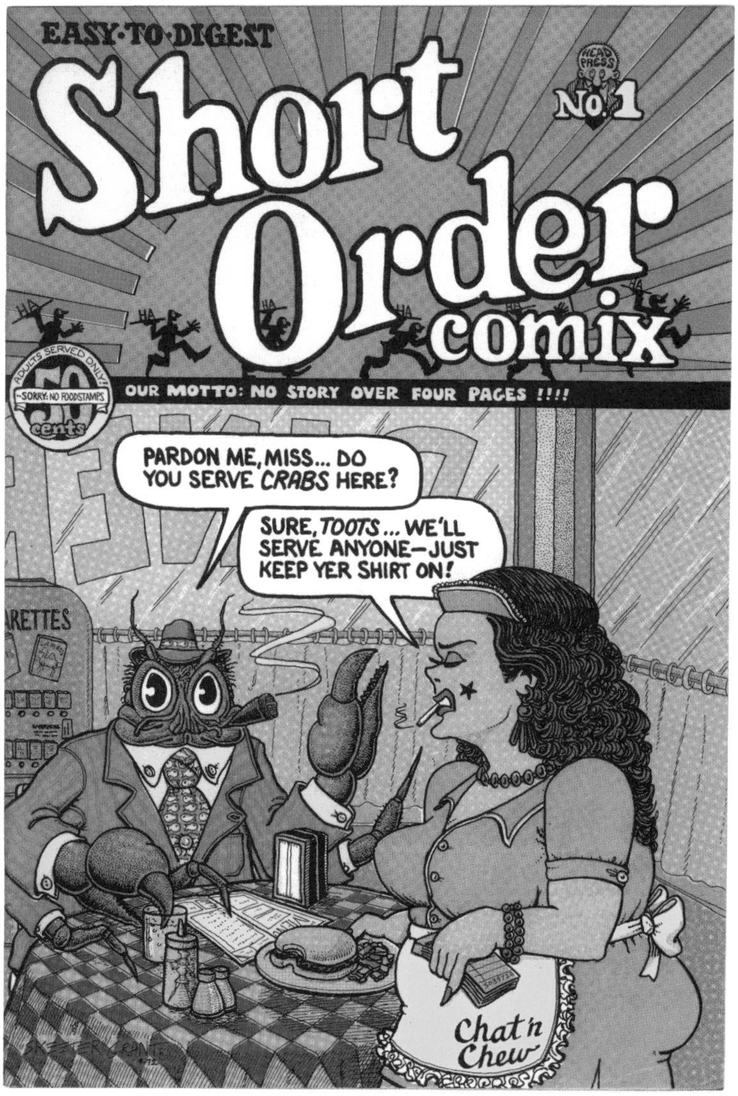
EASY-TO-DIGEST
Short Order comix
No 1
ADULTS SERVED ONLY! 50 cents SORRY: NO FOODSTAMPS
OUR MOTTO: NO STORY OVER FOUR PAGES !!!!
PARDON ME, MISS... DO YOU SERVE CRABS HERE?
SURE, TOOTS... WE'LL SERVE ANYONE—JUST KEEP YER SHIRT ON!
RETTES
Chat 'n Chew

RIGHT: *Short Order Comics* #1, 1973 (first publication of "Prisoner on the Hell Planet")

BELOW LEFT: *Zip-a-Tunes* booklet, 1972 (here super-imposed on a Zipatone instruction card)

BELOW RIGHT: Zipatone overlays for cyan, magenta, yellow and black plates used in preparing the covers and endpapers of *Breakdowns*

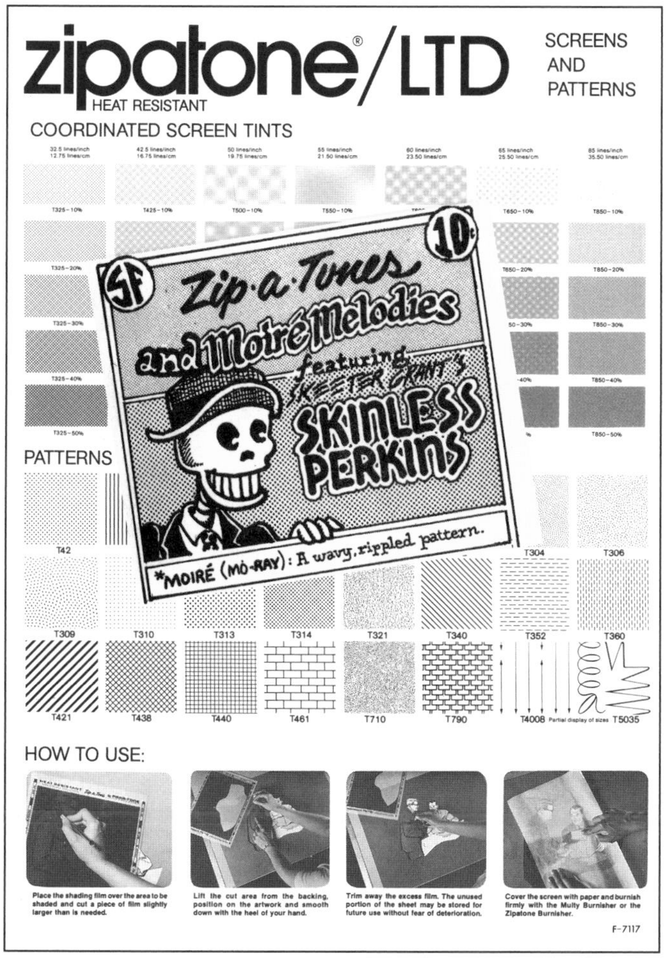
zipatone®/LTD
HEAT RESISTANT
SCREENS AND PATTERNS
COORDINATED SCREEN TINTS
PATTERNS
HOW TO USE:
10¢
SF
Zip-a-Tunes and Moiré Melodies featuring Skeeter Grant's SKINLESS PERKINS
*MOIRÉ (MO-RAY): A wavy, rippled pattern.
F-7117

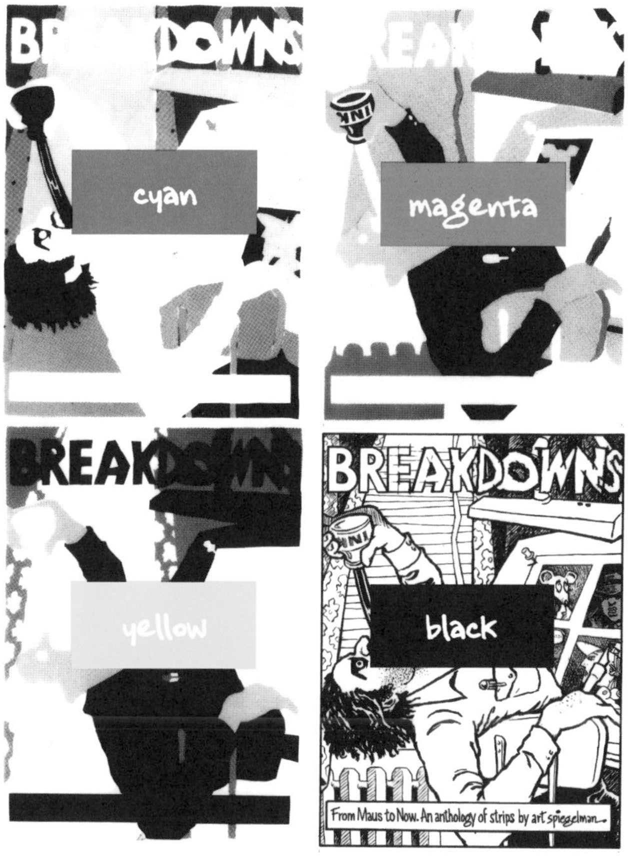
cyan
magenta
yellow
BREAKDOWNS
black
From Maus to Now. An anthology of strips by art spiegelman

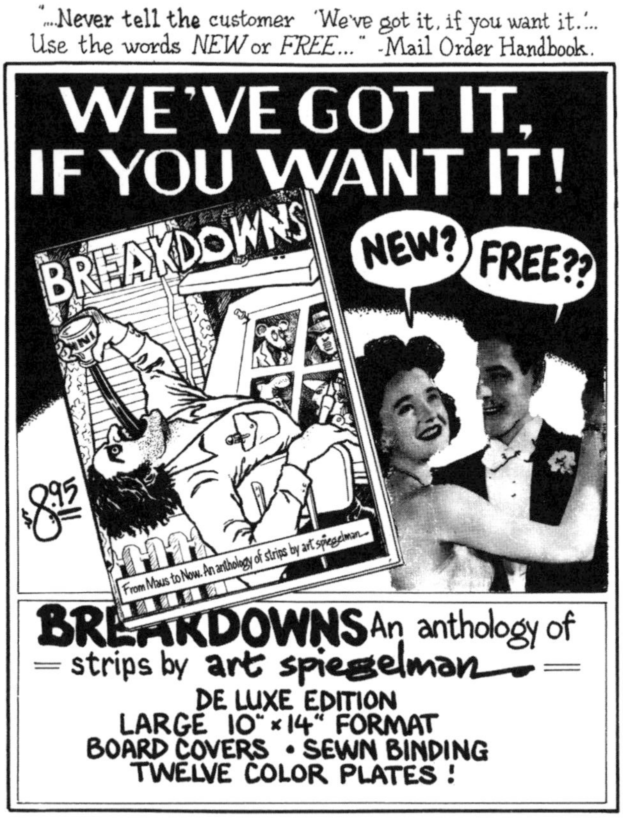
"...Never tell the customer 'We've got it, if you want it.'... Use the words NEW or FREE..." -Mail Order Handbook.
WE'VE GOT IT, IF YOU WANT IT!
BREAKDOWNS
NEW?
FREE??
$8.95
From Maus to Now. An anthology of strips by art spiegelman
BREAKDOWNS An anthology of strips by art spiegelman
DE LUXE EDITION
LARGE 10" × 14" FORMAT
BOARD COVERS • SEWN BINDING
TWELVE COLOR PLATES!

hit the underground comix "business" in the early Seventies, just when I'd hit my stride. A new head comix publisher, who hadn't yet heard the bad news, committed himself to the second issue of *Short Order Comix,* and I thought it might be my last and best chance to do an extended piece, unfettered, before the whole system tanked. I crammed all the scattered notes and notions about comics that I'd been squirreling away into one eight-page story—one of the longest pieces I ever did before the 300-page *Maus*. I changed the tagline that had been on *Short Order*'s first cover ("Our Motto: No Story Over Four Pages!") to acknowledge the achievement.

In 1970, I'd contributed a dank one-pager about necrophilia to the first issue of *Young Lust*, a popular X-rated parody of Romance genre comics. Four years later, I returned to the magazine, site of that youthful indiscretion, with "Little Signs of Passion." The full-color issue, a rarity at the time, attracted first-rate work by an A-list of underground comix artists. But even in that context, my "deconstruction" (to use a word I didn't know back in 1974) of love stories was not something its Adults Only audience seemed adult enough

DON'T GET AROUND MUCH ANYMORE
A GUIDED TOUR by art spiegelman

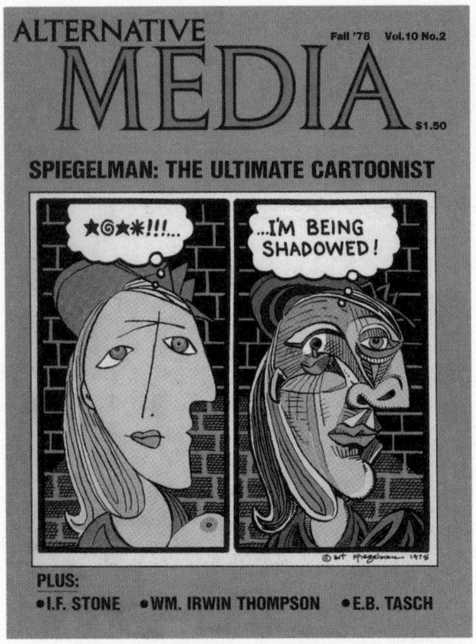
ALTERNATIVE MEDIA
Fall '78 Vol.10 No.2
$1.50
SPIEGELMAN: THE ULTIMATE CARTOONIST
★@★✳!!!...
...I'M BEING SHADOWED!
PLUS:
•I.F. STONE •WM. IRWIN THOMPSON •E.B. TASCH

"Better to be thought a fool and remain silent than to write and remove all doubt."
— Abraham Lincoln

I've been told that "Don't Get Around Much Anymore" is depressing. I don't see it that way. "DGAMA" is, among other things, a meditation on depression and alienation.

The text was written in a single flash—an excretion into a notebook, not originally conceived as material for a comic strip. Since it is primarily descriptive, it might seem unpromising for a medium noted for frantic action. Perhaps this is what drew me to it. The text afforded me an opportunity to expand on the idea that comics represent time spatially. That is, an interval of time is usually implied between each panel, though they all exist simultaneously on a page. The only motion (the only frantic action) when one reads a comic strip is in the reader's eyeballs. One is trained to read a comic strip from left to right, top to bottom, one panel at a time. "DGAMA" attempts to derail this training.

I tried to adopt drawing techniques and mannerisms—a style—appropriate to the subject matter. The rapidograph pen, a tool used for mechanical rendering that creates lines of unvarying width, seemed a good choice, as did the parallel-line shading and general starkness of the black and white. I did want something angular about the artwork—a metaphor for feeling "boxed in," a visual pun on the title, "Don't Get AROUND Much Anymore."

The drawing is very diagrammatic. All comic-strip drawings must function as diagrams, simplified picture-words that indicate more than they show. The first two panels, the first row of panels, are diagrams of the rest of the strip—diagrams of diagrams. I often try to synopsize my strips in the first panel or so before the beginning. They function like "splash" panels in more traditional comics—the lead panel that depicts the theme or high point of the action to follow.

Panel 1 shows the narrator in relation to most of the objects focused on in the rest of the page—a long shot of which the other panels are details. The Floorplan is a further abstraction, situating the objects and space that serve to define the narrator.

Panel 3, the title, is from a Duke Ellington blues song. The lettering is based on a specimen in an obscure 1920s lettering book. The square shape of the letters, the initial difficulty in decoding them, the mechanical tone sheets, all reinforce the themes of the strip. The detail of the narrator's face is redrawn from the panel above in a small box almost the same size as the letters, and can function as the word "I."

Many parallels are made between comics and film (both are popular art forms that synthesize other media, both are children of late nineteenth century technology, etc.) The differences between them must be respected, but I have occasionally regretted that, unlike film, comics have no soundtrack. Referring to the Ellington song is a step toward providing a mental soundtrack; asking for a dripping faucet as accompanist is an even more emphatic one. The dripping faucet line is meant to be both taken seriously, yet also function as a self-conscious joke about my avant-garde aspirations.

Panel 4, referring to the cable television, is a close-up of the space between the narrator and the television in Panel 1. The bars of the window create subdivided panels.

The text in Panel 5 is out of sync with the visual. It more directly refers to the picture in the previous panel pulling the reader's eye back, or at least making one mentally connect the two panels. (This device—disengaging the picture from the text it illustrates—is a reaction to the many unsophisticated comic strips in which the picture is little more than an illustration of the text above it.) The figures on the collaged *Life* cover have been squared off to satisfy visual harmony and a personal penchant for graffiti. The collage impulse, a tactic borrowed from Cubism, is fundamental to the strip's pervasive references to media as extensors of experience.

In Panel 6, once again the text appears to be out of sync, referring the reader back to the *Life* magazines depicted in the previous panel—although the *Life* magazine logo in the lower left leaves an ambiguity. The double-image record player sets up a back-and-forth eye movement within the panel, in an attempt to create a visual equivalent to the sound of a skipping record (more on this later.)

Now that a new pattern has been established—a block of text appearing one panel after the picture it describes—it is my obligation to rupture the pattern. Therefore, Panel 7. The text at the top refers to the television in Panel 8 (while the text in Panel 8 once again refers back to Panel 7. The text at the bottom of Panel 7 brings one back again to the record of Panel 6).

to embrace. And in 2008, when *Breakdowns* was reissued, my editor at Pantheon, Dan Frank, had to allay my fears that the "hardcore," sexually explicit panels—though not exactly prurient in their context—could still keep the book off-limits for many mainstream booksellers years later. His response, "Huh, you mean the *naughty* bits?" left me feeling like a hick.

Many of the artists in that issue of *Young Lust* (Robert Crumb, Kim Deitch, Justin Green, Bill Griffith and Spain Rodriguez) became the core of *Arcade*, a short-lived (1975–1976, R.I.P.) quarterly I co-edited with Bill Griffith, that tried to function as a lifeboat when the San Francisco comix schooner started to sink. Almost all the pieces I did for *Arcade*—like "Cracking Jokes," the nonfiction comics-format essay on humor that appeared in the first issue and "The Malpractice Suite," an appropriation (another term I didn't know back then) of inert *Rex Morgan* newspaper strips in the penultimate sixth issue—ended up in *Breakdowns*.

In fact, the only thing I did for the magazine that did not make it into the book was "Some Boxes for the Salvation Army," a stillborn project, the remains of which I dumped into *Arcade #5*, laying it out like a sketchbook of random panels when the deadline loomed. Jealous of my independent filmmaker pals who could shoot footage and edit it after, I wanted to do the same in comics. I reasoned that I could shuffle panels and sequences around after drawing them as long as I used same-size panels on a grid. The panel would become the basic unit of thought rather than the page. I could interweave memories, story fragments and ideas in different styles to mimic the non-chronological way the mind works. It sounded like it was worth a try, but unfortunately, I was too scattered a young %@#$!! to draw enough "footage" to quite find out at the time. (At least that failed experiment di-

TOP LEFT: Mail-order ad for *Breakdowns,* 1978

BELOW: *Alternative Media*, Fall 1978, volume 10, no. 2 (Virtually the only notice *Breakdowns* got at the time was from a friend, Bob Singer, the editor of the magazine who wrote the cover story, "James Joyce, Picasso, Stravinsky and Spiegelman." He also invited me to write the "Guided Tour" essay below, a panel-by-panel analysis of "Don't Get Around Much Anymore." More "communicator" than "shaman," I couldn't resist.)

The cupboard in the upper left of Panel 7 is empty.

The laterally mismatched face on the TV in Panel 8 was found, as is, in a *Life* magazine ad pointing out the virtues of a larger picture tube. I am amused by the connection between her vacuously smiling face and the line, "The refrigerator is empty."

In Panel 9, for the first time, the words and picture are firmly connected. The upper box of text refers to the crackers and cupboard boxed directly beneath. Note that the cupboard now has a box of crackers, probably Ritz. The water pours onto the text box describing the faucet.

Panel 10: text and image are again unmoored. The image is a return to Panel 4. The text in Panel 11 directs one's attention to both Panels 10 and 11. The phrase, "he's been bouncing that ball for hours" gives duration to the "action" of the strip—it has been hours since the reader first encountered the kid at the beginning of the page; our narrator has been stationary for quite a while. The closest thing to an event in the strip is the kid bouncing his ball, the ROUNDest object in the strip, the one most emphatically represented as alive/in motion. It exists outside the narrator's room.

By keeping the two images almost identical in Panels 10 and 11 the eye—always scanning for differences—is focused on the "movement" of the ball. The back-and-forth motion already established in the strip makes the ball bounce repeatedly (to the accompaniment of a dripping faucet, slowly.)

The repetition of image in the next two panels provides counterpoint to all this activity. The Modigliani print used to illustrate the Ann-Margret article also comes from a *Life* magazine ad. At the top of Panel 13, the man from the Lark ad is placed on the cover of *Life* ... to put more flavor in it.

The teeth in the last panel provide a startling contrast with the stylized teeth of the Lark man. The middle row of teeth, incidentally, is a toothbrush. The text and image both are means of making the strip swallow its own tail; sending one back again—with a grin or a grimace—to earlier panels, to find more than was made available on first reading... or in this article.

Buy my book.

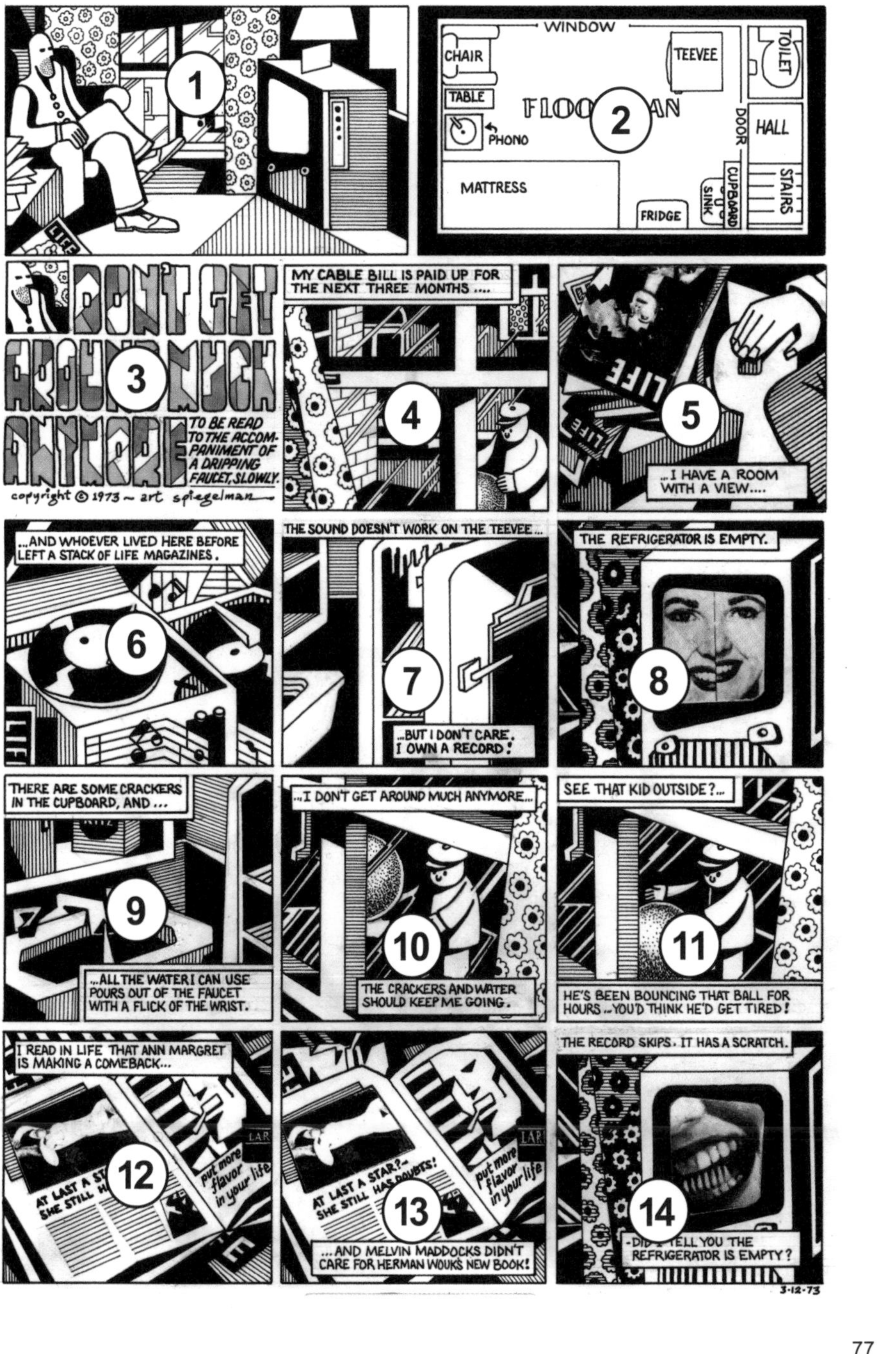
1
WINDOW
CHAIR
TABLE
TEEVEE
TOILET
PHONO
2
DOOR
HALL
MATTRESS
FRIDGE
CUPBOARD SINK
STAIRS
DON'T GET AROUND MUCH ANYMORE
TO BE READ TO THE ACCOMPANIMENT OF A DRIPPING FAUCET, SLOWLY.
copyright © 1973 ~ art spiegelman
3
MY CABLE BILL IS PAID UP FOR THE NEXT THREE MONTHS....
4
LIFE
5
...I HAVE A ROOM WITH A VIEW....
...AND WHOEVER LIVED HERE BEFORE LEFT A STACK OF LIFE MAGAZINES.
6
THE SOUND DOESN'T WORK ON THE TEEVEE...
7
..BUT I DON'T CARE. I OWN A RECORD!
THE REFRIGERATOR IS EMPTY.
8
THERE ARE SOME CRACKERS IN THE CUPBOARD, AND...
9
...ALL THE WATER I CAN USE POURS OUT OF THE FAUCET WITH A FLICK OF THE WRIST.
..I DON'T GET AROUND MUCH ANYMORE...
10
THE CRACKERS AND WATER SHOULD KEEP ME GOING.
SEE THAT KID OUTSIDE?...
11
HE'S BEEN BOUNCING THAT BALL FOR HOURS ..YOU'D THINK HE'D GET TIRED!
I READ IN LIFE THAT ANN MARGRET IS MAKING A COMEBACK...
12
put more flavor in your life
AT LAST A STAR?- SHE STILL HAS DOUBTS!
put more flavor in your life
13
...AND MELVIN MADDOCKS DIDN'T CARE FOR HERMAN WOUK'S NEW BOOK!
THE RECORD SKIPS. IT HAS A SCRATCH.
14
TELL YOU THE REFRIGERATOR IS EMPTY?
3-12-73

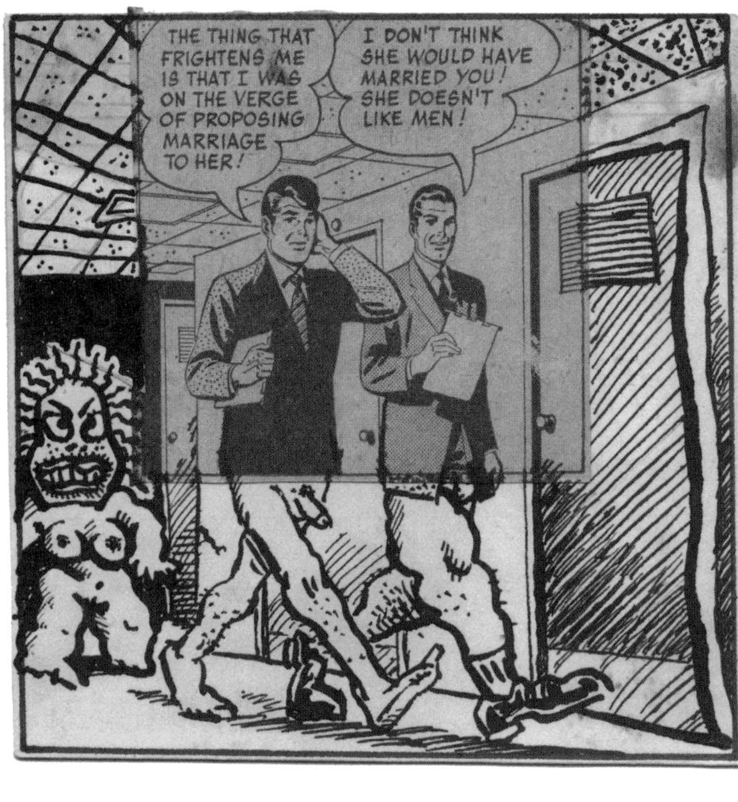
THE THING THAT FRIGHTENS ME IS THAT I WAS ON THE VERGE OF PROPOSING MARRIAGE TO HER!
I DON'T THINK SHE WOULD HAVE MARRIED YOU! SHE DOESN'T LIKE MEN!

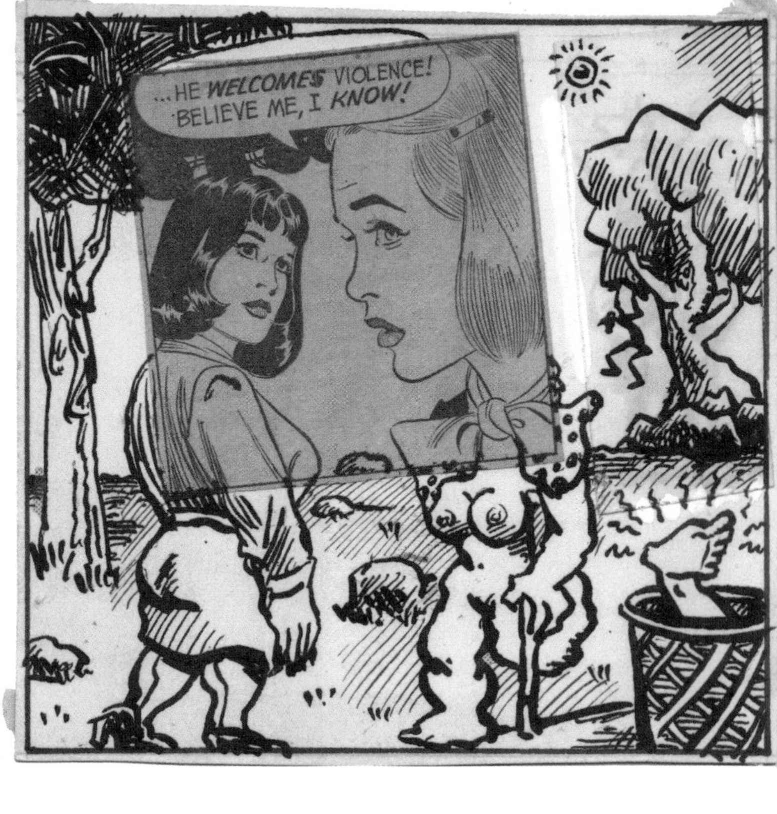
...HE WELCOMES VIOLENCE! BELIEVE ME, I KNOW!

"Once a poet has known the excitement of conceiving a poem and taking it through various drafts, still under the same excitement, the craving will always be with him. When it becomes oppressive he often puts himself into a receptive posture, keeps pen and paper handy, and waits for the miracle of the Muse Goddess's appearance; then grows impatient, begins doodling with words (as you give the planchette a little push to make it start), and soon finds a promising rhyme or phrase. Thus he contrives a visitation—not of the Goddess, but of one of those idle foolish earthbound spirits that hover around the planchette board, or the pillows of sick men. Every poet knows in his heart which are the necessary and which the unnecessary poems. But too often he tries to fool himself that all are necessary...

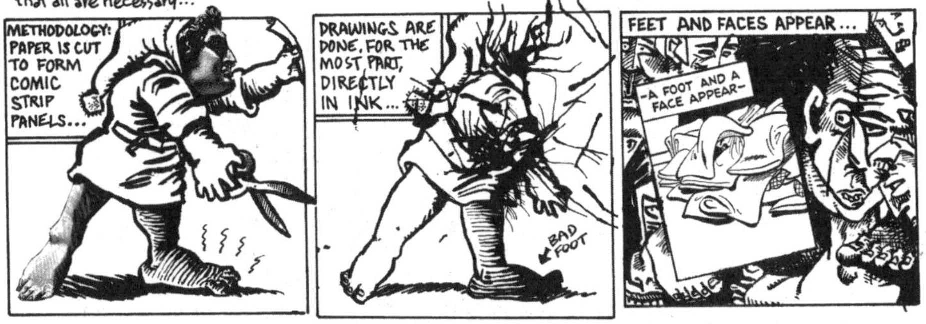
METHODOLOGY: PAPER IS CUT TO FORM COMIC STRIP PANELS...
DRAWINGS ARE DONE, FOR THE MOST PART, DIRECTLY IN INK...
BAD FOOT
FEET AND FACES APPEAR...
—A FOOT AND A FACE APPEAR—

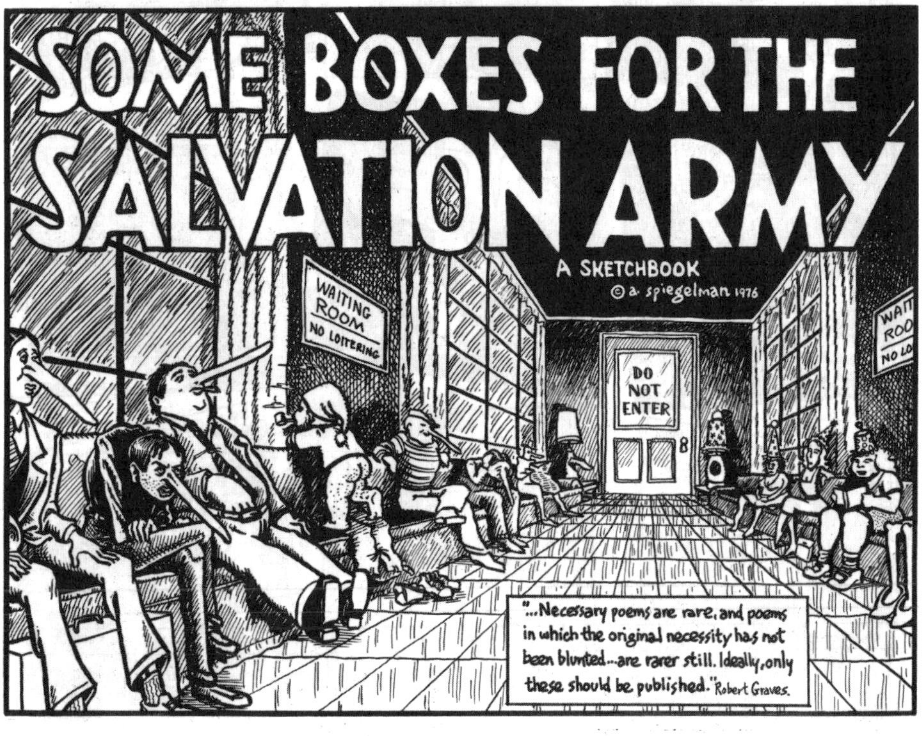
SOME BOXES FOR THE SALVATION ARMY
A SKETCHBOOK
© a. spiegelman 1976
WAITING ROOM
NO LOITERING
DO NOT ENTER
"...Necessary poems are rare, and poems in which the original necessity has not been blunted...are rarer still. Ideally, only these should be published." Robert Graves.

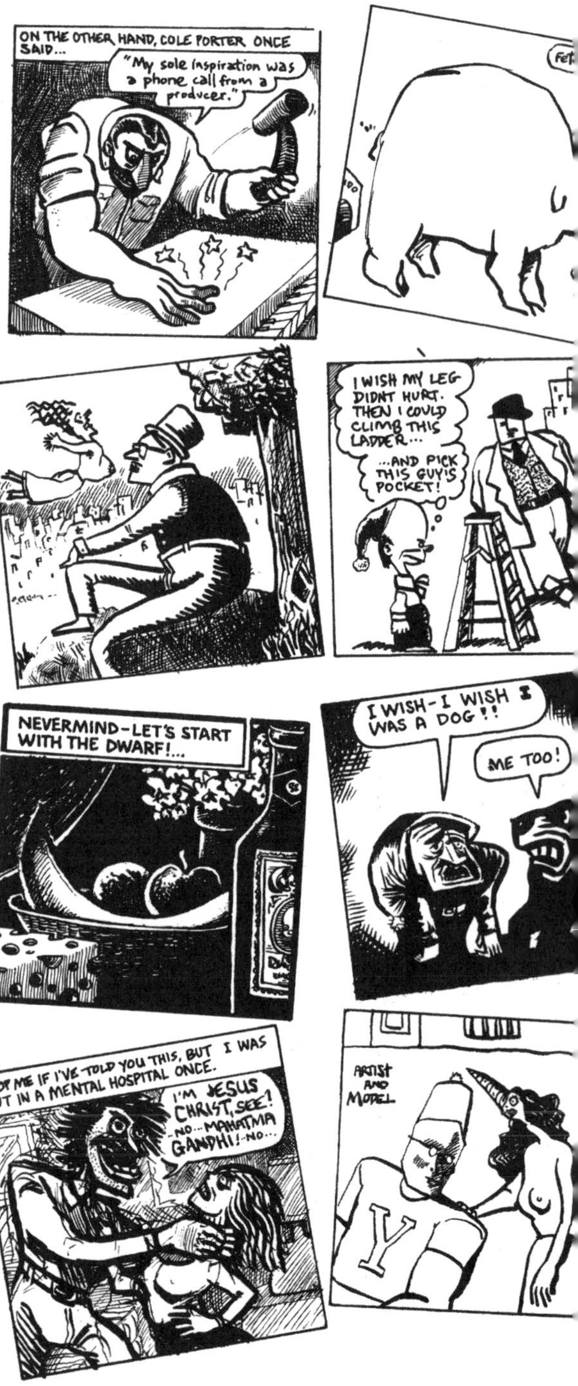
ON THE OTHER HAND, COLE PORTER ONCE SAID...
"My sole inspiration was a phone call from a producer."
I WISH MY LEG DIDNT HURT. THEN I COULD CLIMB THIS LADDER...
...AND PICK THIS GUY'S POCKET!
NEVERMIND-LET'S START WITH THE DWARF!...
I WISH-I WISH I WAS A DOG!!
ME TOO!
STOP ME IF I'VE TOLD YOU THIS, BUT I WAS PUT IN A MENTAL HOSPITAL ONCE.
I'M JESUS CHRIST, SEE! ...NO...MAHATMA GANDHI!...NO...
ARTIST AND MODEL

rectly led to my *Rex Morgan* collage piece, "The Malpractice Suite," in the very next issue of *Arcade* three months later. And decades later, I returned to the Boxes for the Salvation Army notion to make what became "Portrait of the Artist As a Young %@#$!!" introduction to the book now in your hands.

Back in the Seventies, in the middle of *Arcade*'s brief run, I moved back to New York City and resumed a weekly relationship with Topps Gum. In 1977, Woody Gelman, still the Creative Director of Topps, decided to expand Nostalgia Press, the small publishing house he ran on the side. He asked me if there was any book I ever dreamed of doing, and *Breakdowns* got rolling. But the dream got smashed—like so many American dreams—when Elvis Presley died. Woody, believing he could sell a billion copies of a quickie Elvis memorial poster book, invested in a forest of paper. By the time it became obvious that he'd vastly over-extended himself, *Breakdowns* was already printed. An embarrassed Woody was reluctant to pay the bill and bring the book out. I was devastated, but Jeff Rund, a purveyor of fine bondage and pornography books who had just published a Crumb anthology, generously came to my rescue, explaining to the printer: "I don't understand two thirds of the shit in this book, but anyone who could do that 'Maus' strip and the thing about his mother's suicide deserves a break."

So, with an errata sticker explaining the change of proprietorship, *Breakdowns* got published in 1978. Though to say it was "published" is an exaggeration: five thousand copies had roiled off the press, but almost half of those were unusable. The printers, in a woozy all-nite session, distractedly let black ink glop all over the "Little Signs of Passion" pages,

LEFT: **Out-takes from "Some Boxes for the Salvation Army"**

BELOW: **"Some Boxes for the Salvation Army," three pages for *Arcade* #5, Spring 1976**

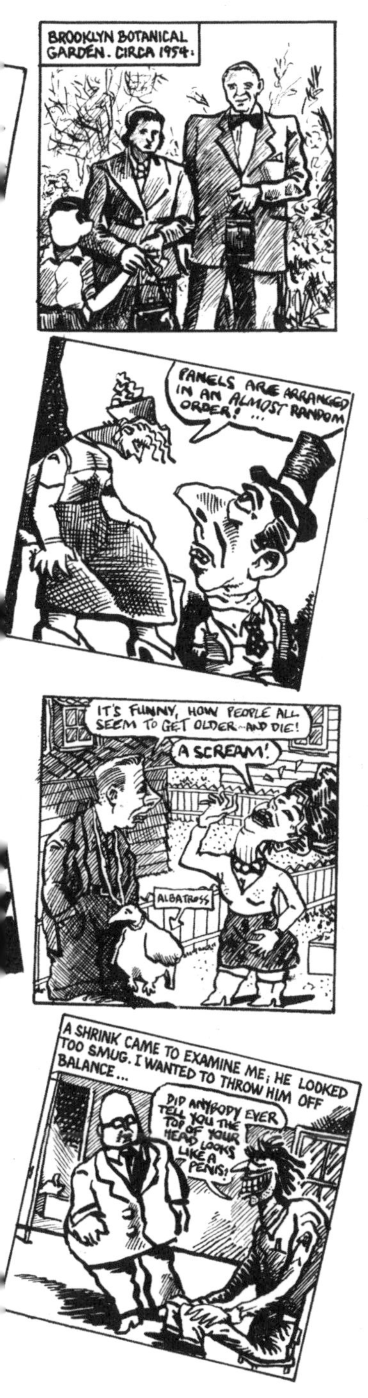

BROOKLYN BOTANICAL GARDEN. CIRCA 1954:
PANELS ARE ARRANGED IN AN ALMOST RANDOM ORDER! ...
IT'S FUNNY, HOW PEOPLE ALL SEEM TO GET OLDER...AND DIE!
A SCREAM!
ALBATROSS
A SHRINK CAME TO EXAMINE ME; HE LOOKED TOO SMUG. I WANTED TO THROW HIM OFF BALANCE...
DID ANYBODY EVER TELL YOU THE TOP OF YOUR HEAD LOOKS LIKE A PENIS?

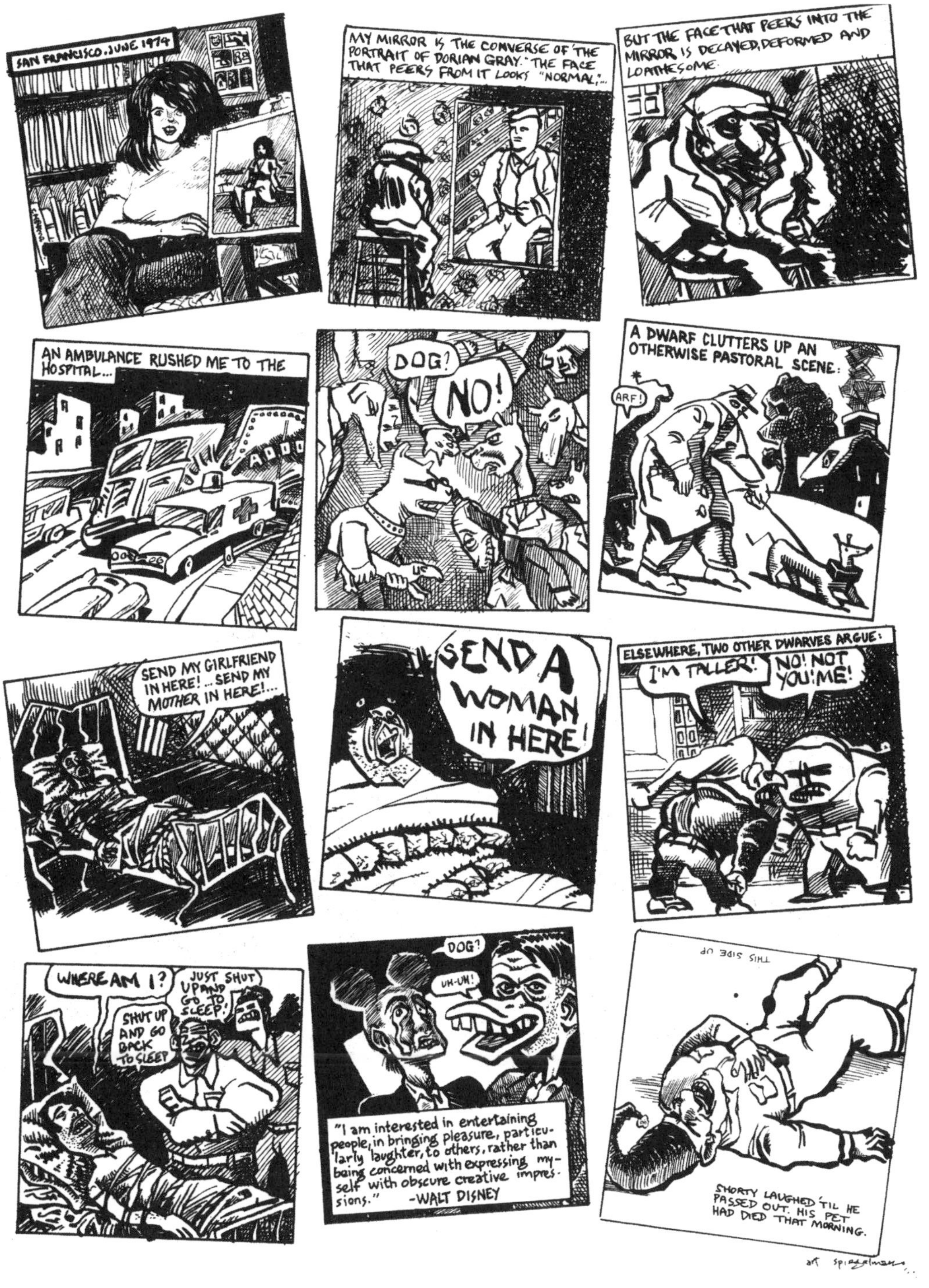

SAN FRANCISCO. JUNE 1974
MY MIRROR IS THE CONVERSE OF "THE PORTRAIT OF DORIAN GRAY." THE FACE THAT PEERS FROM IT LOOKS "NORMAL,"...
BUT THE FACE THAT PEERS INTO THE MIRROR IS DECAYED, DEFORMED AND LOATHESOME.
AN AMBULANCE RUSHED ME TO THE HOSPITAL...
DOG?
NO!
A DWARF CLUTTERS UP AN OTHERWISE PASTORAL SCENE:
ARF!
SEND MY GIRLFRIEND IN HERE! ... SEND MY MOTHER IN HERE!...
SEND A WOMAN IN HERE!
ELSEWHERE, TWO OTHER DWARVES ARGUE:
I'M TALLER!
NO! NOT YOU! ME!
WHERE AM I?
JUST SHUT UP AND GO TO SLEEP!
SHUT UP AND GO BACK TO SLEEP
DOG?
UH-UH!
"I am interested in entertaining
people, in bringing pleasure, particu-
larly laughter, to others, rather than
being concerned with expressing my-
self with obscure creative impres-
sions." -WALT DISNEY
THIS SIDE UP
SHORTY LAUGHED 'TIL HE PASSED OUT. HIS PET HAD DIED THAT MORNING.
art spiegelman

screwing up the mechanical reproduction while ogling the hardcore images of human reproduction. In any case, there was barely any demand for the copies that were bound and offered for distribution. Years later they were still being peddled through small ads in *Raw*, the magazine of avant-garde comics that I co-edited with Françoise Mouly in the Eighties.

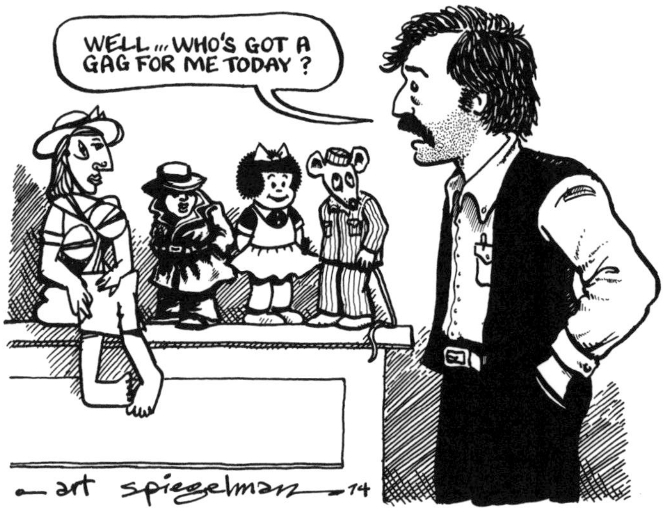
WELL... WHO'S GOT A GAG FOR ME TODAY ?
art spiegelman '74

The long *Maus* book that followed after *Breakdowns* was originally serialized in the pages of *Raw*. The magazine was shaped by the aesthetics and format of *Breakdowns*, combined with Françoise's sense and her sensibility. It was she who dragged me, kicking and screaming, to start *Raw* as a showcase for what comics could be after I'd vowed never to do such a thing again in the wake of *Arcade*! I had first met Françoise when I was putting *Breakdowns* together and she got curious about its production. She mastered the arcane art of hand-cut zipatone separations after the cursory two-minute explanation I gave her before heading out for a day at Topps. I returned that evening to find that she had flawlessly completed the separation I was working on. Naturally, dear reader, I married her.

Breakdowns figures prominently in my life and my development as an artist, but I was still surprised when Dan Frank asked to see the book in 2004 and was eager to have Pantheon republish it despite the "naughty bits." We were putting together *In the Shadow of No Towers* at the time, a collection of the broadsheet comics pages that I'd made in the aftermath of September 11. I explained that the fragmentation and structural concerns that had preoccupied me in *Breakdowns* came to the foreground again when I tried to find a way to deal with my shattered brain after seeing a plane crash into a 110-story structure about fifteen blocks from our home.

I told Dan that the 300-page *Maus* had grown directly out of the resounding lack of response to *Breakdowns*. Believing that comics were a medium designed for print, I thought that if I kept following the trajectory I was on, I would again be reduced to passing out leaflets on street corners. I dreamed of a comic book that was long enough to need a bookmark and there was one story—the one about my parents' experiences in WWII—that seemed compelling enough to devote myself to telling it for what I anticipated would be three or four years. (It took me thirteen years to complete. I applied the lessons I'd learned while thwarting narrative, spinning them in reverse to make a flowing story.)

Though I'd been braced for resistance to my 1970s work, it never occurred to me that *Maus* would eventually become "canon-fodder" in today's culture wars—banned by a school board in McMinn County, Tennessee. The implications are horrifying, though as a card-carrying underground cartoonist, I somehow feel honored.

I'm glad *Breakdowns* is getting one more spin around the block as a deluxe paperback fourteen years after the Pantheon hardcover edition and about forty-five years(!) after the original edition. Some may look at my first book as a mere artifact of its time—with all the failings that changing perspectives may bring to any work. But for me, *Breakdowns* is a manifesto, a diary, a crumpled suicide note and a still-relevant love letter to a medium I adore.

—art spiegelman, nyc.
2008/2022

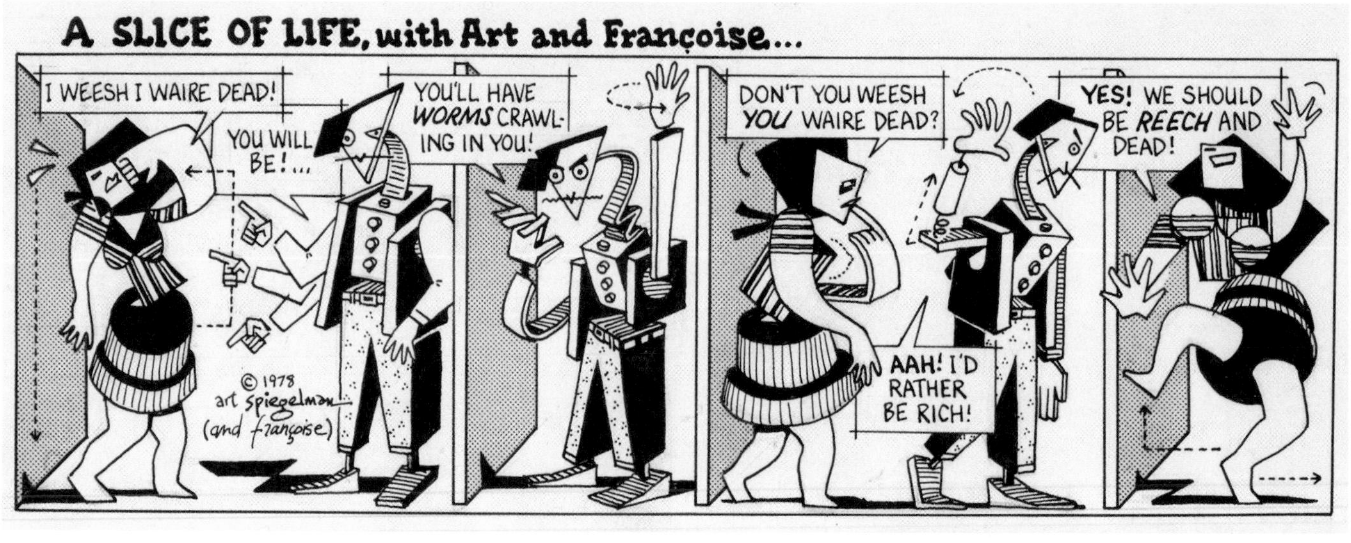
A SLICE OF LIFE, with Art and Françoise...
I WEESH I WAIRE DEAD!
YOU WILL BE!...
YOU'LL HAVE WORMS CRAWLING IN YOU!
DON'T YOU WEESH YOU WAIRE DEAD?
YES! WE SHOULD BE REECH AND DEAD!
AAH! I'D RATHER BE RICH!
© 1978 art spiegelman (and françoise)

TOP OF PAGE: Self-portrait, *The Apex Treasury of Underground Comics*, 1974

ABOVE: "A Slice of Life," published in *Snarf* #8, 1978

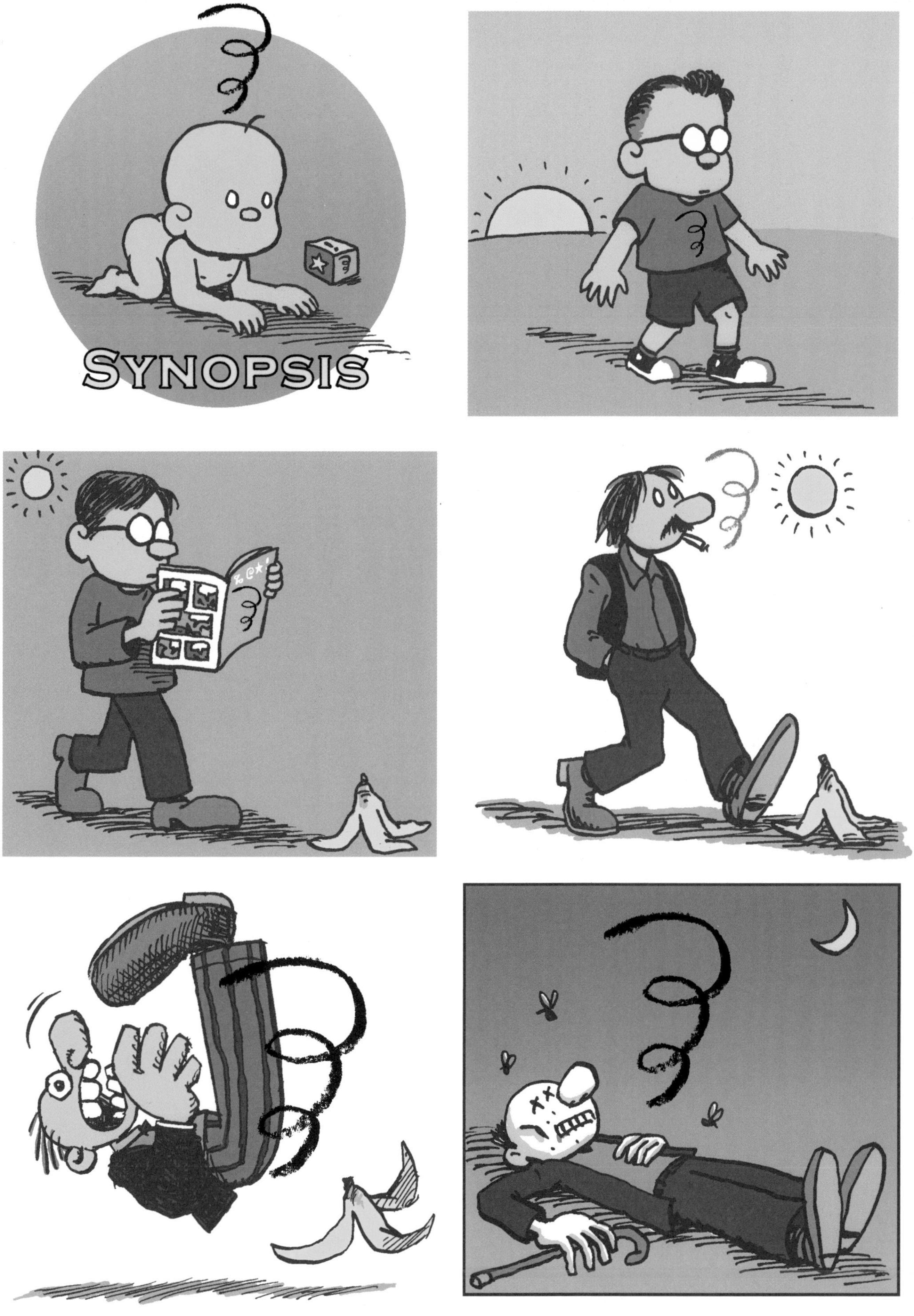
SYNOPSIS

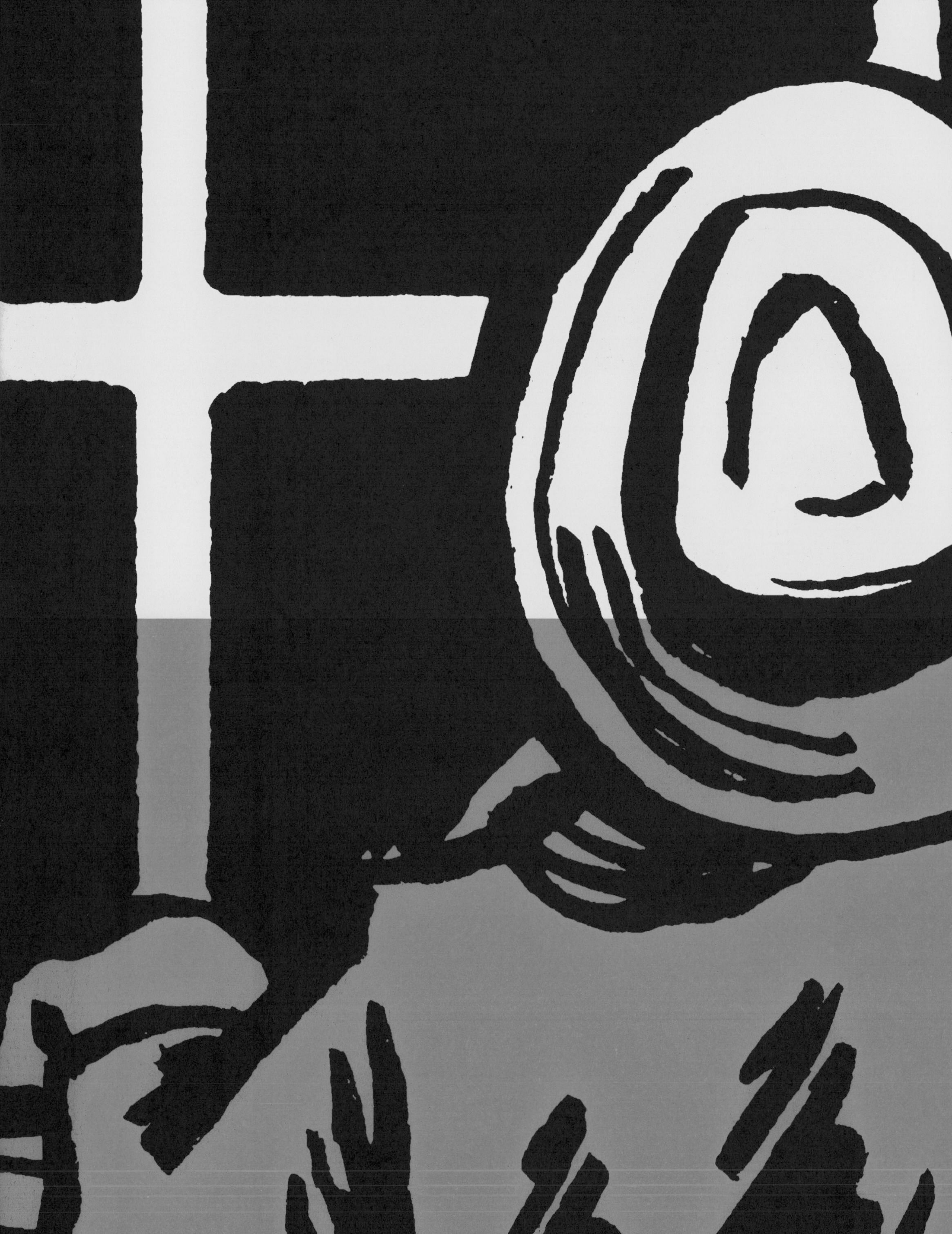